AF440658

PRO$PER
THROUGH
TAX
PLANNING

Also by ROBERT BUECHNER:

Accumulating Wealth With Before-Tax Dollars (with David L. Manzler)

Why Universal Life (with David L. Manzler and Isaiah M. Goodfellow)

PRO$PER THROUGH TAX PLANNING

Robert Buechner

COWARD-McCann, Inc.
NEW YORK

Library of Congress Cataloging in Publication Data

Buechner, Robert.
    Prosper through tax planning.

    Includes bibliographical references and index.
    1. Tax planning—United States.   I. Title.
KF6297.B84   1982   343.7304   82-8145
ISBN 0-698-11196-6   347.3034   AACR2

Printed in the United States of America

Acknowledgments

Writing this book was both more fun and more work than I expected. Fortunately I was assisted by many excellent people, whose efforts helped me enjoy more of the fun side of my efforts. For her assistance in editing, I would like to thank Leslie Major. For their review of certain technical areas of the book, I am indebted to Richard B. Rothman, Dale Williams, Larry Blau, John Vogelgesang, and my very talented associate, Frank Marnell. For their careful assistance in helping me footnote the book, I am grateful to William Hesch, Douglas Brendamour, Thomas Vergamini and Richard Grant. For her tireless typing and very helpful comments, I thank Nancy Brun. For her revisions and constant copying of the chapters, I thank Cathy Mullis. For the sense of direction he gave me, I thank Aron Mathieu. For the creative artwork, I am indebted to Dale Justice. For her valuable comments and encouragement, I am grateful to Janet Stuhlreyer.

Many of my students at Samuel P. Chase College of Law were instrumental in putting together some of the initial material for this book. In particular, David Garretson, Douglas Miller, Greg Kilburn and Tony Brinker gave this book a very helpful push in its infancy. Finally I would like to thank my literary agent and friend, Betty Marks, for her encouragement, and my editor, Thomas Miller, for his expert guidance.

The 1982 updates would not have been possible without the excellent assistance of the Cincinnati and Dayton Touche Ross and Company offices, especially the help of a former crackerjack student and good friend, William Hesch.

The specifics of a tax planning program vary according to the tax laws in effect in a given year. This book was written primarily before the 1982 Tax Act took effect, but has been partially updated to reflect the new tax law: passages in the book relating to the new law are marked by rules in the margins.

Mr. Buechner has offered to make available a free tax update to readers of this book. The update includes an extended discussion of the 1982 Tax Act, plus other recent tax matters, and is keyed to the format of the book. To receive your update, simply send your name and address to Robert W. Buechner, *Prosper*, 105 East 4th Street, Suite 1405, Cincinnati, Ohio, 45202.

Contents

PART II—ESTATE-TAX PLANNING   111

Why This Book Was Written

Our system of taxation is in trouble. Former IRS Commissioner Mortimer Chaplin estimates that the following go unreported:

30–40% of all self-employed income
17–22% of capital gains
35–50% of royalty and rental income
8–16% of dividend and interest income

In 1979, the IRS estimated that between 75 billion and 100 billion of legal income went unreported.

Voluntary compliance is the hallmark of our tax system. Voluntary compliance is based on two factors: fear and morality. Since the number of IRS audits this year is decreasing, the fear factor is becoming less important. Morality is practically all that is left to hold our tax system together, and that does not seem to be working very well.

Many people choose not to comply with our tax system because they perceive the system to be unfair and inequitable. For example, nearly everyone can cite the reported cases of individuals who have made over $200,000 in income yet paid no income taxes. Some people use this as a reason for failing to report their own income properly. It seems people do not see themselves as being lawbreakers simply because they cut a few corners of a system they perceive to be corrupt.

But our tax system is not corrupt or unfair. It is complex, it is confusing, it is poorly written, but it is ethical and fair. The tax breaks that are taken advantage of by the wealthy are, in most cases, readily available to those of modest wealth. The deductions people receive, such as for interest payments and charitable contributions, do make sense. Our system is worthy of voluntary compliance.

It is true that you may need a tax expert to help you take full advantage of our tax laws. But why should that be an indictment of our tax system? If your faucet leaks, you call a plumber. If your car breaks down, you take it to a mechanic. If your ear aches, you see a doctor. We live in an age of specialization, and tax planning should be given the same kind of respect as a pain in the neck.

This book is written for all the people who have not recently received a complete checkup from a tax expert. It will tell you what others are doing to cut their taxes and help you make your own tax-planning decisions. This book does not take the place of a tax expert; it simply puts you in the position of knowing what one would tell you if you were to pay for ten to fifteen hours of general tax advice.

If you cheat on your taxes, *stop*. If you don't cheat, don't start. Our system of voluntary compliance and limited audits is far superior to any other tax system in the world. If this system fails, you will have your tax return audited every year and the balance of your bank accounts will be reported regularly to the IRS.

Moreover, cheating doesn't pay. My experience has been that cheaters do not know the first thing about tax planning. They could save far more through legitimate tax planning than they could ever save through cheating. Plus, if they do get caught, it can mean penalty taxes and a jail sentence.

Through reading this book, you will learn that you do not have to cheat to avoid taxes. I predict you will become so excited about the tax-planning opportunities available to you that you will be both happy and proud to continue to report every last penny of income.

Introduction

The Economic Recovery Tax Act of 1981 offers an unprecedented opportunity to build and conserve wealth. It was founded on the premise that massive tax cuts coupled with tax incentives for saving and investing would stimulate vigorous economic growth, resulting in greater productivity and less inflation.

The 1981 act definitely enables you to pay less in taxes. It does not, however, eliminate the need for bona fide tax planning; it enhances this need. If you are able to combine tax cuts with an overall tax planning strategy to minimize your personal tax liability, you can be a recipient of the new wave of prosperity that has been planned for this country.

This book is not a compendium of tax shams or innovative brainstorms. It is a simplified presentation of proven tax-saving strategies, written by an attorney for his clients, to help people like you understand the basic techniques of reducing taxes and developing the tax-planning habit. The key to tax planning is knowing the alternatives. Once you know what you want, your tax adviser can help you put the details into practice.

Tax planning should be approached holistically. Personal income-tax planning cannot be considered without evaluating how tax savings in this area affect tax liabilities for your personal estate. Similarly, business tax planning must take into account alternatives that may be available through personal family-tax planning. For these reasons, this book presents the three basic areas of tax planning—personal, estate and business—and suggests how they can work together most advantageously. An understanding of all the ideas expressed in this book should be gained before the reader embarks on any one tax savings program.

Several concepts appear in all three parts of this book. Interest-free loans create an excellent opportunity for transferring income from a high-tax-bracket taxpayer to a low-tax-bracket taxpayer. In addition, the interest-free loan can be used in estate-tax planning to transfer wealth tax-free from one generation to the next and is often a fundamental part of business tax planning. The ownership of life insurance is a very important aspect of tax planning for most of us. If we die, we want to make certain our family is well provided for and that the government does not benefit from our decision to protect our family. However, while we live, we want to pay for life insurance in the most tax advantageous manner possible.

Qualified plans, such as pension and profit-sharing plans, would receive the most valuable concept (MVC) award hands down if one were to be given. Not only are qualified plans the best income-tax-savings vehicle going, they are also an instrumental part of estate-tax planning. Thus if you own your own business and are in a position to control your level of participation in qualified plans, you would be well advised to read the qualified-plans chapters (Chapters 21 and 22) before tackling other parts of this book.

There is one rule you should always follow in tax planning: when in doubt, pursue the safest course of tax reduction. For example, before you consider an oil and gas lease to reduce your income-tax liability, be certain you have no further opportunities to maximize qualified-plan contributions. Before you use interest-free loans in the intrafamily tax savings area, consider the use of a short-term trust. Your world will soon be filled with tax-savings ideas that you must organize based on your current level of tax planning. If you are a tax-planning novice, be sure to read Chapter 25, Whom Do You Trust?, before you take your first tax-planning step. Tax planning is an ongoing process, and it is important to begin that process with someone who can provide substantial assistance to you in the long run.

After the biggest tax cut in history in the Economic Recovery Tax Act of 1981, Congress followed it up with the biggest tax increase in history with the Tax Equity and Fiscal Responsibility Act of 1982. The 1982 Act claims to go after a few abuse situations, when in fact it takes a step backwards with regard to some of the benefits given to business from the 1981 Act and decreases the ability to save dollars in the qualified plan setting. I find the 1982 Act especially repugnant because it is drawing savings out of the capital formation markets of our country when capital formation is crucial for our future prosperity. In any event, the 1982 Act simply emphasizes the fact that you cannot rely on the government to do your tax planning for you. You must act today on viable tax planning ideas because they may be gone tomorrow.

This book does not attempt to teach you all the details of sophisticated tax planning. Your time is too valuable for that. The purpose of this book is to give you a knowledge of the basics so that you can understand the options available to you and make an informed decision about what your next tax planning step should be.

Robert W. Buechner

part I
Income-Tax Planning

chapter 1

Introduction to Personal Income-Tax Planning

If you had $20,000 of after-tax income to spend in 1974, you would have needed $40,200 of after-tax income in 1982 just to stay even—an increase of 101 percent. Yet in order to have after-tax income of $20,-000 in 1974 and $40,200 in 1982, your income (assuming you were married and had two children) would have had to increase from $25,-220 for 1974 to $57,050 for 1982—an increase of 126 percent. Why, when your after-tax dollars have had to increase 101 percent since 1974, have your before-tax dollars had to increase 126 percent? Because the government, even with its tax cuts, has not reduced taxes enough to keep up with what inflation has done to push your income dollars into higher and higher income tax brackets.

The 1981 Economic Recovery Tax Act attempted to remedy the problem of tax-bracket creep caused by inflation. It provided for a minimal 1981 tax reduction and 10 percent tax cuts to take effect July 1, 1982, and 1983. After 1984, the individual income-tax brackets, zero-bracket amount (see following) and personal exemptions are to be adjusted for inflation based on increases in the Consumer Price Index. The tax reduction from 1982 to 1984 is not as large as it might initially appear. If you earned $56,700 in 1982 and 1984, your after-tax income will increase from $40,200 to $41,800. That is only a 4 percent increase in after-tax income over two years. You will still be paying over $15,000 in taxes, not including your state and city taxes. Moreover, if all else fails in the government's effort to balance the budget, taxes may be raised once again, either through direct repeal of the cuts or through repeal of the indexing of tax brackets.

In fact, if Congress were really serious about tax cuts, it would have made the indexing of the tax brackets concurrent with the tax cuts. The way the system is now, if we have 8 to 10 percent inflation for the next three years, the tax cut will be made meaningless. For example, if you made $50,000 in 1981 and are married with two children, your tax liability, not taking into account itemization, was approximately $14,500 (calculating Social Security at 6.5% of $29,700). If 10 percent inflation continues through 1984, then in 1984 your income will be approximately $66,000 and your tax liability for 1984 would be $19,000 (calculating Social Security at 7% of $40,000). In 1981, you have $35,500 to spend after taxes. At 10 percent inflation, you would need $47,250 in 1984 after taxes just to stay even. Based on $66,500 of income and $19,000 of taxes for 1984, you would have after-tax dollars of $47,500 in 1984. You judge whether there is a significant tax cut that takes place between 1981 and 1984.

Moral: Do not look to the government to provide satisfactory tax relief in the long run.

What can you do about higher and higher taxes? First, make sure you pay no more in taxes than you are legally required to. Each year, you should employ a bona fide tax return preparer to make certain you are taking advantage of all permissible deductions, credits, income averaging and the like.

Second, develop your own income-tax planning strategy, based on the next seven chapters. Create a balance in your tax-planning program and attempt to use at least one idea from each of the next seven chapters (except for the chapter on marital discord, which you want to avoid if at all possible). But before you start developing your own tax-planning strategy, consider what tax planning is all about and how it ties in with the manner in which taxes are computed.

The Basics of Tax Planning

Personal income-tax planning consists of (a) reducing or shifting income (such as transferring income to children), or (b) increasing deductions (such as by investing in a tax shelter that generates losses, or by making charitable contributions at the end of December). One of the keys to effective planning is understanding the essential steps of computing income and deducting certain expenses.

In spite of the complexity of Internal Revenue Service (IRS) tax forms, learning the mechanics of calculating your personal income tax is like learning the soft shoe with a couple of side steps.

1. Add up all your *gross income*—include wages, interest, dividends, capital gains—and reduce any business income by business expense.[1]
2. Subtract from item 1 the following expenses: alimony, 60% of long-term capital gains, Keogh and IRA contributions, moving expenses, employee business expenses (such as car expenses). The

result of item 1 minus item 2 is your adjusted gross income. At this point, you can either go to the tax tables (see Appendix A) to calculate your tax liability (taking into account the number of dependents you claim), or you can itemize your deductions.[2]

3. Itemizing your deductions means that you subtract further from your adjusted gross income the following: interest payments, state and local taxes, charitable contributions, tax-advice payments and medical expenses.[3] Medical expenses, except health-insurance premiums and drugs, are only deductible to the extent that they exceed 3% of your adjusted gross income.* One-half of health-insurance premiums are deductible up to $150. The remaining balance of health-insurance premiums and drug expenses in excess of 1% of adjusted gross income are combined with all other medical expenses in computing the amount subject to the 3% limitation.[4]

4. Once you have calculated your itemized deductions, you must add back in the zero-bracket amount that pertains to your filing status. For example, the zero-bracket amount for single taxpayers in 1982 was $2,300 and for married taxpayers filing jointly was $3,400. The zero-bracket amount functions as the equivalent of itemized deductions for people who do not itemize. Thus it does not help you to itemize deductions unless your itemized deductions exceed the zero-bracket amount applicable to your filing status.

5. Subtract your net itemized deduction (item 4) from your adjusted gross income (item 1 minus item 2).

6. Go to the tax tables in Appendix A to calculate your tax liability in item 5, taking into account your number of dependents.

7. Add Social Security taxes at an approximate 9% rate on income up to $32,400 for 1982 if you are self-employed. If you are not self-employed, Social Security will be approximately 7% of income up to $32,400.

8. If you have been involved in a tax shelter during the year, you may have some additional tax to pay on tax-preference items (see Chapter 7). Also, if you had a very large amount of long-term capital gains, you may have an alternative minimum tax to pay (see Chapter 4).

Naturally there are complexities involved in determining such matters as a taxpayer's filing status, who can be taken as a dependent, what

---

* The 1982 Tax Act increased the 3% limitation for medical expenses to 5%. This makes medical-reimbursement plans more valuable than ever. (IRC §213)

is a medical expense, whether there is any limit to the amount of charitable contributions that can be taken, what exactly constitutes income and on and on. These knotty little questions and others like them are *not* discussed in this book. They can be answered by your tax-return preparer, by the IRS's own Publication 17 (which is free) or by an income-tax preparation guide such as J. K. Lasser's *Your Income Tax*.

You will be looking forward in this book, not backward. Tax planning is a process of gaining some control over your tax liability; it is not being a passive planner. In order to reduce your personal income-tax liability, you must take action. This book provides you with some action-oriented ideas that, if they are properly implemented (and in most cases you will need your attorney or tax adviser to help you with this), will have you paying less taxes each year.

You may have heard of the advantages of having a balanced portfolio of investments. This same principle works in income-tax planning. Compare the following with your own portfolio of ways to reduce your income tax:

1. Purchase your own home.
2. Pay charitable contributions at the end of the year, not at the start of the next.
3. Acquire enough life insurance to take care of your family if you check out early.
4. Make an interest-free loan to your children or to a trust established for their benefit.
5. Put some of your investment money into a single-premium deferred annuity.
6. Get into at least one tax-shelter investment, such as residential real estate or an oil and gas lease.
7. Make a gift of appreciated stock to your children.
8. Set up an IRA even if you are already covered by a qualified plan maintained by your employer.

If you are not already doing all these things, the next few chapters of this book should be valuable reading for you.

chapter 2

How to Pay for College

Suppose you are making a comfortable living but are concerned about the cost of college for your ten-year-old daughter, Amy. You anticipate that when she is ready to go to college, tuition will cost $10,000 to $14,000 per year. One of the things you would like to do is start saving now for Amy's college education.

Here's what you can do. Set up a trust for Amy's benefit that will last for ten years and one month, over which you will have no control. If your spouse combines with you in making a gift to the trust, you can contribute up to $45,289 this year without any estate- or gift-tax consequences. At the end of the ten years and one month, the property you contribute to the trust will revert back to you. During that period of time, income generated by the trust property will be taxed to Amy, at her tax bracket. Amy will also have the benefit of the exclusions for interest and dividends, and she will be entitled to a $1,000 personal exemption. Thus the income paid for the trust to Amy will be subject to very favorable income tax rates.

Moreover, if you want to increase further the trust income, you can make an interest-free loan of cash to the trust, payable back to you on demand. However, there is some risk involved with any interest-free loan.

As long as Amy saves the income paid to her to apply to future college needs, you can still deduct her as a dependent.

One of the most common dilemmas facing a taxpayer in a high tax bracket is the prospect of financing a college education for children. It is an enormous expense and, with inflation, one that grows agonizingly more so each passing year. Yet there are three ways to plan now so that your dollars will go further each year in building your son's or daughter's college nest egg or in paying an offspring's current college expenses. The three ways we will discuss here permit you to retain ownership or use of the assets you have so that you do not have to give up property totally to finance your children's college education.

The most prudent way to save tax dollars for the payment of college tuition is to take advantage of something called a Clifford or short-term trust.

The Clifford Trust

What a Clifford Trust Can Do for You

A Clifford Trust is a trust that lasts for at least ten years and one day.[1] Income generated by trust assets is distributed to the beneficiary you name, who should be in a lower tax bracket than you are.[2] This enables you to have more after-tax dollars for yourself and your beneficiary than if you had received the income and paid the tax at your own tax rate.

At the same time, you retain for your own future needs a "reversionary" interest in the property that makes up the trust; this means that after a minimum of ten years and one day—perhaps when your income is less—the property and its income will be yours again. This enables you to limit your current tax burden at a time when your income from other sources is high but still to retain a future interest in these properties, so that when you need them later, they will be there. This is a great way to help save money for your child's college expenses and still have your hard-earned assets when you need them. You can also use a Clifford Trust to support an aging relative who is in a lower tax bracket than you.

To decide whether a Clifford Trust would work well for you, ask yourself:

1. Do I have a secure present income that places me in a high tax bracket?
2. Do I have income-producing property that I do not need now, but that I would like to hang onto for the future (such as when I retire)?
3. Is there someone in my family who depends on my support or who may need my financial aid in the future and who is in a significantly lower income tax bracket than I?

If your answer to each of these questions is yes, the Clifford Trust can help you out.

A point of interest—the contract to receive royalties from this book has been assigned to a Clifford Trust for the benefit of the author's children. In the author's opinion, tax planning begins with the family unit. No child is too young to benefit the family by serving as a taxpayer—at the lowest tax rate available. Money accumulated in the children's names may be used for extraordinary expenses such as camp or a college fund.

Clifford Trust Technicalities

There are several legal requirements you must beware of in setting up this trust. For example, in establishing the trust, you must be careful not to retain any discretionary control over it; if you do, the IRS will label you the true owner of the income and defeat your tax-saving purpose.[3] In order to stay within the IRS requirements, you yourself should not be trustee of the trust unless income is required to be distributed currently and certain other requirements are satisfied. Otherwise, the IRS may claim that you never divested yourself of the income earned by the trust. Nevertheless, you may want to name yourself or your spouse as trustee, but in this area, you must consult an attorney who is experienced in drawing up Clifford Trusts. See Appendix B for a model Clifford Trust.

Whatever you do, be sure that you allow enough time for the effective transfer of property to the trust so that the trust is in fact alive for at least ten years and one day. Always leave extra time for potential delays that could occur in getting the property effectively transferred. If the intended trust property has not been transferred effectively in the eyes of the IRS for the full ten-year-and-one-day period, you will end up being taxed on the income generated by the assets in the trust.

You should also be careful to avoid the use of Clifford Trust income to provide the essentials of life for a person you are legally required to support (such as a minor child). Shelter, clothing and food are essentials; camp, private education and college expenses probably are not, although this varies from state to state. Clifford Trust income applied to essentials for a person you are required to support will be taxed to you.[4]

When you transfer property into the trust, you may have to file a gift tax return for this property. The gift generally will be 44 percent of the value of the property you transfer into trust for the ten-year-plus period. Each person can now make a tax-free gift of $10,000 per beneficiary, or a husband and wife can join together to make a tax-free gift of $20,000.[5] With a Clifford Trust, you and your wife could make a gift of up to $45,289 (44% × $45,289 = $20,000) in one year that would qualify as a tax-free gift.[6] If the contributed property is sold and a capital gain realized, you will probably have to pay capital-gains tax on this gain without having access to the trust funds to meet this bill. If you add more funds to the trust, there must be ten years plus still remaining for the trust. To allow you to make additions to the trust rather than establishing a new trust, your Clifford Trust should permit you to extend the terms of the trust each time you make an addition.

The Clifford Trust can be set up to permit you to borrow the money contributed to the trust. However, in order for you to do this, the following requirements must be satisfied:

1. There must be an independent trustee for your Clifford Trust.
2. You must pay a reasonable rate of interest.
3. You must put up adequate security for the amount borrowed.

If you do not comply with these requirements, you will lose the tax benefits of your Clifford Trust.

If you want to take your tax planning one step further, you could create a Minor's Trust (a special trust that generally requires distribution of income and principal when the beneficiary of the trust reaches age 21, as discussed in Chapter 3) as the beneficiary of your Clifford Trust. A Minor's Trust, unlike a Clifford Trust, can either accumulate income or distribute income to the beneficiary.[7] This enables you to use the income-tax bracket of the Minor's Trust to help reduce the total income taxes paid on the income generated by your Clifford Trust. For example, if $6,000 income is generated by the Clifford Trust and paid to your Minor's Trust, you might choose to have $2,000 left in and taxed to the Minor's Trust and $4,000 distributed and taxed to the minor beneficiary.

The Clifford Trust vs. Other Tax-Saving Techniques

If you can afford to give up control of property for at least ten years, the Clifford Trust is a better tax-savings vehicle than the interest-free loan or gift and lease-back, both of which are discussed later in this chapter. Unlike Clifford Trusts, interest-free loans and gift and lease-back are not spelled out in the Internal Revenue Code and do not have the blessings of the IRS; thus, if you can afford a Clifford Trust, you will avoid the risk of IRS hassle that exists with other tax saving ideas.

Interest-Free Demand Loans

An interest-free demand loan is a device by which someone in a high tax bracket (you) lends property to a taxpayer in a low tax bracket (your son or daughter whose college expenses you are trying to muster). The object of this device is to allow your son or daughter to enjoy the use of the property and its income without adverse tax consequences to you. Although the IRS has not accepted the interest-free loan as a legitimate tax savings device, the courts have permitted the desired tax results of interest-free loans.[8] The courts have held that you, the lender, need pay no gift tax on an interest-free demand loan, for you will retain immediate control over recalling the property. Your child then will pay tax on

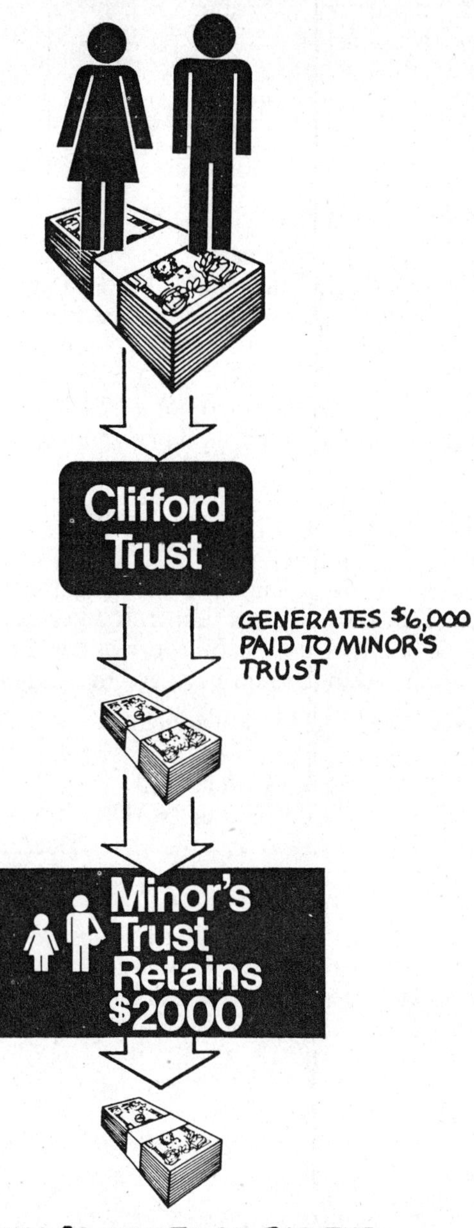
PARENTS $40,000
Clifford Trust
GENERATES $6,000 PAID TO MINOR'S TRUST
Minor's Trust Retains $2000
PAYS $4,000 TO OR FOR THE BENEFIT OF MINOR BENEFICIARY

the income generated by the property at his or her much lower tax rate. In this way, the property remains within the family and generates more after-tax income than it did before. You can use the interest-free loan to provide funds with lower taxed dollars for college educations, supplemental income for elderly relatives or for capital needed by young adults starting in business or buying their first home.

How to Go About Setting This Up

The idea is to lend cash to the person you wish to benefit but still to retain immediate control over the money. The loan must be a *demand note,* which means that the amount lent will be repaid on demand by the lender. Thus you can recall the borrowed money at any time you wish. Because the property is neither in your possession nor generating income for you personally, you should not be taxed on the income actually generated by it; as a result, this will lower your overall income and your tax bill.

Remember, the loan must be interest free, not a low-interest loan, and it must be a demand loan. Furthermore, the person who receives the benefit of the loan must either be of sufficient age and ability to contract a loan agreement or must act through a trustee such as the trustee of a Clifford Trust, discussed earlier. If a loan is made to a custodian of a minor, the IRS may treat the loan as a gift, since under the laws of most states, custodians do not have the authority to borrow money.

Sample Interest-Free Demand Note
with an Adult Child
PROMISSORY NOTE

$10,000.00   December 1, 1981
                                                    Cincinnati, Ohio

The undersigned, for value received, hereby promises to pay to the order of Ralph Small the sum of Ten Thousand Dollars ($10,-000.00) on demand with no interest from the date hereof.

If the loan is not repaid on the date of demand, it shall bear interest at the rate of 20% per annum until paid.

____

Ralph Small, Jr.

When to Act

If your daughter is eighteen and headed for college and you have cash available, should you make her an interest-free loan?

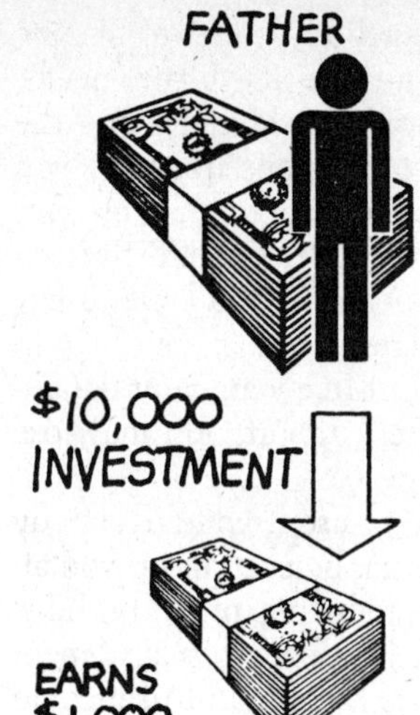

FATHER
FATHER
$10,000 INVESTMENT
$10,000 LOAN TO SON INTEREST FREE
EARNS $1,000
EARNS $1,000
TAX $500
$0 TAX
NET $500
NET $1,000
NET TAXES SAVED $500

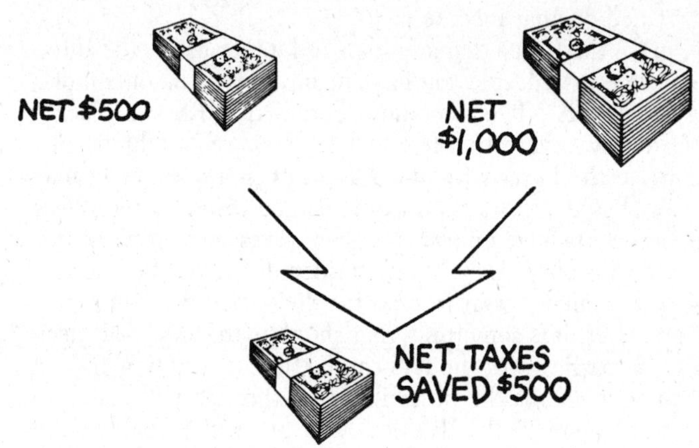

You should consider a number of factors, such as your own income needs, the likelihood of a change in your immediate and future needs, the availability of cash to be lent, the needs of your daughter and the reliability of your daughter. With respect to tax consequences, you should be in a relatively high tax bracket compared to that of your daughter or the trust you establish for her; otherwise, the effectiveness of this device as a tax savings will be lost. Generally if you have to pay for your daughter's college education, the interest-free loan can help finance this cost. However, if, through the interest-free loan, your daughter is able to provide more than one-half of her support, you may lose your dependency deduction for her.

Also, the interest-free loan is a good device to use if you are already supporting a daughter who is in a much lower tax bracket and if you already have a significant amount of income-producing property. This method can provide the same level of financial support to your dependent, but at a considerable tax savings, because the amount of income paid to the "borrower" will not pass through your taxable income—instead, it will go directly to the recipient and be taxed at his or her rate.

Warnings About Interest-Free Loans

Income from the interest-free loan should not be used to provide for the essentials of life (food, shelter and clothing) for a minor child. If it is, you will be taxed on that income.

Unless you make the loan a demand loan and interest-free, the Internal Revenue Service may decide you have made a gift of income, not a loan, taxable to you. (A gift of income occurs if the IRS can place a value on the benefit you have transferred to your son or daughter.) The IRS may challenge the interest-free loan as a gift in any event or may even attempt to charge you on the income earned on the interest-free loan. Yet the tax courts have upheld the tax advantages of interest-free loans in nearly all instances they have considered to date. So the fact that the IRS may challenge your interest-free loan should not stop you from acting. However, it is something that should enter into your decision making, since battles with the IRS can be time consuming and expensive, and there is always the possibility that the IRS will come up with a winning argument. If the IRS does win, you will probably be in no worse position for your efforts except for interest charges for late payment of taxes, which may be substantial.

The IRS has some compelling arguments it could make that would destroy the value of interest-free loans. However, the IRS has chosen not to make these arguments in any of the cases it has litigated to date. If you do make an interest-free loan, keep the risks in mind.

Furthermore, as already indicated, do not make an interest-free loan to a minor son or daughter, since a minor (or in most states even the custodian of the minor) does not have the legal capacity to borrow money, and the transfer may therefore be treated as an outright gift. Use a trust instead as a vehicle to which you can make the interest-free loan.

Finally, you run the risk that something will happen to your principal (your 80-year-old relative may run off with the loot) and that you may never get all your money back. One way to alleviate this risk is to require the borrower to put up adequate collateral.

Gift and Lease-Back or Loan-Back Arrangements

There is yet another way to transfer income to a lower-bracket tax-payer. This method is through something called a *gift and loan-back* (or *lease-back*). Again, there are very rigid requirements as to how this transaction must be structured to avoid IRS problems.

How They Work

Suppose you own an office building, which you use in your business and which is fully depreciated. Your son, age sixteen, will soon be heading for college. Since you do not want to give up control of your office building forever, you establish a Clifford Trust, discussed before, to which you give your office building, and have the trust lend or lease the property back to you. The net effect of this is to transfer income from you to the trust, which will distribute it to your son for tax purposes and give you the use of the building for your own continuing business needs. Plus, with the Clifford Trust, you will get the property back after ten years. You generate an interest or lease deduction on your tax return and lower your overall income (and income tax) by transferring ownership of income-producing property to the trust for your son, who is in a lower tax bracket than you are. And the family as a whole has more money after taxes are paid. Note in the following example that a gift tax return has to be filed to report the gift in excess of the statutory maximum for tax free gifts.

In order to minimize the risk of an IRS challenge to the deductibility of rent paid on the gift/lease-back to a Clifford Trust or any other type of trust, it is very important that the transaction be set up properly.

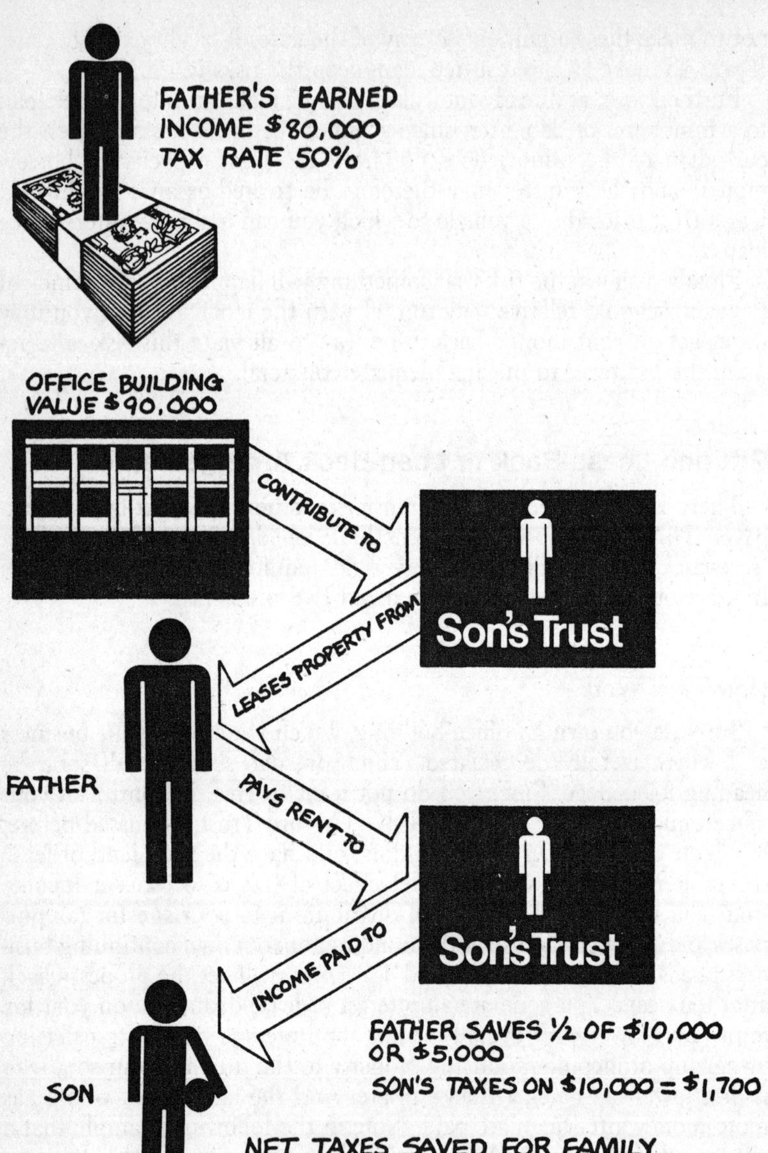

FATHER'S EARNED INCOME $80,000 TAX RATE 50%
OFFICE BUILDING VALUE $90,000
CONTRIBUTE TO
Son's Trust
LEASES PROPERTY FROM
FATHER
PAYS RENT TO
Son's Trust
INCOME PAID TO
SON
FATHER SAVES ½ OF $10,000 OR $5,000
SON'S TAXES ON $10,000 = $1,700
NET TAXES SAVED FOR FAMILY PER YEAR IS $3,330

Tax-court decisions indicate that the following guidelines should be followed:[9]

1. An experienced and independent trustee, such as a corporate fiduciary, should be used. *Avoid* using the grantor, a friend or a relative as trustee.
2. All documents should be executed properly, including the trust instrument, the deed and a written lease.
3. The rental income should be set at a fair market rate—one that is bargained for between the trustee and the grantor of the trust and that they agree is reasonable.
4. The trust document must spell out the powers and duties of the trustee, including specifically the power to lease the property.

If all these items are properly taken care of, the risk of challenge by the IRS will be minimized.

Extra money generated by a gift/lease-back can be used to pay for college, to help an elderly relative with bills or to finance other matters that are not legal support obligations.

Although our example has used a building, the property you transfer may be either as tangible as equipment used in your business or, as mentioned earlier, simply cash. If you transfer equipment or other tangible property, the property should be fully depreciated so that you are not transferring something that has a tax benefit to you.

Any direct transfer in excess of $10,000 will be treated as a taxable gift, and you should examine Chapter 14 to determine what impact this may have on you. Remember that only 44 percent of the transfer to a Clifford Trust is generally treated as a gift subject to allowance for tax free gifts.

When to Act

The best time is when you are in a high tax bracket, with an accumulation of income-producing property and with family members in need of extra financial support. Also, the gift should tie in with your overall estate planning and *not* be something you do solely for the income-tax advantages.

Aspects to Be Wary Of

In making a gift and loan-back or lease-back of income property, two separate transactions are involved. First, you must make a *completed gift*. This means you must completely divest yourself of the property—

you retain no interest—and deliver that property over to the recipient. You can do this, for example, by making a deposit of your check in the bank account of your son or by transferring real property through a general warranty deed. Once you have given him the property, you must make certain you borrow the money back from him via a *bona fide indebtedness*. Use a promissory note, making the transaction an unconditional and enforceable obligation on your part to repay on demand the amount borrowed, plus interest. Or enter into a bona fide lease contract. *You must satisfy the technical requirements of making a gift and then a loan or lease in order to keep the IRS satisfied.*

If the IRS feels you failed to make a completed gift or an enforceable loan with adequate security, it will not allow the interest deduction or deduction for rent on your tax return. Keep the interest rate on your loan or the rental value on a building you transfer in line with market levels, so that the IRS will have no reason to doubt your transaction, and be certain to use an independent trustee if you have made the gift to a trust.

The Business Purpose Requirement

One federal circuit court has indicated that a gift and lease-back or loan-back transaction is valid only if there is a business purpose for the entire arrangement.[10] However, the better line of thinking, which has been adopted by the majority of the federal circuits, is that the business necessity only pertains to the actual lease transaction, which must be considered by itself *after* the completed gift has been made. The Fifth Circuit, nevertheless, has attempted to combine the gift and lease-back into one transaction and has attached a business necessity requirement to the combined transaction. While we think the Fifth Circuit Court of Appeal's thinking is incorrect, you may pay some attention to this approach if you live in the states of Florida, Georgia, Louisiana, Texas, Mississippi or Alabama, all of which were formerly included in the Fifth Circuit.

One Final Caution

If you make an outright gift with the intention that there be a loan-back to you, make sure the family member you choose is someone you can depend on. You do not want the loan to be called at a time that is not beneficial to you. The idea is for you to continue to have use of the property after borrowing it or leasing it back—so make sure you pick a family member who is reliable.

A Tip for People with Young Children

Suppose you have a two-year-old for whom you would like to start accumulating funds for private school or a college education, and you do not have much available cash. What can you do? Lend a portion of the cash available to you (such as $4,000) on an interest-free demand-loan basis to a trust that is established for your child. If the money is invested at 15 percent per year, you will have saved yourself income tax on $600 of additional income, while the trust for the benefit of your child can distribute the income to your child's account, income-tax free. To be on the safe side, demand that the loan be repaid at the end of each December, and if your trustee wants to borrow again, make another interest-free demand loan the following January. After several years, you will have started to build up a nice nest egg for your child.

Other Ideas

If you own your own business, it may make sense to put an older child on the payroll as long as there is a bona fide service that will be provided by your child (see Chapter 20). Also, the establishment of a trust for minor children discussed in Chapter 3 provides an excellent opportunity to make a gift to children of cash that can accumulate for their college expenses and can also serve as a vehicle for interest-free loans and gifts and borrow or lease-back. Finally, if you are insurance oriented, a whole-life insurance policy or annuity owned by your son or daughter can accumulate a cash value that can be used for the payment of college tuition. See Chapter 6 for a discussion of the new "high yield" life-insurance products that provide for a rapid accumulation of the cash value. See Chapter 5 for a discussion of the single-premium deferred annuity, which provides a rapid buildup of interest on a tax-deferred basis.

chapter 3

How to Make Gifts in Style

For Christmas, Don Boardman gave each of his adult children a hundred shares of Chieftain Development Company stock, which at the time of the gift was selling for $18 per share. Don had paid only $3 per share for the stock.

One of Don's sons, Robert, wanted to extend his father's generosity to his own one-year-old daughter, Julie. Robert gave the Chieftain stock to his wife, Angie, as custodian for Julie under the Uniform Gifts to Minors Act.

When Angie, as custodian, sold the stock, Julie was taxed on the gain, which was the difference between the selling price and the $300 that had originally been paid for the stock. The $1,500 of long-term capital-gain income was taxed to Julie at her tax rate, and since Julie had no other income, no income tax had to be paid.

The proceeds of the sale were invested by Angie in high-yield certificates of deposit (which were tax free to Julie in her tax bracket), and a nice little nest egg was started for Julie's college education.

Making a gift means giving up something of value to you for the benefit of another person. Once you realize you have a "giving" spirit, the most important restriction on how you give is how much you can afford. By understanding the tax implications of making gifts, you may find that you are able to afford much more than you originally thought.

Making gifts can cause the shifting of income from a taxpayer in a high bracket to a taxpayer in a lower tax bracket. You can structure the transfer of income-producing property to meet a variety of purposes and needs. You can set aside assets that will continue to build up, to be used later for your children's college education or to support an elderly family member. In addition, making gifts can have a favorable impact on your estate planning.

The Joy of Intrafamily Gifts

If you have accumulated income-producing assets and have a secure salary or other sources of income, you should consider making gifts to

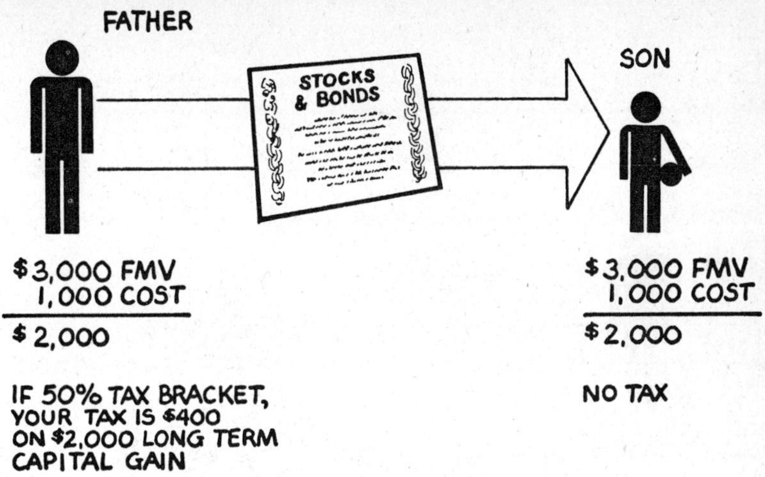

family members who are in a lower tax bracket. If possible, you should make a gift of appreciated property so that the capital gain on the property will be taxed at a lower rate than if you had sold the property.

Suppose you acquired 100 shares of stock in 1976 for $10 per share that appreciated to $30 per share in 1981. If you are in a 50 percent tax bracket and think it is time to sell the stock, making a gift of the stock to your son will save you $400 in taxes, assuming your son has no other income.

The primary advantage of making gifts to family members is that the tax paid by your son or daughter on the income earned on your gift will be much less than the tax you would have paid. For this reason, any property you give should either be high-income-yielding property or converted into such property. Let's take a look at the gift of an interest-bearing bond to a son who is in a zero tax bracket.

When making the intrafamily gift, do not overlook the requirements for a valid gift under IRS guidelines.[1] Be sure to meet the following requirements:

1. You have the capacity to make the gift.
2. You intend to make a complete transfer of ownership.
3. You completely divest yourself of the property.
4. You make full delivery of the gift to your donee, who accepts control.

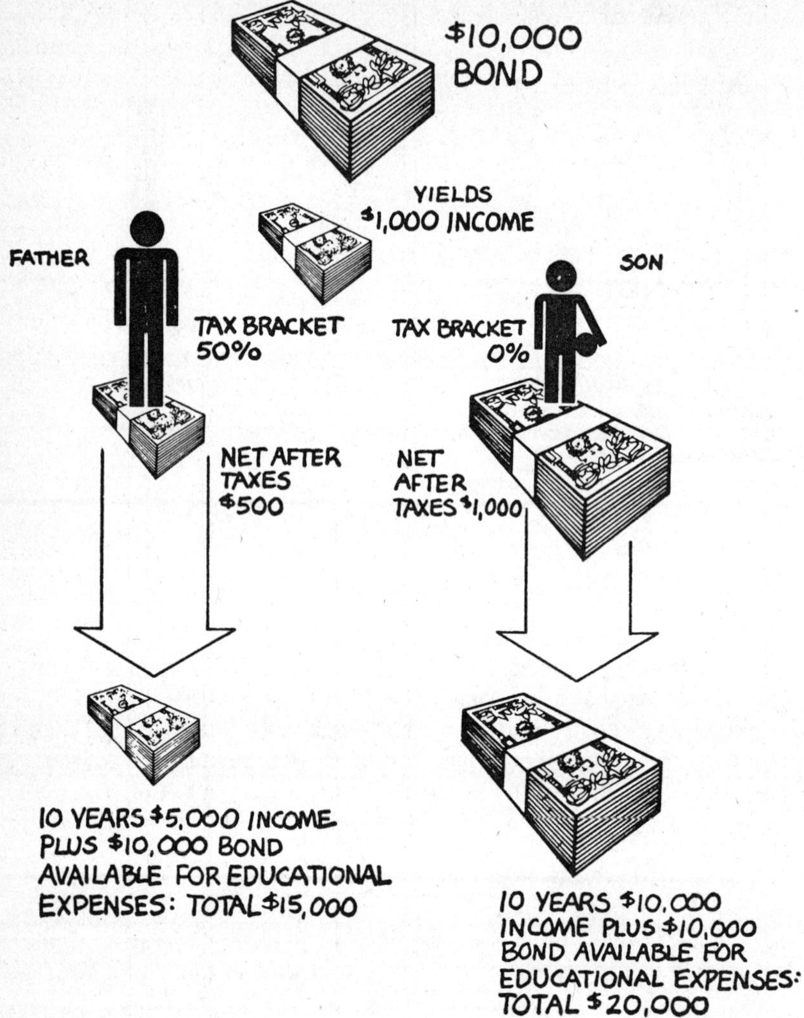

In addition, make certain that your gifts are tied to your estate plan. Under IRS rules, you can now give up to $10,000 worth of property each year to each of your "donees" without incurring tax.[2] By having your wife join in your gift, the limit becomes $20,000 per year per person.[3] Therefore, if you spread your giving over a period of years, you may limit the gift each year and avoid any gift tax. If you are in a position in which you can make annual gifts, consider making gifts of up to $10,000 per year to each child. Over a period of years, this can result in very substantial income tax savings and help your estate-tax situation.

For a more complete discussion of the estate-tax advantages of making gifts, see Chapter 14.

Also, the 1981 act now permits you to give an unlimited amount to children for the actual payment of college tuition. This used to be a problem for people whose children had college expenses exceeding the amount that would qualify as a gift. One possibility this creates for the elderly or dying parent is to make a contractual arrangement with a college for the prepayment of four years of tuition for a child. This obligation would reduce the size of the parent's estate while providing a substantial benefit to the child.

In any event, do not use the income taxed at your child's lower tax bracket for an expense (such as food, shelter and clothing) you are obligated to pay. If the income is used for such a purpose, the income will be taxed to you at your tax rates.[4]

Gifts to Minor Children

Gifts to minor children are generally made to a custodian for the child under the Uniform Gifts to Minors Act. The custodian holds legal title to the property, but the child is taxed on any income generated by the property. In most cases, the spouse of the donor should be the custodian, although in community-property states, the custodian should be a brother or sister (see Chapter 17). If you plan to make gifts to minor children over a period of time or want to be able to borrow back the gift as discussed in the previous chapter, the establishment of a trust should be considered.

Gifts in Trust

Through a trust, you can transfer property or investments for the benefit of family members but retain control over the ultimate disposition of the property itself. The Clifford or short-term trust discussed in the prior chapter is an example of how a trust can be set up for your gift giving. By establishing a trust for your intended beneficiary, you are able to determine with the trustee the manner in which the income is either distributed or accumulated. Also, the trust is a separate tax-paying entity; therefore, the trust income will be taxed either to the trust (if the income is accumulated)[5] or to the beneficiaries (if they receive the income).[6] In either event, the beneficiaries receive the benefit of the income and you do not have to pay tax on the income generated at your tax rate.

In order to create a valid trust to accomplish the intended income tax savings, you must relinquish certain rights. If you retain the right to revert the income or principal interest to yourself or to change the beneficiaries or their interests, the trust may not be recognized by the IRS, and the income will be taxed to you.[7] Also, the trust must specify that it is not for the "support" of your dependents, or the income will continue to be taxed to you.[8]

There are three basic types of trusts you can use for gift-giving purposes, all of which are irrevocable, meaning they cannot be changed once they are set up. The Clifford Trust, discussed in the previous chapter, permits you to make a gift of property that will revert back to you at the termination of the trust, which must be at least ten years and one day after property was contributed to the trust. The two other types of irrevocable trusts are a Minor's Trust and a Crummey Trust.

The Minor's Trust

There are usually two objectives to keep in mind in setting up an income-tax-saving trust. First, you want the income generated by the trust assets to be taxed to someone other than yourself. Second, you want the contribution to the trust to be treated as a gift of a present interest (eligible for tax free gift allowance) so that you will get the benefit of the $10,000 exclusion ($20,000 if you are married and your spouse joins with you in making the gift). In order to accomplish both these objectives with minor children, a Minor's Trust should specify the following:

1. Income may be accumulated in the trust or paid out for the benefit of the child.
2. Any accumulated income and principal must be payable to the beneficiary upon reaching age 21. If the beneficiary elects, the trust can continue past age 21 but only with the option of the beneficiary to terminate it at any time.
3. If the child dies before age 21, the trust assets must be paid to the minor's estate or the person appointed under the minor's will if the minor has made a valid will.

Because of the requirements of a Minor's Trust, a separate trust should be established for each child.[9] The Minor's Trust can be used as the recipient of an interest-free loan or for the gift and lease-back or loan-back transactions discussed in Chapter 2. In either case, the trust document should give broad powers to the trustee, so that the trustee can either borrow or lend money, as the case may be.

Some tax practitioners like to make the grantor of a trust that is to be the recipient of an interest-free loan *different from* the lender of the money. The reason for this is that the IRS might argue that a *revocable* trust situation exists if the grantor and lender are the same person.

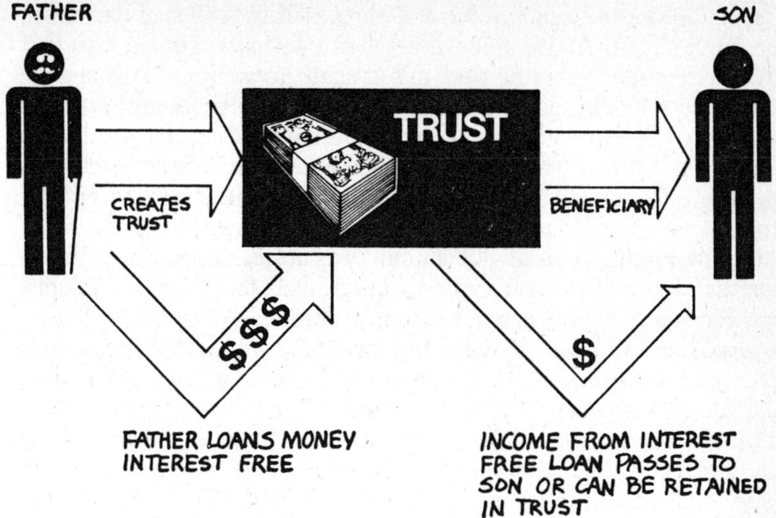

Under a *revocable* trust, the grantor is always taxed on the trust's income. To avoid this result, all you have to do is make your spouse the grantor of the trust (if you plan to be the lender of the interest-free loan).

If income is accumulated in the trust, it will be taxed to the trust at the trust's tax rates. If the income is distributed to the beneficiary, the income will be taxed to the beneficiary at the beneficiary's tax rate. (Thus, the creation of a trust results in another taxpayer, who can be used to minimize income taxes.)

It is also possible for a Minor's Trust to be designed so that all the income will be distributed on an annual or more frequent basis. If this is the case, the trust does not have to terminate when the beneficiary attains age twenty-one and thus could be established to last for the lifetime of the beneficiary or for any lesser period of time. Also, when the principal is distributed from this trust, it does not have to go to the original beneficiary but could go to another sibling or person designated by the income beneficiary.

The Crummey Trust

The drawbacks to a Minor's Trust are: (a) inability to benefit more than one child from the trust, (b) mandatory payment of principal and accumulated income at age 21 unless the distribution of income is mandatory, and (c) payment of principal to the estate of a deceased child unless, again, the payment of income is mandatory.

One way around these problems is through the creation of a so-called Crummey Trust. A Crummey Trust derives its name from a case that permitted annual gifts to a trust to be treated as a present gift (eligible for the $10,000 annual exclusion) as long as the beneficiaries of the trust were able to withdraw the contribution made to the trust each year.[10] This right of withdrawal should not exceed $5,000 each year (even if your spouse joins with you in the gift); the reason for this is that the beneficiary is deemed to make a gift by not exercising his or her withdrawal rights. This $5,000 amount was not increased when the annual gift exclusion was increased from $3,000 to $10,000. Congress may remedy this discrepancy in the near future.

In addition to being designed to provide the withdrawal rights, your Crummey Trust can also be designed to provide for income on the trust assets to be taxed to (a) the trust; (b) one or more beneficiaries, including later-born children; (c) a combination of items a and b; and (d) yourself. You would only want the income in the trust to revert back to yourself if there were tax advantages to be gained. (This would be the case if you set up the Crummey Trust to purchase life insurance on your life, as is discussed in Chapter 11.)

In any event, the Crummey Trust can provide for income to be distributed to beneficiaries or accumulated in trust and does not need to terminate upon the attainment of any age by a beneficiary.[11] In other words, the Crummey Trust creates more flexibility for you than a Minor's Trust and still has all the advantages. See Appendix C for a model Crummey Trust for a minor.

All the trusts that have been discussed—Clifford, Minor's and Crummey—are irrevocable trusts. This means that once the trust is established, it cannot be amended or revoked. Thus, great care must be taken in the drafting of such a document. Also, the income-tax treatment of trust income depends on the language used in the trust, so an experienced attorney is a must for helping you implement your tax-savings trust. (See Chapter 25, Whom Do You Trust.) Generally your irrevocable trust must provide (a) that income will not be used to pay for an obligation you have to support minor children; (b) that income will not be used to purchase life insurance on your life or on your spouse's life; and (c) that you have no right to substitute assets for trust assets or to purchase assets from the trust for less than adequate consideration or to borrow money without giving adequate security.

None of the Above

If you are not concerned about the payment of estate taxes, you can establish a trust that does not comply with the requirements of a

Minor's Trust or a Crummey Trust but that will still provide the same favorable income tax results. However, it must contain the special provisions discussed already, and a gift-tax return must be filed each time you make a gift to the trust. Such a trust will enable you to transfer appreciation on the property contributed to the trust out of your estate. However, your contribution to the trust will not be treated as a present gift and will not be covered by the $10,000 gift exclusion.

Gifts to Charities

One of the best methods to meet your social or moral obligations and at the same time accomplish income-tax savings is to give appreciated property to charities.[12] You can deduct from your taxable income the full value of most gifts to charity. Because of the tax saved by this deduction, the actual cost of the gift is only a fraction of the value.

Suppose you purchased stock ten years ago for $1000, which has appreciated to $11,000. Assume you are in the 50% tax bracket. If you sell the stock, your tax will be 50% × $4,000 (40% of $10,000) or $2,000. Your net cash gain will be $9,000. If you give the stock to charity, you will save $5,500 in taxes (from the $11,000 deduction). Your net cash gain will be $5,500. The actual cost to you of the $11,000 gift is $3,500.

NOTE: You only get to deduct the fair market value of an appreciated capital asset if you have held the asset for twelve months or more. Also, there are limitations on the amount you can deduct in a calendar year, if you are considering a very large gift.

The next time you think of calling someone to haul away your used appliances or furniture, consider donating these items to charity. The fair market value of these items will be deductible from your taxable income.[13] If the appraised value is more than $200, you will want receipts or an appraisal to preserve your deduction if it is questioned by the IRS.

If you have items of art or of an educational nature, consider donating these to a charity that is specifically designed for such use, such as donating a painting to an art museum. The fair market value of any of these would be deductible against your taxable income.

In making gifts to charities, it is important that you keep records of the date, description of property, fair market value, original cost, agreements as to the use of the property and the amount you claim as a deduction. Be sure you give to a valid charity that has been set up for religious, scientific, literary, educational or other charitable purposes.

Charitable giving can be a significant part of your estate-tax planning. If you are contemplating making a large gift but are hesitant to do so during your lifetime, read Chapter 16 to learn how you can benefit in both an income-tax and estate-tax manner from charitable giving during your lifetime.

You might also consider a gift to a *charitable remainder trust*, which permits you to retain an income interest in the property conveyed while still receiving a present charitable deduction. If you do not have a present need for income but may have a need for your principal later on, you should consider the *charitable lead trust*, which distributes income to a charity and returns the principal to you or to your designated beneficiary upon termination of the trust. See Chapter 16 for a more detailed discussion of the charitable remainder trust and charitable lead trust.

Charitable Contributions if You Do Not Itemize

Taxpayers who do not itemize deductions on their tax returns are now permitted to make a limited deduction for charitable contributions. The deductible amount is based on both a percentage of the contribution and a maximum amount that is permitted in accordance with the following table:

Tax Year Beginning	Percentage of Contribution	Maximum Contribution Taken into Account
1982	25%	100
1983	25%	100
1984	25%	300
1985	50%	no limit
1986	100%	no limit

For example, if you do not itemize and make a charitable contribution in 1983, you would be permitted a charitable deduction of $25. This deduction expires for tax years beginning after 1986 unless it is renewed by Congress.

Charitable Giving by the Corporate Owner

If you are the sole shareholder of a corporation, you have an extraordinary opportunity to use your corporation to help you with your charitable giving. By making a gift of a portion of your stock to your favorite charity, you receive a tax deduction equal to the fair market value of the stock. Since the charity really would prefer cash over stock in a closely

SOLE SHAREHOLDER
100 SHARES XYZ
CORPORATION
VALUE $100,000

20 SHARES GIVEN AS
$20,000 CHARITABLE DONATION

$20,000 PAID
BY CORPORATION
FOR STOCK
CHURCH SELLS STOCK
TO CORPORATION

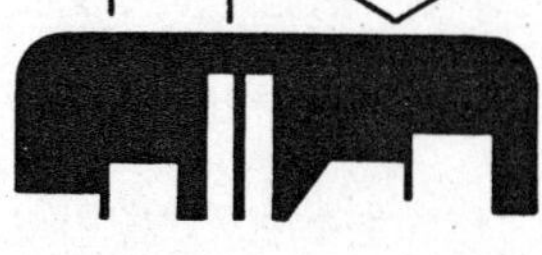

XYZ CORPORATION

STILL SOLE SHAREHOLDER

held corporation (and since you really do not want the charity to own stock in your company), your corporation in most cases can redeem the stock from the charity. In this way, you have been able to use corporate cash for charitable giving *and* get a personal income tax deduction.

When this transaction is completed, you are in the same position as before as the sole shareholder of the corporation. If you are in the 50 percent tax bracket, the $20,000 charitable contribution would save you $10,000 in taxes. If instead of making the charitable contribution and redeeming the stock, you had paid the $20,000 from the corporation to yourself as a bonus, you would have paid a tax of $10,000 and been in exactly the same position as though you had made the $20,000 charitable contribution (but your favorite charity would have nothing). The only difference is that the $20,000 paid as a bonus is deductible to the corporation, whereas the $20,000 paid to redeem stock is not deductible.

Do not get any type of firm commitment from the charity that it will redeem your corporation's stock before you actually transfer your stock; if you do, the IRS may challenge the tax benefit of your charitable gift and maintain that your corporation has made a dividend payment to you when it redeems your stock.

chapter 4

How to Time Income and Deductions

You are having the best income year of your life but are feeling nauseated just thinking about all the income tax you will have to pay. What can you do?

First, you can plan to use income averaging to lower the effective tax rate on your income. Second, you can take some of your short-term losses (if possible) or long-term capital losses to create a tax deduction of up to $3,000. Third, you can pay all your charitable contributions for next year at the end of this year. Fourth, you can pay your January mortgage at the end of December. Finally, to the extent possible, you can push a portion of your additional income into next year.

If, after following all these suggestions, you still calculate that you will pay far too much in income taxes, read Chapter 7 and learn about tax shelters for further tax savings.

Unless you have your own business which accrues income and expenses (an accrual-basis taxpayer), you are a cash-basis taxpayer and are required to report income in the year in which it is received and to deduct expenses in the year they are paid.[1] Although this method seems inflexible, in fact, it creates some substantial planning opportunities for you. You do have control over your tax liability and can do a number of things to reduce your current year's projected tax liability.

Shifting Income and Deductions

Generally you should shift taxable income from the present year to the next year because taxes are to be reduced through 1984, after which indexing of tax brackets to account for inflation is supposed to take effect.[2] Also, it is always better to defer paying tax dollars as long as possible so that you have use of those dollars for that time. Any money saved in the present year can be invested and earn a rate of return that will increase your net worth.

However, you may be faced with circumstances that change this basic rule. If, during the current year, you have an extremely large amount of itemized deductions (see Chapter 1), you may want to take the additional income this year. What you need to do is subtract from this year's income your itemized deductions in excess of the zero bracket amount ($2,300 for single taxpayers, $3,400 for married taxpayers)[3] and compare with your projections for the following year. If next year's income less itemized deductions in excess of the zero bracket amount is significantly greater than this year's, it may be advantageous for you to take more income this year. However, you have to compare next year's tax bracket for your income with this year's tax bracket.

Generally you will want to pay the charitable contributions that you would normally make early next year (plus any other deductible payments, such as for real-estate taxes, interest, deductible medical expenses) during but as late as possible in the current taxable year. The reason for this is that the current tax savings associated with the payments will be immediately available to you, and you will get the advantage of having made the payment as soon as you receive your refund check or, if you have to pay additional taxes, by April 15 of the following year.

> Every year in April, Paul gives $1,000 to Michigan University. He is in the 50 percent tax bracket, so he figures his contribution costs him only $500 net. However, he does not get the benefit of his contribution until April of the following year. If he had been able to invest his $500 on a 10 percent after-tax basis, he could have made an additional $50. Thus, his contribution actually costs him $550.

If instead Paul makes his contribution on the last day of December, he has given up the $500 he gets back in tax savings for only three and a half months, and his net cost is then only $512.50 ($500.00 plus $12.50 for the loss of the $500 during 3½ months).

Paul could also get a more immediate advantage from his $1,000 gift by having his withholding adjusted to reflect his decreased tax liability. This method should be combined with the end-of-the-year giving to maximize the benefits of charitable giving.

If you are in a marginal position with regard to whether to itemize (if your deductions are nearly equal to your zero bracket amount), you might consider combining all your deductible expenses in one year so that you itemize one year and take the zero bracket the next.

> Ted and Mary Jane own a home that creates about $2,400 in interest deductions each year. Also, they have property, state and city taxes of $500 and make charitable contributions of $500.

In 1982, they pay thirteen months of their home mortgage and pay the next year's charitable contributions in advance. Also, they withhold from their paychecks their full obligation for state taxes. For their efforts, they have increased their itemized deductions to $4,100 and now it is well worth their effort to itemize.

In 1983, they pay no charitable deductions, underpay to the extent possible on their state withholding (they get the advantage of paying the 1983 underpayment on their 1984 tax return) and pay only eleven months of their mortgage. In 1983, they minimize their tax liability by *not* itemizing.

There are times, also, when you will want to shift income as well as deductions from one year to the next. A change in tax rates as we have recently experienced is one important reason to shift income between years. When you know the tax rates are going to be lower the subsequent year, you should shift your income and deductions so that your taxable income is higher in that year. The idea is to reduce taxable income in the present year when the higher tax rates are in effect, and then pay the tax at a lower rate the following year. To use this money-saving technique, it is imperative that you stay abreast of all the changes in the tax laws relative to your situation.

Similar to this reason for shifting income and deductions into another tax year is a change in the taxpayer's status (single, married, head of household, surviving spouse) or exemptions (reaching age 65, blindness, change in dependents). A change in any of these will result in a change of rate or amount of tax. For the same reasons already discussed, you should shift income and deductions to a year that will result in the higher income being taxed at a lower rate. It is always best to arrange transactions so that taxable income is greatest in the year in which it will be taxed at the lowest rate.

How to Shift Income

For the most part, salaries and wages are not controllable by you unless you are self-employed and thus have a much wider degree of control over the receipt of income. However, you can control the timing of income from other sources. Thus the sale of stock or property that results in a gain or the receipt of a pension can be controlled by you so that it is received in a year when tax dollars can be saved. If you are contemplating the receipt of income you can control, see whether it should be received in another year. Delaying the receipt could greatly enhance the value of what you receive.

One option that is readily available to you for the shifting of income is to transfer some of your money-market assets to Treasury bills that mature next year. By doing this, you will defer the receipt of income on the cash invested until the T-bills mature. Otherwise, you would be taxed this year on the interest earned from your money-market investments.

Also, you can invest borrowed funds in deeply discounted bonds that mature next year or in future years. Since these bonds are government issued, you could obtain financing approaching 100 percent of the cost of the bonds. Part of your interest would be deductible this year, but you would not be taxed on the income until the maturity date of the bonds. Moreover, if the maturity date of the bonds is more than one year after you acquired them, you could be eligible for long-term capital-gain treatment on your income from the bonds. In order to be eligible for long-term capital-gain treatment, the discount (if original issue) must be less than .25 percent of the redemption price times the number of years to maturity.[4] If the discount is greater than this, the entire discount will have to be amortized over the life of the bond as interest income. If you are not buying an original issue, this rule does not apply.

Treatment of Capital Gains and Losses

You can achieve significant tax savings by carefully timing your capital gains and losses. Capital gains and losses are derived from the sale of capital assets such as stocks, bonds and investment real estate. Long-term capital gains and losses are those gains and losses that result from the sale of capital assets that have been held for more than one year.[5] Sixty percent of your net long term capital gain is not taxed. One half of long-term capital losses are deductible from your income, up to a total deduction of $3,000.[6] Short-term capital gains and losses are treated as income and losses dollar for dollar, with the net of short-term capital losses over gains being limited to $3,000 in one year. Also, when net long-term capital losses are combined with net short-term capital losses, the total deduction is limited to $3,000 in one year and the short-term capital losses are taken first.

There are two different dates to watch when considering the sale of capital assets. The first is the one-year anniversary of the purchase of the asset. This date will determine whether the gain or loss is short term or long term. The second is the end of the taxable year. Near the end of the year, you must decide whether to sell any capital assets in order to take advantage of the offsetting effects of gains and losses. It is at this time that the tax-planning strategy is effective.

If you have sold assets at a gain during the year, you may want to consider selling some assets at a loss near the end of the year. The result of this is that the loss will offset the gain, and no tax or a lesser tax will result from the transactions. Conversely, if you have incurred a capital loss during the year, you may want to take a gain on the sale of another asset so that the loss may be taken full advantage of in the taxable year. However, you do not want to use good income dollars (long-term capital gains of which only 40% are subject to taxation) to cancel out good loss dollars (short-term capital losses that are deductible dollar for dollar from ordinary income). But you do want to use long-term capital losses (which are deductible only fifty cents on the dollar up to a total deduction of $3,000) to offset short-term capital gains (which are included in your income on a dollar-for-dollar basis). To summarize, if possible, follow these rules to maximize your tax savings.

If You Have Already Taken	*Take Only*
short-term capital gain	long-term capital loss
short-term capital loss	DO NOTHING!
long-term capital gain	long-term capital loss
long-term capital loss	short-term capital gain or long-term capital gain if loss is more than $6,000

Warnings About Capital Asset Transactions

Suppose you want to sell some stock in order to take a capital loss, but you also want to retain ownership of the stock. If this is the case, you should purchase the same stock more than thirty days either before or after the contemplated sales date. Repurchasing the same stock within thirty days or less is known as a *wash sale* and will result in the loss being nondeductible. If the repurchase is made more than thirty days before or after, your loss will be deductible and your new basis in the stock will be the new purchase price. Therefore, in any future sale, the gain or loss will be reflected as a result of this new basis.[7]

NOTE: This thirty-day rule formerly did not apply to the sale of tangibles such as gold or silver. However, the 1981 tax act apparently has changed this by directing the IRS to issue regulations that would apply to wash sales of straddle positions (straddle positions here would include ownership of commodities).

As mentioned earlier, capital losses over and above capital gains are deductible up to $3,000. Therefore, any short-term capital loss larger than $3,000 or any long-term capital loss larger than $6,000 (because of the 50% exclusion) will not be deductible if there are no offsetting gains but will be carried over to subsequent years.

Any loss incurred on the sale of a personal asset such as a residence, an automobile or jewelry is not deductible.[8] Only losses on "investment assets" are deductible. However, any gain received on the sale of a personal asset should be included in income.

Alternative Minimum Tax*

When you are dealing with long-term capital gains, you must be aware of the alternative minimum tax provisions. Generally this tax is computed by adding to the taxpayer's gross income, less deductions, the taxpayer's itemized deductions in excess of 60 percent of the taxpayer's adjusted gross income (excluding medical, casualty losses, state and local taxes) plus the untaxed portion of his long-term capital gain. This total amount, reduced by a $20,000 exemption, is subject to the following tax rates: 10 percent on the first $40,000; 20 percent on the second $40,000; and 25 percent on the excess over $80,000.[9] If this tax is higher than your regular tax, you must also pay the excess over your tax liability or, in essence, you pay the higher tax. Be sure to have this tax calculated by your tax adviser before proceeding with the sale of property that will spin off very large long-term capital gains.

Disposition of Property

There are special tax savings pertaining to the disposition of property that can result in favorable tax benefits. They are the installment method of accounting and the tax-free exchange.

The *installment method of accounting* is used any time a capital asset is sold and the payment received in the year of sale is not 100 percent of the sales price. The *nontaxable exchange method* is utilized when property is exchanged for property of a like or similar nature. Either of these methods may save tax dollars when you are selling property.

Taxable income from an installment sale is computed by multiplying the gross profit percentage by the amount received during the year.[10] The gross profit percentage is computed as follows: (a) Subtract your adjusted basis (cost of the property less depreciation) in the property

---

* The 1982 Tax Act has combined the add-on minimum tax with a new alternative minimum tax that is essentially a 20 percent flat tax on the amount of alternative taxable income (adjusted gross income before net operating losses plus tax preference items generally associated with tax shelters) exceeding $40,000 (for married taxpayers filing jointly). Investment tax credits are not allowed as a deduction against this tax. (IRC §55)

from the sale price less any selling expenses. This results in the gain on the sale. (b) Divide this gain by the sales price less selling expenses. The resulting percentage becomes the gross profit percentage. This percentage is constant over the life of the payback period. If the sale originally resulted in a long-term capital gain, then the final result is multiplied by 40 percent. The amount received each year multiplied by your gross profit percentage is your taxable income resulting from the installment sale. The beauty of the method is that it lets you pay tax on the gain over the life of the installments, which results in the income being taxed in a lower tax bracket than if it were all bunched in one year.

You own a piece of farmland you paid $20,000 for over ten years ago. You decide to sell it for $200,000, payable at the rate of $40,000 per year for five years with interest on the unpaid balance of 14 percent per year.

Each year, of the $40,000 you receive, $4,000 will represent a return of your initial $20,000 basis and $36,000 will represent a long-term capital gain subject to the 60% deduction. Any interest you receive will be treated as ordinary income.

Like the installment-sale method, nontaxable exchange reporting is mandatory. It must be used if the circumstances warrant. Under a nontaxable exchange, no gain or loss is recognized when property held for productive use in a business or investment is exchanged only for property of a "like kind" that will also be held for use in a trade or business.[11] This can be of enormous benefit to a taxpayer who is "trading up" properties. It allows you an opportunity to dispose of your property, invest in new property and not be taxed on the transaction. In order to qualify, there must be an exchange of like properties that were and will be used for a business or investment. It is important to note that your basis in the new property for resale or depreciation purposes will be the same as your basis in the old property increased for any additional cash you pay for the new property. Also any "boot" (cash or property other than like kind) received in the exchange will result in recognition of gain to the amount of the boot received. It is not essential that the property that is exchanged be of a similar grade or quality. Thus apartment buildings can properly be exchanged for farm property. The only requirement is that the property be similar in nature and be held for a business or investment purpose.

A like-kind exchange can be created out of unlikely circumstances. Suppose you have owned a summer home in Michigan for fifteen years and have reached the age when you would rather have a winter home in Florida. In order to avoid the long-term capital gain on your Michigan property, find a buyer for the Michigan property and have him buy the

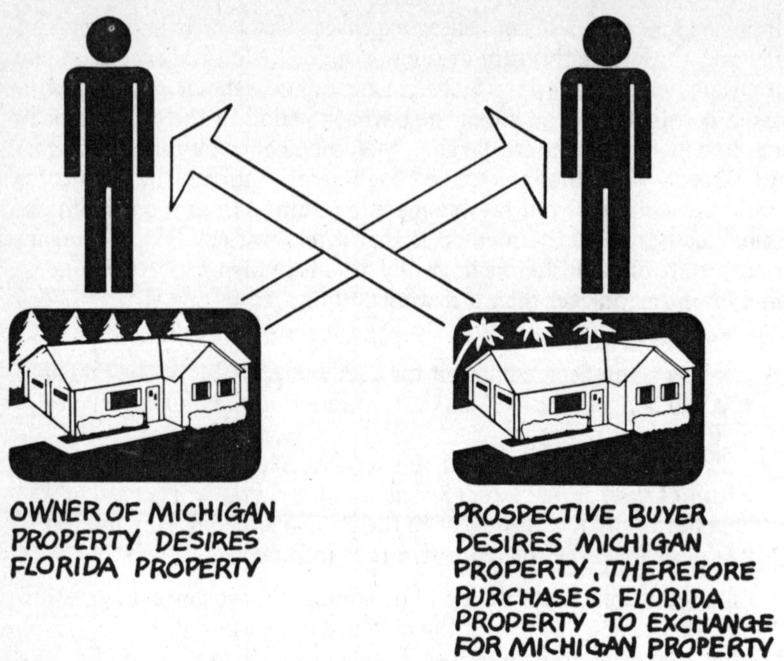

Florida property. Then you can exchange your Michigan property for his Florida property, all tax free to you.

Of course, any cash you receive on the deal in addition to the Florida property will be taxed to you as a long-term capital gain.[12]

Income Averaging

Someday you may find yourself in a situation where your income has increased substantially in one year as compared to previous years. In this situation, the benefits of income averaging allow you to apply a specific method for computing your income tax that has the effect of taxing the higher income as though it were earned over a five-year period.[13] This tax-computation method can result in significant tax savings, and you should always be aware of it when planning taxable transactions.

When You Should Consider Income Averaging

The provisions of income averaging are elective. You must make a choice in order to benefit from income averaging in a taxable year. However, you must meet certain requirements in order to qualify for income averaging. Usually, whenever you qualify for income averaging, it will be to your advantage to use it.

To be eligible, your averagable income (as explained later) must be greater than $3,000. When this occurs, you will save tax dollars by electing to income average. For instance, property dispositions may cause you to incur a large gain in one taxable year. Or the additional income of a previously nonworking spouse may result in additional taxable income. Any year in which a significant increase in taxable income occurs is a time to check the benefits of electing income averaging.

The procedure for income averaging is simply a methematical computation. Once your taxable income has been determined, it is merely a matter of following the different steps to find if income averaging can be used and if it will be advantageous. First, you must compute your averagable income. This is equal to the difference of the current year's taxable income over a base period income. The base period income is equal to 120 percent of your average taxable income for the four preceding years. As mentioned earlier, this averagable income must be greater than $3,000.

Using the tax rate schedules, the tax on the base period income is computed. Next, the tax is computed on the base period income plus 20 percent of the averagable income. The difference between these two taxes is then multiplied by 5 in order to compute the tax on the averagable income. This figure is then added to the tax on the base income in order to arrive at the total tax due. While this procedure may sound difficult, it is easily followed by filing Schedule G of Form 1040.

Tony, single, had taxable income of $18,000 in the previous four years. Because of a large capital gain, his taxable income for the present year, 1982, is $40,000.

base period income = 120% × $18,000 = $21,600
averagable income = $40,000 − $21,600 = $18,400

Since averagable income is more than $3,000, Tony can income tax average.

Twenty percent of averagable income is added to base period income.

20% × $18,400 + $21,600 = $25,280
tax on base period income ($21,600) = $3,938
tax on $25,280 = $5,110

The difference is multiplied by 5 and added to tax on base income to arrive at the total tax liability.

5 × ($5,110 − $3,938) = $9,798

Tax for Tony on $40,000 without income-averaging would have been $10,968.

Limitations on Income Averaging

Only residents or citizens are eligible for income averaging. Corporations, trusts and estates cannot benefit from these provisions.

In order to use the benefits of income averaging, you must have provided 50 percent or more of your own support during each of the four base period years. However, this support requirement does not apply if any one of the following conditions is met: (a) during the computation year, you attained age twenty-five, and during at least four of your taxable years beginning after you attained the age of twenty-one, you were not a full-time student; (b) more than one half of your taxable income for the computation year is attributable to work performed by you in substantial part during two or more of the base period years, or; (c) you file a joint return for the computation year, and not more than 25 percent of the adjusted gross income on the return is attributable to the otherwise disqualified individual.[14]

A change in marital or filing status during the base years or the taxable year will affect your ability to income-average and the computation of the amount. There are complicated rules that govern such situations, which you should review with your tax adviser.

chapter 5

How to Plan for Retirement

Henry Stennett was an independent plumber all his life. At age 65, he decided to retire and to receive his $800 per month tax-free Social Security dollars.

But more important, with all his children out of the nest, he and his wife sold their home for a $100,000 profit and purchased a much smaller home in Indianapolis and a condominium in Florida with the proceeds, without paying any tax on their profit.

Henry also elected to withdraw $1,500 each month from his single-premium tax-deferred annuity, which he had purchased six years ago for $40,000 and which had doubled in value.

Finally, Henry terminated his Keogh plan and, on a $100,000 distribution, paid a tax of less than $18,000. The remaining amount he placed in a money-market fund, using the interest to supplement his other retirement income.

If you are like most people, you have too many current obligations to be bothered with the thought of retirement. Yet there are investment opportunities that should fit in with your current tax planning objectives while at the same time enabling you to accumulate some additional wealth for retirement. Whatever you do, do not count too heavily on Social Security. If it is still around when you are ready to retire, it may be available in a very different form from what is available today. The savings incentives we are about to discuss were, in part at least, created to remove some of the burden from Social Security.

How Much Money Will You Need for Retirement?

The inflation of the 1970s and early 1980s has dramatically altered everyone's retirement plans. Because inflation has such a significant effect on how much money you will need for retirement, you must plan for how you can live with it. If inflation does not continue at the same high levels, you will still be better off as a result of your planning.

The first step in retirement planning is to calculate how much retirement income you will need, taking into account inflation. Here are the steps you should follow to make that determination.

1. Calculate in today's dollars how much retirement income you would need if you were to retire today.
    a. Take your current after-tax dollar income and subtract temporary expenses (child support, education, savings, and other expenses you will not have at retirement). This will give you your minimum retirement income.
2. Multiply this number by the inflation factor based on your years to retirement. Let's assume an 8 percent inflation factor for illustrative purposes. (If inflation is lower than 8 percent, other assumptions used throughout, such as the investment return on your money, will also change.)

Years to Retirement	Inflation Factor			
	6%	8%	10%	12%
5	1.338	1.469	1.611	1.762
10	1.791	2.158	2.594	3.106
15	2.396	3.172	4.177	5.473
20	3.206	4.661	6.727	9.646
25	4.291	6.848	10.834	16.998
30	5.742	10.062	17.449	29.958
35	7.684	14.784	28.101	52.794

Suppose your after-tax needs are $15,000 per year and you would like to retire in twenty years. At 8 percent inflation, you will need $69,900 per year of after-tax dollars to maintain your present style of living (4.661 × $15,000).

Where will all these dollars come from? If you refer to the part of this chapter that discusses Social Security, you will observe that if your present income is $35,000, you can expect to have 17 percent of that replaced by Social Security if the system is still around in basically the same form in twenty years. The same inflation factor of 4.661 must be applied to Social Security also, which means that we will assume Social Security will provide approximately $27,700 of the $69,900 you need (4.661 × .17 × $35,000).

The remaining $42,200 of after-tax income must be provided through your company's retirement plan, your own IRA account and your own savings.

The prospect of having to provide that much additional income each year when you are presently making only $35,000 per year is mind boggling. However, it may not be as difficult as it seems.

If inflation stays as high as 8 percent per year, interest paid on investments should also stay high and you should be able to receive a net after-tax return on your investments at age sixty-five of at least 10 percent. This would mean that you should plan to accumulate savings and retirement-plan monies that total $422,200 in twenty years. You could then live off the interest on your monies and save the principal to be used as a further aid in your retirement years to combat inflation.

Although the $442,200 amount looks large now, if you could invest $50,000 today at 12 percent compound interest, in twenty years, it would grow to more than $482,000. If you had started your planning ten years ago, you could easily have saved that $50,000 today and would have no worries about your retirement needs—as long as Social Security continues in its present status. If you are inclined to assume the worst, for example, that Social Security will not be available to you in any form when you are ready to retire, then today you would need to have about $75,000 to secure your retirement needs, all other assumptions remaining constant. Of course, one of these assumptions is that you can invest your money to earn after-tax interest of 12 percent or more. This brings us to the key to retirement planning and why it is so important for you to begin your savings program today.

The Magic of Compound Interest

During a period of high interest, you have a tremendous incentive to save. That is because the dollars you save can grow at a compound rate of interest and double in value every five or six years. Suppose, for example, you have $10,000 to invest at 13 percent compound interest. Take a look at what happens to your $10,000 savings over a period of twenty-five years:

End of Year	Value of $10,000 Investment with Compound Interest of 13%
1	$ 11,300
5	18,424
10	33,946
15	62,543
20	115,231
25	212,305

It takes some searching to find an investment opportunity that will pay you after-tax 13 percent compound interest for just one year. Moreover, it is extremely difficult if not impossible to find an investment opportunity that will guarantee that after-tax 13 percent compound interest for twenty-five years. Yet we have been living in an era of high interest that may continue, and concern that high interest yield opportunities may disappear is no reason not to save. In any event, whatever you are able to save now will add significantly to the funds that are available to you at retirement. The more years you have until retirement, the more meaningful your present savings will be.

You say savings are great, but what about the fact that inflation is eating away at the value of the dollars you save. It is true that inflation decreases the purchasing value of your dollar in the future. However, if you can earn a higher after-tax rate on your savings than the current rate of inflation, you will come out ahead in the long run.

> Suppose you are able to invest your money so that it will grow at 16% per year, and the inflation rate is 10% per year. Every 12 years the true value of your money will double. If the inflation rate were only 4%, and you can still make the same 16% investment, the true value of your money would double every six years.

The key to savings is the after-tax interest that you earn. That is why your retirement planning should focus on those investment opportunities that permit your money to accumulate on a tax-deferred or tax-free basis. If you own your own business, you have at your disposal the most powerful retirement planning tool available: qualified plans (see Chapters 21 and 22 before reading any further if you do own your own business). Let us take a look at the types of tax-favored investment opportunities available to you.

Deductible IRA Contributions

It used to be that you could only set up an IRA (Individual Retirement Account) if you were an employee who was not covered by a qualified plan. Now any person who has earned income can make an annual deductible contribution to an IRA of $2,000 or 100 percent of earnings, whichever is less.[1] If a contribution is also made for a nonworking spouse, the total contribution can be as high as $2,250, but in this case, two separate IRA accounts will have to be opened, one for you and one for your spouse.[2] The contribution to the IRA for the nonworking spouse must be at least $250. You must be under age seventy and a half through the year in order to deduct your IRA contribution.

An IRA for 1982 can be set up anytime during 1982 or even in 1983 up to the time your 1982 income tax return is due (including extensions). Only cash can be contributed to an IRA. If you have the cash available, you may want to begin an IRA as early in the year as possible to maximize the benefits to you of the tax-deferred income.

If your company's qualified plan permits deductible employee contributions, you can contribute to both your company's plan and to an IRA, but you will be limited to a total contribution of $2,000 ($2,250 if you contribute to an IRA for a non-working spouse). Thus you will have to keep track of your voluntary contributions so that you do not exceed the maximum deductible amount permitted.

Contributions to an IRA accumulate on a tax-free basis. Thus the IRA contribution of $2,000 per year grows to $91,524 in twenty years, assuming an interest rate of just 8 percent. Unfortunately the money cannot be withdrawn without penalty from an IRA until you are at least fifty-nine and a half, and withdrawals must begin before age seventy and a half. The penalty on a premature distribution is 10 percent of what you receive, plus you may be penalized on your investment rate of return for an early withdrawal, plus you will be taxed at the ordinary income rate on the amount you receive.[3] However, if you are having a terrible income year and have a desperate need for your IRA dollars, they are available to you. Retirement planning is ridiculous if you are starving today, so do not think that your IRA contribution is necessarily locked up forever.

If you have your own corporation, you might consider putting your spouse on the payroll (if he or she is not already working) to create an additional $2,000 IRA deduction. If the additional Social Security taxes (to cover your spouse as an employee) are too high, you might try compensating your spouse through board-of-director fees. However, in either case, do not get greedy—whatever you pay your spouse should be supported by documentation of hours worked and services performed. Do not make board-of-director fees excessive, or the IRS may be inclined to treat these as dividends to shareholders.

The manner in which you invest your IRA is a very important decision. Primarily you should look for a high-yield investment that is very safe. When you are evaluating the yield on your investment, be sure to find out how often the interest is compounded and what the front-end charges are. Life insurance companies, banks, savings and loans and brokerage houses all offer IRA accounts. An IRA cannot be used for the purchase of life insurance, since the money used for life-insurance premiums will not qualify as a deductible contribution. Moreover, it is no longer possible to use your IRA account for collectibles, such as gold, art, stamps and jewels.[4]

Is there any time you should not contribute to an IRA? *Yes.* Suppose you are putting in your last few years with the phone company before you start up your own phone-accessory business. In this case, you should hold onto every dollar you can so that you will have more dollars with which to start up your business. Also, if you are young, have your own business and are thinking of incorporating, you might want to wait until you have your own corporation before you start qualified-plan contributions. In a corporate setting, you can be trustee of your plan and borrow from the assets allocated to your account, plus you are not limited to the same size contribution as you are with an IRA. Corporate qualified plans are the best bet going and create much more flexibility for you than the modest $2,000 IRA contribution.

Single-Premium Deferred Annuity*

An annuity is traditionally thought of as an investment that returns fixed periodic payments for the duration of an individual's life. However, an annuity can simply be an investment vehicle.

A single-premium deferred annuity is a tax-favored investment that may be attacked at any time by the IRS or by Congress. It works this way. An investor puts up a large sum of money, say $50,000, which earns interest within the annuity contract at a high rate, say 14 percent. The interest is not taxed until it is distributed. While the interest accumulation within the annuity is income-tax free, the investor generally has the right to withdraw without any surrender charges up to 10 percent of the total value of the annuity each year. As long as the investor is withdrawing principal, no tax need be paid on the money.[5] Thus the single-premium deferred annuity can give the investor a return that has much the same appearance as a high-yield tax-free municipal bond for many years. After the entire initial investment has been withdrawn, future withdrawals will be taxed as ordinary income. However, when you are ready to start receiving taxable distributions, you may be in a lower tax bracket, especially if the indexing of tax brackets is not changed. Nevertheless, at some point when the earned interest is paid out (even if on account of death), the recipient will be taxed on the amount received.[6] Thus the single-premium deferred annuity is a vehicle of tax deferral and not a vehicle of tax avoidance.

A wraparound annuity permits the investor to determine the underlying investments of the annuity. The return on the annuity will then be

* The 1982 Tax Act has changed the taxation of the single-premium deferred annuity for policies purchased after August 13, 1982, so that loans and withdrawals will be taxed to the extent of income within the contract and may also be subject to a 5 percent penalty tax. Loans from the single-premium whole life policy may, at the discretion of the Secretary of the Treasury, be subject to the same tax treatment. (IRC §72)

based on the return of the underlying investments. It used to have the same tax advantages as the single-premium deferred annuity, but the IRS ruled unfavorably on the typical wraparound annuity in September, 1981, disallowing its tax-deferred status.[7] We mention this because the IRS could act to challenge the tax characteristics that have been promised on the single-premium deferred annuity.

Tax-Free Municipal Bonds

A tax-free municipal bond earns income that is income-tax free at the federal level and may also be exempt at the state and local level.[8] If you have a large chunk of cash that is creating income that is taxed at a high rate, you might consider an investment in tax-frees, either on an individual basis or through a tax-free mutual fund. The only problem is that during a time of volatile interest rates, your tax-free investment might fluctuate wildly in value as interest rates rise and fall. Thus the purchase of tax-frees is not just a legitimate means of avoiding taxes; it creates the same type of investment risk as all similar investments (such as stocks and bonds). Choose your time to buy tax-frees wisely and, if possible, buy when you and your broker believe interest rates are at their peak.

Single-Premium Whole Life

A new type of single-premium whole life (SPWL) product has been developed that can help you accumulate wealth for retirement. The SPWL accumulates interest on a compound basis at a high rate (13.1% in the spring of 1982) and is reported to have enough of a pure-death benefit in it to cause the policy to qualify as life insurance. Because it is a life insurance policy, the proceeds received from an SPWL on the death of the insured will generally be received tax free. Also, money can be borrowed from an SPWL, usually at favorable interest rates, if the need arises.

The SPWL is similar to a municipal bond in that it pays tax-free interest. It differs from a municipal bond in that the interest paid accumulates within the policy on a compound basis, the policy provides a pure-death benefit on the death of the insured and money can be borrowed from the contract. The policy may provide the most utility for you if the insured under the contract is someone other than yourself.

James, age 40, has $20,000 of cash to invest. He buys an SPWL on his father's life. When his father dies in six years, James receives over $50,000—all income-tax free.

Because the SPWL is a newly developed contract, check with your tax attorney to make certain the contract you want to purchase will provide you with the tax benefits you expect.

Tax-Sheltered Annuity

If you are employed by a charitable organization such as a church or university, the best retirement planning vehicle for you is the tax-sheltered annuity. In this type of plan, your employer may contribute to the plan for your benefit or you may have to make the contribution out of your own salary or a combination of both. The amount of contribution that you are permitted to make depends on your level of compensation and the size of contributions you have made in the past. The tax-shel-

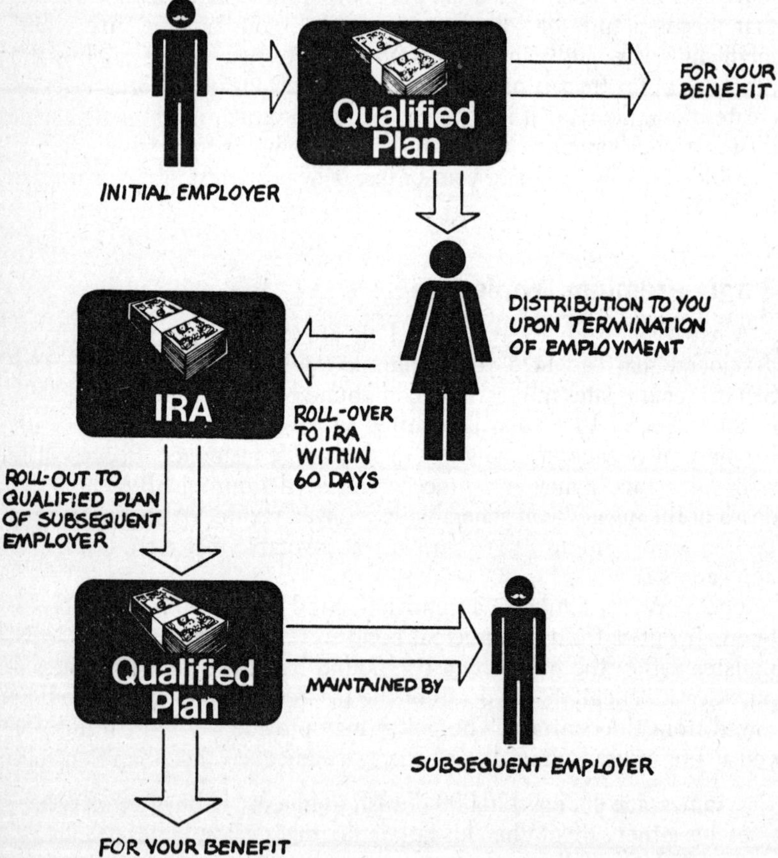

tered annuity program has the same advantages as an IRA—the contributions are tax deductible and are permitted to accumulate income-tax free.[9] Yet it has the same disadvantages: you cannot receive the benefit of these contributions, without penalty, until you have reached at least age fifty-nine and a half.

IRA Rollover

Suppose you receive a distribution from a qualified plan of your employer upon termination of the plan or upon termination of your employment. You have two choices. You can pay a tax on the distribution (which may be at favorable tax rates if the distribution qualifies as a lump-sum distribution) or you can roll over the distribution to an IRA account. The rollover to an IRA account must occur within sixty days of the distribution to you and enables you to defer tax on the distribution until you start receiving money from the IRA (which generally must happen after age fifty-nine and a half and before seventy and a half). Also, the IRA assets continue to grow on a tax-free basis and can provide a very sizable sum for you at your actual retirement.

When an IRA account is the recipient of qualified-plan assets, it is called a *conduit IRA*. This means that the assets rolled over to the IRA can be rolled out of the IRA to another corporate qualified plan. This gives you the advantage of maintaining control of these assets if you, for example, should start up your own business. Banks, savings and loans, insurance companies and investment companies all have IRA account possibilities for you, including the conduit IRA.[10]

Purchase of Home

If you have not already done so, you should purchase your own home. Since our tax system makes it extremely favorable for you to own your residence, you do not want to wait any longer than absolutely necessary to become a home owner.

Interest on your mortgage payment and real estate taxes is deductible if you itemize deductions on your tax return (see Chapter 1).[11, 12] Rent for an apartment is not deductible. You never have to pay tax on the appreciation of your home as long as you purchase an equally expensive or more expensive home within twenty-four months (either before or after) of the sale of your current home.[13] Finally, when you are ready to sell your home and buy something smaller or go back to renting because all your children are out on their own, you can receive up to $125,000 of profit income-tax free if you are age fifty-five or over.[14] What more could you possibly ask for?

The only consideration you should give to the purchase of a home is cash flow. Do not commit yourself to so large an investment that you cannot enjoy it. In any event, if you do purchase a home, have the withholding on your federal income tax adjusted to reflect the fact that your taxes will be reduced because of the deductibility of the mortgage interest and related taxes. Estimate how much your deductible expenses will reduce your income subject to tax (see Chapter 1) and claim as many additional dependents on your withholding form as the thousands of dollars in reduction of income. For example, if the purchase of a new home will reduce your taxable income by $3,000, claim three additional dependents.

Social Security

A chapter on retirement planning would not be complete without some discussion of Social Security. Social Security has been the whipping boy of the federal government for the last five years because (a) payments to recipients bear no correlation to what they paid in; (b) payments to recipients bear no correlation to what their needs are; (c) the program is drastically underfunded; and (d) since 65% of today's work force is 35 or under, it places an unfair burden on the younger generation of workers in this country, who believe the system will not and perhaps should not be around when they are ready to retire.

Social Security was initially designed as supplemental income for retirees. Yet it has grown to the point where many people are living entirely on Social Security. Thus it has become a Catch 22—we can not afford to live with it, and many, many Americans can not afford to live without it.

Social Security replaces a much higher proportion of pay for lower-income workers than for higher-income workers. The following chart gives you some idea of what you can expect to receive from Social Security based on your present yearly earnings:

Your Present Yearly Earnings	*Estimated Percentage of Earnings Replaced*
$10,000	38%
$15,000	34%
$20,000	28%
$25,000	24%
$30,000	20%

$35,000   17%
$40,000   15%
$45,000   13%
$50,000   12%

This table assumes you have been working
regularly and that your earnings have been
and will continue to increase with the average for the country.[15]

Since Social Security is received income-tax free, it is a benefit you
should not ignore. Yet you may have to do some planning to receive it.
One of the real tragedies of our system is that an individual is penalized
for earning money between the ages of sixty-five and seventy-two. For
these ages, every two dollars of income earned above $5,500 reduces the
Social Security an individual is eligible to receive by one dollar. This
means that our older Americans who want or have to work are essentially subject to a tax of over 50 percent on their first dollars of income
earned over $5,500. This creates a terrible injustice to the individual
who wants to continue to work past age sixty-five.

What Can You Do to Receive Social Security?

If you are approaching retirement age and have your own business,
do not get caught in the Social Security income trap at age sixty-five. If
your business is unincorporated, consider forming a corporation so that
you can control how much income is paid to you at age sixty-five. In
this way, you can continue to work as hard as you want and still be eligible to receive your hard-earned, tax-free Social Security dollars. The
dollars you earn that are not paid out as income can be left to accumulate in the corporation (but watch the accumulated-earnings tax—
$150,000 for professional service corporations, $250,000 for all
others),[16] can be contributed to a qualified plan or can pass through to
you as dividends. The last idea is most desirable when you have made a
Subchapter S election (see Chapter 19), although the IRS may object
to this type of planning, especially if your salary seems way too low.

If you do not own your own business, what can you do? You can talk
with your employer about converting your employment status to that of
a consultant so that you would then be considered to have your own
business. Or you can let your employer drop your salary to $5,500 and
make up the difference to you through income-free loans and stock options. In any event, do not give up your Social Security retirement dol-

lars without exhausting every possible avenue short of actually retiring—unless this is what you really want to do. You have earned your Social Security retirement dollars, whether you want to continue working or not, and it is up to you to make sure you receive them.

Retirement Planning in Perspective

Anything you do to save taxes now, whether it is within the family setting or through legitimate tax shelters, will enable you to accumulate wealth for your retirement years. By applying the principles discussed in the last four chapters plus considering the tax-sheltering investment ideas discussed in Chapter 7, you will develop a valuable portfolio of tax-saving ideas that should have a very favorable impact on the dollars available to you at retirement. Make tax planning one of your interests and you will be rewarded with substantial dividends at retirement.

chapter 6

How to Create an Instant Estate

Lloyd Sampson, age 26, purchased a $250,000 term life insurance policy on May 1, 1980, to protect his wife and children in the event of his premature death. He paid one quarterly premium before he died on June 8, 1980, in a boating accident.

For an investment of less than $200, Lloyd's wife and children received $250,000 to help them continue life without him.

Unfortunately the scenario you have just read is a true story with the name changed. Fortunately there is such a thing as life insurance to protect your family in the event something happens to you before you have lived a full and fruitful life.

Life insurance may be the most important investment you will ever make. Yet there are many different types of insurance contracts, and the decision as to what to buy and how much to buy can be difficult to make.

Types of Insurance

There are two basic types of life-insurance contracts that you can purchase—term and whole life, which is also called ordinary insurance. *Term insurance* provides pure death protection, and its premiums in most cases will increase every year. This increase reflects the fact that the chances of death increase as you get older and further away from whatever physical exam you may have taken initially to qualify for the insurance. (Some companies will drop the cost of your term coverage if you can requalify under a new physical exam.) *Whole life insurance* is a combination of pure insurance coverage and an investment side fund. As the investment side fund increases (this fund is called the cash value of the policy), the amount of pure insurance coverage decreases. The premium for whole life coverage is generally a level premium (the same for each installment).

WHOLE LIFE CONTRACT

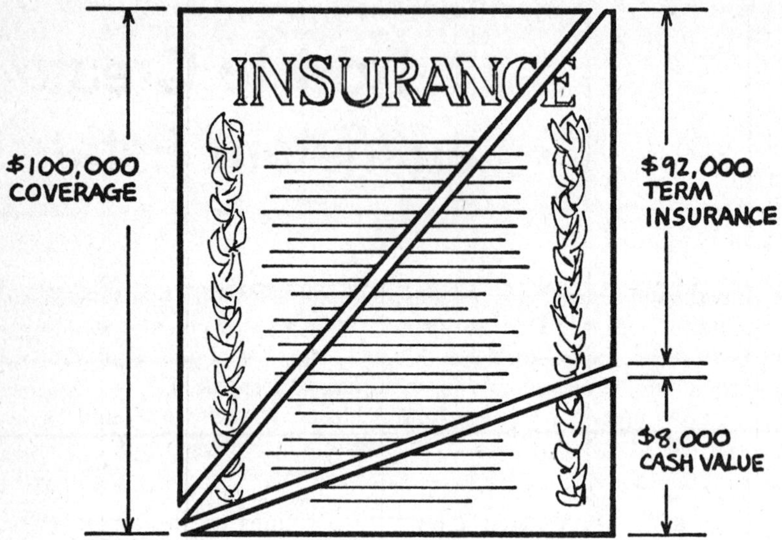

There are other insurance contracts that provide for variations in premium payments. An *endowment contract* is a whole life insurance policy that matures at a stated age, such as sixty-five. *Maturity* here means that the face value of the contract will be available to you at the stated age even if you are alive. The face value of the contract will also be available to your family if you die prior to attaining the stated age. A *graded premium whole life contract* has a premium structure that increases each year until it levels off after a period of approximately ten years. This type of contract is a hybrid whole life contract and is meant to ease the customer into a regular whole life premium structure. A *vanishing premium whole life contract* provides for higher premiums than the regular whole life contract but also provides that the insurance is *paid up* after a certain number of years. *Paid up* means that the contract will always pay its face amount coverage upon death, even if no future premiums are paid.

Finally, a *single premium whole life contract* provides for the payment of a large premium on a one-time basis only. Because the single-premium policy eliminates the insurance company's administrative costs of collecting and processing additional premium payments, the return on a single-premium policy can be very favorable. Also, certain single premium policies are now paying the same high interest on the cash value of the policy as is true with the universal life insurance contracts (see the later section of this chapter titled Universal Life Insurance) and thus are very attractive as a combination investment–life insurance contract.

Annuities, which are also marketed by life insurance companies, and the single-premium whole life policies, are discussed in Chapter 5.

Tax Advantages of Life Insurance

At death, proceeds from a life insurance policy are paid to the named beneficiary on a tax-free basis.[1] This means that a very large estate can be made available for loved ones without that estate having to pass through the income-tax wringer. The only exception to the tax-free payment of the proceeds occurs when the policy is sold or otherwise transferred during the holder's lifetime for valuable consideration.[2] This so-called transfer-for-value rule does not apply in many situations, because there are some important exceptions, such as when ownership of the insurance policy is transferred to the insured. Nevertheless, you should consult your tax adviser or life-insurance agent before you attempt to change the owner or beneficiary of a policy in any situation in which you receive some value for making the change. A gift of a policy to a spouse or into trust is not a transfer for value.[3]

In addition to the proceeds of an insurance policy being income-tax free, the payment of dividends by a mutual insurance company to a policyholder also occurs income-tax free. These dividends are treated as a return of premium.[4] Mutual insurance companies are companies owned by the policyholders, and the payment of a dividend is simply treated as a return of premium payment. The rates for insurance coverage with a mutual company may or may not be lower than the rates of a stock company (an insurance company owned by its shareholders). The rates depend on each individual insurance company and not on whether the company is a mutual or a stock company.

The receipt of tax-free dividends can be an important advantage. Suppose you acquire a policy from your corporation, which has paid premiums for eight years on the policy. As you become the owner of the policy, you will benefit from future dividends on the policy, *even though* much of those dividends may be attributable to the prior premiums paid by your company. Thus you may be able to acquire life insurance on your life at a very low cost by having your corporation pay for the initial years of premiums before you acquire actual ownership of the policy. For a general discussion of who should own a life-insurance policy for estate-tax purposes, see Chapter 11.

The cash-value accumulation in a whole life insurance contract occurs income-tax free.[5] This cash-value accumulation is readily available to you. You can either borrow the cash value at a rate that is now 8 percent in most contracts or you can obtain the cash value of the policy upon surrender of the policy to the insurance company. Income taxes would have to be paid upon the surrender of the policy only if the cash value were in excess of the premiums paid. This will generally not happen for many years with most typical whole life insurance contracts (excluding universal life), since a significant portion of each premium is used for the pure term insurance coverage. Also, the return on the investment portion of a whole life insurance policy is generally at a low guaranteed rate.

If you borrow money from your life-insurance policy, you will be entitled to deduct the interest paid to the insurance company as long as you pay without borrowing at least four of the first seven years' premiums.[6] When a contract is set up to provide for systematic borrowing for the payment of premiums, it is called a minimum deposit contract. *Minimum deposit* means that you pay as little money as possible to keep the life-insurance coverage in full force and effect.

The ability to borrow on a whole life insurance contract can be very advantageous to the policyholder. The reason for this is that the borrowed funds continue to be credited with interest by the insurance company at an income-tax-free rate (such as 5%), while the interest paid by the borrower is deductible (except in the case of borrowing on a single-premium policy).

Suppose you are in the 50 percent tax bracket and you borrow from your whole life policy at 8 percent. The net cost to you is 4 percent. If the borrowed funds are credited with tax-free interest of 5 percent, you achieve a net gain of 1 percent by borrowing.

What Type and How Much Life Insurance Should You Purchase?

The primary purpose of life insurance is to provide a death benefit at your death. Thus the first and most important thing to do in purchasing life insurance is to make certain that you have enough life insurance coverage. Obviously the least expensive way to provide a pure death benefit is to purchase term insurance. This will at least take care of your most immediate and pressing needs. Once your immediate needs are met, then it is time to consider whole life insurance.

If you are purchasing insurance to protect your family, you might consider sufficient insurance as being enough to provide the same income for your family upon your death as they had before your death.

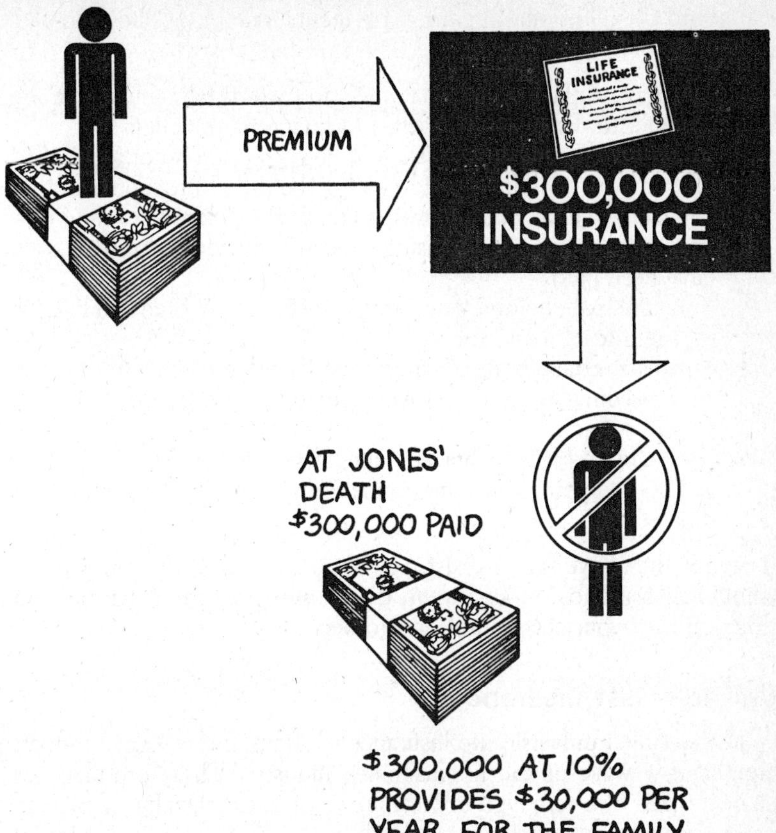

There is always the question of what inflation will do to the value of the dollars you leave for your family. This is an important consideration and one that you should fully discuss with your life insurance agent. In any event, the production-of-equivalent-income test can be used as a starting point for your determination of how much insurance you should have. Also, there are additional factors (such as age of your children, total family assets, ability of your spouse to work, future needs of your family, etc.) that must be taken into account in determining your insurance needs.

When to Pay More for Insurance Coverage Than You Have To

Suppose you have enough insurance coverage. When should a portion or all of that coverage be whole life insurance?

You should consider the purchase of whole life insurance when you can afford the additional premium payments and any of the following factors exist:

1. You have difficulty saving money and would use the whole life contract to discipline yourself into saving more dollars.
2. You can find some entity (such as your corporation or a qualified plan in your corporation) to pay for the initial premiums so that you can eventually obtain ownership of the policy after the front-end costs (commissions, insurance company administrative costs) have been paid.
3. You anticipate holding onto the policy for a long time and like the idea of a level premium.
4. You have attained an advanced age, and the cost of term insurance becomes more expensive than the whole-life coverage in a very few years.
5. You are in a high tax bracket, and the minimum-deposit concept can enable you to buy insurance cheaper over a long period of time.

If any of the above factors exist, you should consider the purchase of whole life insurance. In any event, do not shy away from sharing your thinking with your accountant or attorney.

Universal Life Insurance

The so-called universal life insurance contracts and similar products are the new wave of the life-insurance industry. These products are characterized by a very high interest return on the cash value of the policy and usually include a variable death benefit that can be revised from time to time by the policyholder. The cash value return in these policies is represented to be about 10 to 12 percent, versus 6 percent or less in typical whole life contracts.

These policies are like any typical whole life insurance policy. They consist of an investment portion and a pure death benefit portion, which together create the total death benefit. Since the cost of the pure death benefit is paid from the investment portion of the contract, there is a direct correlation between the pure death benefit selected under the contract and the interest return on the investment portion of the contract. The higher the pure death benefit, the lower the interest return on the investment portion. The policyholder is permitted to increase or decrease the pure death benefit under the policy at certain times and upon meeting certain conditions. Thus the universal policy is represented to be the only life insurance policy an individual will ever need and can be used in any situation—therefore its name. During the years when your children are young and you have heavy family responsibilities, the pure death benefit would be very high to cover the significant life insurance needs of the insured. Then, in later years, after the kids are self-supporting, the contract could be used as more of an investment vehicle and the pure death benefit significantly decreased.

The cash value of the contract, like any typical whole life insurance contract, can be borrowed by the policyholder at an interest rate that is usually 8 percent. Since the borrowed funds are credited by the insurance company with an interest rate that may be 5 to 5½ percent, there can be a net gain to the high-bracket taxpayer by borrowing as discussed before. Thus there may be a real incentive to the policyholder to borrow funds. In any event, the cash values of the contract are earned tax free by the policyholder, and the ability to borrow makes the policy attractive both as a savings vehicle and as a life-insurance contract.

Where the High Interest Comes From

The key to the universal-life contract is the high interest return on the cash value. It is intriguing to discover why certain insurance companies can now pay such a high return on the cash value of a whole-life policy.

Traditionally state laws have limited the amount of interest that can be guaranteed on a whole-life contract to 5.5 percent (or 4.5%, depending on the state). This is the maximum interest that can be guaranteed by law under a whole-life contract. Mutual insurance companies, which earn more than the guaranteed rate, have paid out a portion of their profits (earnings in excess of the guaranteed rate) in the form of dividends to the policyholders. However, the dividend that is paid generally represents the mutual company's after-tax profits, and thus the size of the dividend must be limited.

The new high yield policies, on the other hand, are offered by stock companies that claim that the excess interest (interest in excess of the maximum interest permitted by state law) is a deductible expense and not a dividend. Consequently, because the payment of excess interest is made with the stock insurance company's before-tax dollars, the stock companies have more dollars to credit to the cash value of whole life insurance contracts. As you can imagine, the mutual companies are feeling threatened by the high-return policies and are vigorously resisting the ability of stock companies to offer a higher return on cash value than the mutual companies can possibly offer.

What Might Change the High Interest

If the mutual companies are successful in challenging the deductibility of the excess interest credited on the new high yield policies offered by stock companies, the excess interest that can be offered will dramatically decrease and will probably approach the dividends offered by mutual companies. Also, if the interest rates start decreasing, the money earned by universal life insurance companies on their investments will decrease, thus causing a drop in the excess interest they can profitably offer. *Remember*—only the interest permitted by state law (4.5% or 5.5%) is actually guaranteed under the contract. Thus the excess interest initially promised may be changed at the discretion of the insurance company.

Tax Effects of Universal Life Contracts*

The tax effects of the universal-life contract are represented by universal life insurance companies to be the same as any typical whole life insurance policy, namely:

1. The death benefit, consisting of both the cash value plus pure death benefit protection, will be received income-tax free at the death of the insured.
2. The interest paid on the cash value will not be taxable to the policyholder unless the policy is surrendered, at which time the policyholder would be taxed on the difference between the cash paid to him or her, less what he or she paid in premiums.[7]

Although a favorable private-letter ruling (a ruling made on an individual basis) has been issued by the IRS on the tax effects of a universal-life contract offered by E.F. Hutton (called CompleteLife),[8] this private-letter ruling, like all private-letter rulings, only binds the IRS with respect to the one policyholder who requested it. Thus this private-letter ruling is not legal precedent for the tax effects of any other universal-life contract.

The universal-life contract has certain aspects that could be attacked by the IRS. The contentions that could be made by the service are the following:

1. The cash value in the contract is a separate side fund investment and cannot be received income-tax free as a death benefit.

---

* Universal Life is now on very solid ground until at least 1984 because of the 1982 Tax Act. (IRC §101(A))

2. The excess interest paid under the contract is taxable to the policyholder as an investment return.
3. Any borrowings from the cash value of the contract in excess of the premiums paid are taxable income to the policyholder.

Of these three possible points of attack, we believe item 3 is the one at which the IRS is most likely to aim its arsenal of weapons.[9] Yet all the promised tax effects of the universal-life contract rest on firm legal footing, and it may well take an act of Congress for universal life to lose its tax-favored status. In any event, it is important for the potential buyer of the universal-life contract to understand that there may be some risks involved with this policy that are not inherent in other whole life insurance contracts.

New Policies Designed to Compete with Universal Life

The life-insurance industry has been offering new products at a previously unparalleled pace. Many companies have come up with their own products, both to meet the criticism leveled against traditional life insurance and to locate a special niche in the marketplace. These policies are worth noting because, like universal life, they are designed to provide greater flexibility for the policyholder and a better return on the policyholder's investment dollar.

Variable Life

This is a whole life insurance product that invests the cash value of the contract in equity accounts. The objective of the contract is to provide increasing benefits for the policyholder to keep up with inflation. Because the contract consists of a securities element, it has been registered with the Securities and Exchange Commission. The death benefit increases or decreases annually depending on the investment results. However, it will never decrease below a guaranteed amount.

Adjustable Life

Under this policy, policyholders may increase or decrease the amount of premium payments, pure death benefit and periods of protection. Coverage can switch between term and whole life to meet the policyholder's changing needs. The policyholder has the option of two types of insurance coverage: lifetime protection with a shorter premium payment or protection that expires at the end of the premium-paying period.

Increasing Whole Life

This policy is actually keyed to the Consumer Price Index to enable the death benefit to keep pace with inflation. Under some policies, the amount of death benefit will increase automatically each year while the policyholder will have the option to increase the death benefit each year to correspond with the percentage increases in the Consumer Price Index.

Buy Term and Invest the Difference

A number of opponents of universal life advocate buying term insurance and investing the difference in annuities or in single-premium whole life (SPWL). The primary drawback to this arrangement is that annuities or SPWL generally require a minimum premium of $5,000.

Deposit Term

This product is a ten-year level term insurance product that requires a one-time deposit in the first year, which averages about $10 per $1,000. At the end of the ten years, if all premiums have been paid, the deposit is refunded plus interest. If premiums are not paid for ten years, the deposit will be forfeited. This feature locks the policyholder into the contract. Opponents of this policy maintain that yearly renewable term insurance is less expensive and does not require the policyholder to commit to the same insurance company for a ten-year period. Deposit term has been severely criticized because of its ability to mislead the consumer.

Selecting the Right Agent

More important than what you have read in this chapter is your selection of a life-insurance agent. Most agents can represent more than one company, so the quality agent can find the life-insurance company that has the best policy for your situation and can recommend the best manner for you to purchase the policy as well as advise you on how much life insurance to purchase.

How do you go about selecting your life-insurance agent? First, most people seem to be chosen by their agent rather than the other way around. Just because an agent has knocked on your door does not mean you are required to work with that person. You should choose to do business only with an experienced agent whom you believe is a true professional and genuinely concerned about you and your present insurance needs. If you do not have an agent, ask your friends or business acquaintances whom they recommend.

There are several things you should look for in evaluting an agent's quality. First, is he or she interested in you and your situation. Second, your agent should appear to you as more of an educator than a salesperson. Any decisions that are made about the purchase of life insurance are your decisions, and you should be fully informed about what you are doing so that you can make the correct decision for you. Also, ask your agent for references and find out the areas in which he or she specializes. You do not want an agent who works primarily in the family market to be responsible for setting up your business insurance. Finally, get a sense of your agent's background and training. The CLU designation means that the agent has completed an experience requirement and has passed a series of tests sponsored by the American College located in Bryn Mawr, Pennsylvania. If your agent does not have a CLU, find out what training she or he has had to takes its place. There are many, many competent agents who do not have a CLU designation, but the ones who do have proved that they have a commitment to advanced training—a factor that should be important to you in selecting your agent.

In any event, ask your accountant or attorney what he or she thinks of your agent and your agent's proposals. Another professional's viewpoint may be helpful in making your insurance decision.

What Not to Do

Do not attempt to line up three or four agents to bid against one another. You will only be confused by trying to compare insurance companies and the cost of insurance coverage. Most important, you will wind up selecting an agent based on what you think is the least expensive insurance contract and not on whom you think is the best agent to advise you with regard to your insurance needs. Remember, the purchase of life insurance is something you may do many times during your lifetime, and you want to be certain that when you call your agent with a question or ask for a recommendation, you will get a correct and helpful response.

chapter 7

How to Shelter Income Through Wise Investments

Doug James, a 50% taxpayer, purchased a $65,000 duplex for $10,000 cash down. The first year his rents equaled all his deductible expenses associated with the property (interest on his mortgage, repairs, property taxes, insurance and advertising). On his tax return, Doug allocated $5,000 of the purchase price to land and depreciated the $60,000 allocated to the building over a fifteen-year period on a straight-line basis. The annual $4,000 depreciation deduction saves Doug $2,000 in taxes, resulting in a net after-tax return on his $10,000 down payment of 20%.

In addition, Doug gets the benefit of the appreciation of the property and can increase his rental income over a period of time without any corresponding increase in his expenses.

There are many ways for you to invest so that your money generates a tax savings as well as investment income. Yet you should bear in mind that such tax shelters are not for the fainthearted. The tax savings ideas expressed in this chapter involve risk and may in some cases entail a time commitment. Tax shelters are seductive because you do save money in taxes, at least initially, but in the long run, you must analyze both the projected tax savings and the expected investment return, if any, to determine whether a contemplated tax shelter is the best place for your money.

Before you read on, if you have your own business, go directly to Part III of this book, Business Tax Planning. You should maximize the tax savings available to you in a business setting, especially the savings available through qualified plans, before you consider a risky tax shelter. Also, establish your own IRA (see Chapter 5) before you look for a risky shelter. To the extent that it is possible, your tax planning options should be organized in the order of degree of certainty of the tax savings and of the underlying investment. And a qualified plan or an IRA offers you an opportunity that is virtually 100 percent guaranteed as to both.

Most tax shelters consist of a leveraged investment that permits you to get the benefit of a much larger investment for depreciation purposes than the cash you initially have to invest. But the leverage investment aspect of a tax shelter, in many cases, creates the risk that you will have to pay the amount that you borrowed at the end of the shelter's useful life—or it may mean that you will incur a significant tax liability upon the disposition of your interest in the shelter. In any event, be certain to determine the *complete* economic effects of any shelter investment you make. The tax effects that are promised to take place up front may not balance the back end costs.

About All Tax Shelters

Do not buy a shelter on the sole recommendation of the person who stands to benefit personally from your business. Get at least a second opinion from someone who can be objective. The price of running the shelter past your accountant or attorney or both is generally small in comparison to the size of the investment you are being asked to make.

Real Estate Investment—The Safe Way

The safest tax shelter by far is real estate. The rules regarding deductibility of expenses and depreciation write-off for real estate are hard and fast. In addition, if you are the sole owner or a member of a small partnership (such as with one or two friends) that owns the property, your investment risk is minimized. The "hands on" approach to real estate is the best one to follow. This approach makes *you* directly responsible for controlling the following key elements of your real estate investment:

1. selection of tenants
2. terms of rental agreements
3. maximization of rental return
4. maintenance and improvements
5. determination of most advantageous time to sell

The only problem with the hands-on-approach is that you may spend much of your valuable time renting and maintaining your property and collecting rents. Also, there is the possibility of the midnight phone call complaining about the furnace. Many of these concerns can be handled by hiring a competent manager—but, of course, there is a cost to doing this.

The beauty of the real estate investment is that even though you fully hope and expect your property to appreciate in value, you are allowed to depreciate the portion of your investment allocated to the improvements on the land.[1] Depreciation is deducted dollar for dollar from your income. Then, when you eventually sell, the gain attributable to the depreciation that has been taken on a *straight-line* basis is taxed to you as a long-term capital gain.[2] Straight line depreciation is an equal spreading of your building investment over fifteen years—an abbreviated period representing the useful life of the building established by the 1981 act (effective for real property purchased after 1980).[3] Depreciation that is in excess of straight line is called *accelerated depreciation* and increases deductions in the initial years of property ownership. If accelerated depreciation is taken with respect to nonresidential property, upon its sale, all the gain up to the amount of depreciation taken will be taxed as ordinary income.[4] In the case of residential property, upon its sale, the difference between the depreciation taken and what straight-line depreciation would have been will generally be taxed as ordinary income.

A. J. Rice purchases an apartment building for $130,000. He allocates $10,000 of the purchase price to land and elects straight-line depreciation of $8,000 per year for a fifteen-year period. If he sells the property five years later for $160,000, his basis will be reduced by the $40,000 of depreciation taken. His gain (the difference between the selling price—$160,000—and his basis—$90,-000) of $70,000 will be taxed as a long-term capital gain.

If A.J. had taken accelerated depreciation on the property, his total depreciation for the five years of ownership would have been approximately $55,000. Upon the sale of the property, his gain would be $85,000 (increased by $15,000 because his basis is $15,-000 lower) and would be taxed as follows: $15,000 ordinary income, $70,000 long-term capital gain.

Although accelerated depreciation is more difficult from a record-keeping standpoint and does result in ordinary income upon the disposition of the property, it is still advantageous to the taxpayer in the case of residential property to take accelerated depreciation. The taxpayer gets the present tax benefit and gets the use of the tax dollars saved for all the years of ownership of the property. However, in the case of nonresidential property, the taxpayer's decision must be based on how long he or she expects to own the property before selling it.

One of the drawbacks to purchasing a vacation home as a real estate investment is that there are substantial limitations on deductions that can be taken if the property is used for fourteen days or more during the year as a vacation home. However, if the property is purchased by a partnership, this limitation does not apply.

David and Jim, two attorneys, form a partnership to purchase a condo in Naples, Florida, as an investment. They write off interest, condo fees, depreciation, utilities, travel expenses once a year to the property, and the cost of advertising the unit for rent. The deductions to the partnership are not jeopardized even if one of the partners occupies the condo for over fourteen days.

The Add-on Minimum Tax

Accelerated depreciation on real property subject to a lease is subject to a 15 percent add-on minimum tax.[5] This tax is imposed on your *tax preference items* reduced by the greater of (a) $10,000 or (b) one half of your regular tax liability reduced by most of your tax credits. Tax preference items include:

1. the amount of accelerated depreciation on real estate in excess of straight-line depreciation
2. the amount of accelerated depreciation on personal property, subject to a net lease in excess of straight-line depreciation
3. percentage depletion for oil and gas in excess of the taxpayer's adjusted basis for the property

Suppose your regular tax liability is $30,000, you have investment tax credits of $4,000 and your tax-preference items total $21,000. Your add-on minimum tax is $15\% \times (\$21,000 - \frac{1}{2} \times \$26,000) = \$1,200$. This makes your total tax liability for the year $31,200.

As you can see, this dog of a tax is more bark than bite.

Syndicated Real Estate Investments

The opposite of the hands-on real-estate investment is the syndicated apartment complex or office building. In this investment opportunity, you are asked to purchase a partnership interest that generally limits your liability to your total cash investment. This type of partnership interest is called a *limited partnership interest* and does not permit you to have any say in the management of the investment property or even in when it is sold.

Real-estate syndications are attractive because they spin off substantial losses in their first few years that are deductible from your income. The primary reason for the large losses is that significant depreciation can be taken in the early years, substantially in excess of straight-line depreciation. Unfortunately, at some point, the large depreciation deductions get used up and your investment may start to show gains that are taxed to you as ordinary income. Also, upon disposition of the property, you will be taxed on a portion of the accelerated depreciation (the portion that exceeds straight-line depreciation) as ordinary income.[6]

Most real estate syndications are set up to give the tax results that they promise. However, the terms of the partnership agreement should be carefully reviewed by your attorney before you invest. If the partnership is defective, you could be deemed to have purchased an interest in an entity that will be taxed as a corporation, and you will lose all your tax benefits.

As important as the tax effects is the treatment of profits derived from the investment property. How much of the rental income is paid to the general partner or partners of the limited partnership? What happens on disposition of the property—what percentage of the gain does the general partner get to keep? These aspects have a tremendous impact on the validity of your investment and may have a bearing on its tax effects. If you make an investment solely for the tax benefits, the IRS may call the investment a sham and disallow your deductions.

Norman White has been asked to invest $10,000, along with nine other investors, to purchase an office building. As a limited partner, he will be liable for 1/10 of the borrowings by the partnership. The general partner receives $800 a month for managing the property and does not put up any money of his own.

Upon investigation, Norman finds out that the general partner gets 40% of the gain upon the sale of the property and that the remaining 60% of gain is split among the limited partners. Norman elects to find his own real estate investment.

Tax Credit for Rehabilitation Expenditures*

In order to encourage business to remain in the center cities instead of relocating to newer buildings in the suburbs, Congress, in the 1981 act, sweetened the tax incentives for renovating old structures.[7] There is

* The 1982 Tax Act has combined the add-on minimum tax with a new alternative minimum tax that is essentially a 20 percent flat tax on the amount of alternative taxable income (adjusted gross income before net operating losses plus tax preference items generally associated with tax shelters) exceeding $40,000 (for married taxpayers filing jointly). Investment tax credits are not allowed as a deduction against this tax. (IRC §55)

now a three-tier investment-tax credit for substantial rehabilitation expenditures incurred after December 31, 1981. *Substantial* here generally means the greater of (a) $5,000 or (b) the taxpayer's adjusted basis in the property. For commercial structures that are at least thirty years old, the credit is 15 percent. For commercial structures that are at least forty years old, the credit is 20 percent, and for both commercial and residential structures that are certified historic structures, the credit is 25 percent.

NOTE: The credit is not available for the rehabilitation of residential structures unless the buildings are certified historic structures. Also, rehabilitation of a building more than twenty but less than thirty years old that commenced prior to 1982 will be treated under the earlier law.

In order to be eligible for the new credit, the taxpayer must elect the straight-line method of cost recovery of the rehabilitation expenditures and there must be a "substantial rehabilitation" of the structure, as already discussed. Also, the amount eligible for depreciation deductions is reduced by the amount allowed as an investment tax credit except in the case of certified historic structures.

The following costs do not qualify as bona fide rehabilitation expenditures eligible for the special credit:

1. The cost of acquiring the building to be renovated, or any surrounding property.
2. The cost of constructing a new building.
3. The cost of enlarging a building.
4. If more than 25% of the existing exterior walls of the building are replaced, it is considered new construction and none of the costs will be eligible for the credit.

If a lessee undertakes improvements that would otherwise qualify for the credit, the lessee can only take the special credit if the remaining term of the lease is at least fifteen years.

With regard to certified historic structures, the rehabilitation generally must be done in a manner certified by the secretary of the Department of the Interior to be consistent with the historic character of the property or the historic district in which such property is located. An exception to this requirement is that a building located in a certified historic district that is not a certified historic structure falls outside this requirement if the secretary of the department certifies that the building is not of historic significance to the district. In this case, the rehabilitation does not have to be done in a manner certified by the secretary in order to qualify for the tax credit.

Because of the very large investment tax credit that is available, rehabilitation of old structures should become an increasingly popular investment through the mechanism of a limited partnership.

Equipment Leases—The Safe Way

Investments in equipment that will be leased are transactions very similar to the purchase of real estate, with the following exceptions:

1. Equipment (such as computers, cranes, and printing presses) is not an appreciating asset; thus there is no pot of gold at the end of the lease.
2. Any gain on the sale of the equipment or disposition of an interest in equipment will generally be taxed as ordinary income.
3. a. The purchase of equipment creates an investment tax credit of up to 10% of the purchase price, which may be taken by the purchaser of the property or passed through to the lessee.[8]
   b. An additional first year expense can be deducted up to the purchase price of the equipment if the investment tax credit could be taken.[9] This additional first year expense, created by the 1981 act, is in lieu of the investment tax credit for the amount expensed and is based on the following table:

Year Property Placed in Service	Dollar Limitation
81	0
82 and 83	5,000
84 and 85	7,500
86 and after	10,000

If you own your own corporation and it needs a new computer for keeping track of inventory and accounts receivable, you should consider purchasing the computer personally and leasing it to your corporation. The advantage of this arrangement is that you can make the monthly lease payments to you equal to the monthly payments for the purchase of the equipment. In this way, your cash flow is even and you get an income tax deduction equal to the depreciation of the equipment plus the interest portion of your monthly payments.

If the computer in the example cost $21,000 and was depreciated over a five-year period, the first year of the equipment lease would create an accelerated cost recovery deduction for you of $3,150. At the end of the five-year period, when all the depreciation has been exhausted, you can contribute the computer to your corporation as a contribution of capital. Or, even better yet, give the computer to your children, in trust or

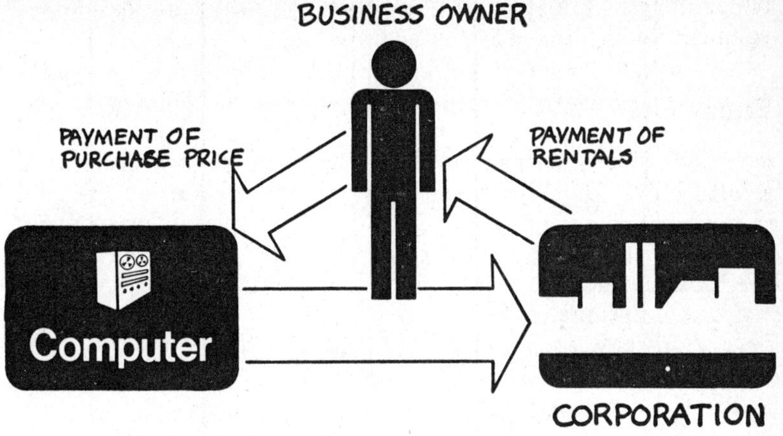

otherwise, so that they will receive the income from the lease and pay tax on that income at their tax rates. (See gift and lease-back discussion in Chapter 2.)

The advantage of the self-contained equipment lease is that you control what happens. Even if the computer you purchased becomes obsolete because of new technology, you can still cause your corporation to make the lease payments.

The Investment Tax Credit*

The investment tax credit (ITC) is a special tax benefit available for equipment purchases. In the previous example, the $2,100 of ITC can be passed through to your corporation or taken by you personally. For property with a useful life of three years, the investment tax credit is only 6 percent.[10] If you want to take it personally, you have to satisfy these requirements:

1. During the first twelve months of the lease, your expenses associated with the lease (not including interest) must be at least 15% of the rentals received during this twelve-month period.
2. The duration of the lease cannot be for more than one half of the property's useful life.[11]

The purpose of item 2 is to keep the risk of the investment with the purchaser. In a situation in which you control the lessee, the IRS may

* The 1982 Tax Act has reduced the investment tax credit by 2% if the taxpayer wants to depreciate his full purchase price.

argue that the risk of the investment has been shifted to your corporation and deny you the ITC.

The best way around the shifting of the risk problem is to bring some nonowners in partnership with you to purchase the equipment. This will destroy the identity between the lessor-owner of equipment and the lessee and reduce the chances that the IRS might be successful should they choose to contest your ability personally to take the ITC. Of course, by bringing in another person (such as a key employee of your company), you have to share the investment tax credit. Your friendly investor should acquire at least 20 to 25 percent, so that IRS will give credence to this interest.

NOTE: If you want to take the additional first year expense discussed before, you cannot also take the investment tax credit with respect to the additional expense.

Syndicated Equipment Leases

A typical syndicated equipment lease (such as for a $2 million computer) will create an opportunity for an investment on a limited-partnership basis. As a limited partner, the investor will be required to accept some personal liability on the borrowings by the partnership for the purchase of the computer. This borrowing is "at risk" and enables the investor to depreciate his or her share of the computer purchase price.[12] However, if the computer becomes obsolete, the investor may be required to come up with some additional dollars. Generally the investment tax credit will pass through to the lessee as an inducement to the lessee to enter into the lease agreement. But the limited partner will still be entitled to significant tax deductions for his or her share of depreciation over the first few years of the lease.

The better types of syndicated equipment leases have a financially strong lessee committed for a fixed number of years. The payments from the lessee will pay for the "at risk" borrowings, so that the investor is protected with regard to her or his at-risk commitment.

With any equipment lease, a limited partner may still be liable for a portion of the borrowing to finance the purchase of equipment even after fully depreciating the at-risk investment. In such a situation, the investor will own a limited-partnership interest that will generate ordinary income upon the disposition of this interest. The amount of income will be approximately equal to the investor's share of the unpaid borrowing.

John Woodson pays $20,000 for a limited partnership interest that lets him write off $80,000 as depreciation over a period of five years. At the end of five years, John's share of the outstanding borrowing is $25,000. If John transfers his interest for $1, he will still recognize ordinary income of $25,000.

Because of the tail-end tax consequences of an equipment lease, you should give some consideration to finding another tax shelter for the year or years in which the income-tax consequences of your equipment-lease investment start turning against you.

Safe Harbor Provisions for Corporate Lessors*

The 1981 act creates a new safe harbor election that can guarantee that a lease of property will be treated as a bona fide lease for federal income tax purposes. The following are the requirements of the safe harbor test:

1. The property must be new investment credit property other than buildings.
2. The lessor must be a corporate lessor other than a Subchapter S corporation.
3. The lessor must have a minimum at-risk investment of 10%.
4. The lease term cannot exceed the greater of 90% of the property's useful life or 150% of its ADR midpoint life. ADR is the table used prior to the 1981 act, which assigns a depreciable period for each asset. The new term is ACRS.
5. Both the lessor and lessee must characterize the transaction as a lease and elect to have the safe harbor provisions apply to the transaction.[13]

Because the lessor is permitted to borrow up to 90 percent of the purchase price and immediately obtain full depreciation allowances and investment tax credits, the new safe harbor provisions may well cause the number of corporations that enter the equipment leasing business to proliferate.

The advantage of the safe harbor provisions is that the IRS cannot maintain that a lease transaction is actually a financing or sale transaction, even though (a) the lessee may be required to purchase the property at the end of the lease; (b) the lessee may guarantee financing for the transaction, except for the minimum 10%; or (c) the transaction only makes sense to the lessor because of the tax benefits.

NOTE: Unless you are considering an equipment lease for your corporation to reduce income taxes, the safe-harbor provisions will not be beneficial to your own personal income tax planning.

* The 1982 Tax Act has repealed the safe harbor leasing provisions beginning in 1984.

Oil and Gas Investments—The Only Way

With real-estate and equipment-lease investments, you can make some predictions about what the total economic effect will be. Also, you can get into each investment on a personal basis. The same is not true with an oil and gas lease investment. Here you are totally at the mercy of the general partners of the oil and gas venture to find productive drilling prospects. See in Appendix D what the SEC said to consumers in April, 1978, about the risks inherent in oil and gas ventures. Because of the risk involved, you should be in the 50 percent tax bracket to consider this type of investment. If you qualify, there are definitely some things you should look for in sizing up the desirability of an oil and gas lease investment.

The tax advantages of an oil and gas investment are based on the fast write-off of your investment and the favorable tax treatment of income from a productive well. First, prepayments of drilling expenses in most cases can be written off in the year they are committed, whether or not actual drilling has commenced. Thus for an investment of $75,000, the investor may be able to deduct a significant portion (such as $50,000) of that investment in the first year—even if the investment is made at the end of the investor's tax year. Certain expenses incurred in drilling operations are deductible, such as intangible drilling and development costs in the year in which such expenditures are made.[14] These expenses include the cost of the contract driller and related expenses that have no salvage value (and thus are not capital expenditures), such as wages, supplies and fuel. The ability to take these costs currently rather than capitalize them is available only to individuals who hold a working interest (as opposed to a royalty interest) in the property.[15] The deductibility is limited to the amount of the investment or dollars at risk. Typically deductible drilling expenses will range from 60 percent to 75 percent of your total investment on a straight promoted interest program (general partner having a carried interest) or 90 percent to 100 percent under a functional allocation program (general partner paying for the capitalized cost). The remaining dollars, except for sales commission, are capitalized and written off over a five-year life.[16] The tangible equipment also receives an investment tax credit of 10 percent.[17]

If oil or gas is discovered, the income for tax purposes is reduced by the greater of the percentage depletion allowance, which for small producers is 18 percent for 1982 (this decreases to 15% by 1984) of the income produced or the taxpayer's share of amortized costs of the partnership properties.[18] The small-producer exemption limits the amount of domestic oil (1,000 barrels of average daily production) and gas (up

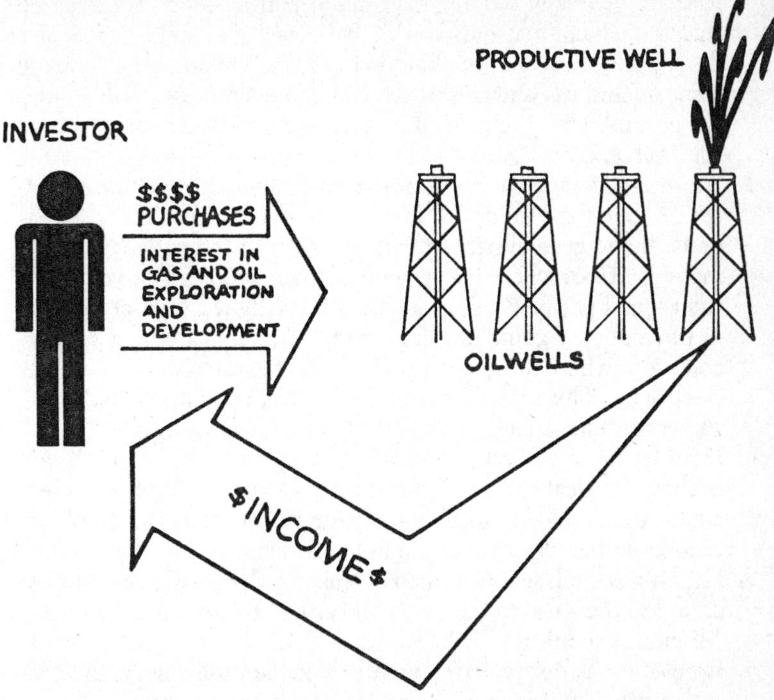

to 6,000,000 cubic feet of natural gas) that qualify for the percentage depletion.[19] Also, a 22 percent depletion rate is allowed for secondary and tertiary production.[20] In any event, the important thing to remember is that any income that is generated by a productive well is subject to favorable income tax treatment.

There are several aspects of oil and gas investments that must be reviewed carefully. Since your investment only makes sense if oil or gas is discovered, you must be certain that your investment dollar is going for drilling that has a high probability of being productive or that the risk-reward is sufficient to justify the investment. These are the most important factors to consider:

1. What is the experience of the general partners—why should you trust their belief that where they drill will produce oil or gas? Can they intelligently handle the amount of money raised with the staff they maintain?
2. How much of your money is going into the ground as opposed to going into the pockets of the general partners? This should be at

least 85%. Many oil and gas limited partnerships are set up so that the general partners are big winners even if oil or gas is not discovered; this is not the kind that you are looking for. There are some oil and gas ventures where 100% of your money will go into the ground, with the general partner taking a larger percentage at the back end.

3. Are the general partners taking a risk, as you are, in the investment? One item to look at in the prospectus to determine this is costs. If the general partner will pay 10% of the costs (typical of many ventures where the general partners are at risk), you know the general partners will be at risk, especially if a high percentage of the money is going into the ground. Be very careful of *turnkey contracts*, where the general partner is agreeing to drill the well at a set price. This may be paying for his or her contribution to the partnership for a large back end interest.

4. How fertile is the region where drilling will take place? Is the drilling "wildcat drilling," meaning it is high-risk drilling? Generally you should try to find a drilling project that is a combination of exploratory and development drilling.

5. How many wells will be drilled? Generally the greater the number of wells, the greater the probability that there will be a strike. Minimum should be 10 to 15 wells.

6. If oil or gas is discovered, how much of the profits go to the general partners and how much go to the limited partners?

7. Are you buying a working interest or a royalty interest? Generally, you do not want to have to capitalize all the drilling costs as you would have to do with a royalty interest.

In a typical oil and gas drilling program, you may be asked to put up a certain amount of cash, say $25,000 over a two-year period, and obtain a letter of credit for $50,000. If the letter of credit is called because a profitable well is not discovered, you are out the additional $50,000. If oil or gas is discovered, the profits will first be used to reduce the borrowings for drilling expenses that are covered by your letter of credit. Since this money is paid to or for your benefit, you may have some income tax consequences before you see any cash flow from your investment. But this is certainly better than having your letter of credit called. One reason to avoid the letter-of-credit approach is that it puts you in an uncertain cash flow position and can put tremendous strain on the drilling operation to try to avoid the embarrassment of calling the limited partners' letters of credit. Remember—you are *at risk* for the amount you have borrowed under the letter of credit.

With an oil and gas investment, your tax benefits are up front, and income and income-tax consequences are incurred later. The liquidity of your investment is extremely low. Even in a very successful project, your after-tax return will probably not be greater than 20 percent per year of your investment. The success of a drilling operation is generally reflected by the longevity of the income flow and not by what the first- and second-year return may be.

If a productive well or wells are drilled, you receive the benefits of the up-front tax deductions plus a stream of income subject to favorable income taxes. Since the energy crunch has caused oil and gas prices to increase dramatically, your oil and gas investment can be a fabulous winner for you from the pure investment standpoint, due to the inflationary potential of the product. Thus your ownership of oil and gas reserves can be a potential hedge against inflation. If the drilling is not productive, you get to keep the tax deductions but lose all your investments, risking $.50 on each $1.00 of investment.

Moral: Make certain you know whom you are depending on before you enter into an oil and gas program. The general partner will make or break the investment.

Red Flags for Oil and Gas Leases

In addition to what was just said about what to look for, the existence of any of the following in the prospectus should cause you to think twice about any oil and gas investment:

1. No limitation exists on general and administrative overhead. Even if the general partner is at risk with you, he can recapture his risks through overhead charges.
2. The general partner has a conflict of interest such as (a) he may be able to drill for his own account; (b) he can farm drilling prospects from one partnership to another (interprogram farmouts)—which is okay if an outside engineering firm is used to determine a fair term between programs; or (c) he is in the drilling business and could charge the partnership a noncompetitive price for a rig.
3. The drilling program will take place on a portion of a prospect (like a checkerboard) rather than over an entire area. In this case, a profitable well could be drilled on your partnership property and then surrounded by wells on property that your partnership does not own. You would not get a return in this situation justified by your risk.
4. The general partner has experienced a very large jump in program

size, say from $2 million in 1980 to $12 million in 1981, and is attempting to raise $20–$25 million in 1982. It is too difficult to grow so large this fast.

5. A change in drilling philosophy or in planned areas of operation occurs.

After Your Dollars Are in the Ground

If your oil and gas investment is successful, the fun begins. To avoid income tax on your profits, you might consider transferring your interest to a Clifford Trust (see Chapter 2) or to your children. If your investment return occurs in your retirement years, take the money and enjoy it. You might even consider rolling it over into another oil and gas investment if your income-tax bracket justifies it. Because of the depletion allowance, you or your children will not have to pay income tax on every dollar received.

If your investment has turned out to be a loser, you might consider giving it to charity. In the early years, you may be able to show enough gas or oil flow to get a reasonable appraisal of your partnership interest and make more money by being charitable than you could by holding onto your investment.

The Stick-to-It Attitude

If you believe in oil and gas investments, do not make one investment and nervously wait for something to happen. Think of going back to the wells for future investments so that you can spread your risk over many different drilling opportunities and improve your chances of coming out a winner in the long run.

Other Types of Shelters

Motion Pictures

Motion-picture investments offer a chance to make a quick profit if a film becomes an instant hit and offer substantial tax write-offs if the film bombs. The beauty of the motion-picture investment is that it can be speedily depreciated under the "income forecast method," which is based on the estimated box office life of the film.[21] Also, investors can take an investment tax credit on the entire cost of producing a film if 80 percent or more of the cost is incurred in the United States (if less than 80% is incurred in the US, a tax credit can be taken only on expenditures made in the US).[22] Nevertheless, although the tax advantages are very appetizing, no one can predict the public acceptance of a film, even for films with proven box office stars. Thus the tax advantages may only serve to soothe the pain of an investment that turns out to be nearly worthless.

Agricultural

In the agricultural area, an investment in crops can result in a 50% to 90% first-year loss, attributable to costs of labor, fertilizer and equipment.[23] Risks include the weather and price fluctuations. The breeding of cattle can also generate very substantial first year losses, attributable to the purchase of an initial herd (and depreciation thereon) and grain costs. The sale of offspring will result in long-term capital gains if the livestock are held more than twelve months (24 months in the case of horses and cattle).[24] The risks here include disease and price fluctuation.

chapter 8

How to Make the Most of Marital Discord

Richard and Susan were having marital problems, not the least of which was their inability to make ends meet. With two kids and a costly mortgage, Richard's $44,000 income did not seem to go very far.

Their attorneys worked out a divorce settlement according to which Richard would keep the small equity in their home but would pay Susan $24,000 each year as family maintenance for her support and the support of the two children. The full amount was deductible from Richard's gross income as alimony and income to Susan. However, Susan was permitted to file her tax return under the more favorable head-of-household rates and to claim her two children as dependents.

Because of the tax savings of over $2,000, Richard and Susan are able to live their separate lives in peace and in comfort.

Not much good can be said about the agonizing process of severing the legal ties of marriage. Feelings of betrayal, resentment and guilt often snuff out a couple's ability to communicate in a productive manner with regard to the economic issues of who gets what and when. That is why so often divorce lawyers have to be brought forth to wage long battles on behalf of their clients. Yet regardless of what your marital situation may be with regard to who is at fault and to what degree, do not let your feelings obscure the importance of proper tax planning in the splitting of property and income.

In most divorces, there are three economic issues that must be resolved: ownership of property, payment of alimony and child support. Each of these has its own specific tax consequences, which must be understood.

Property Settlement

When John transfers property to his wife, Mary, in a property settlement, John is usually treated for income-tax purposes in exactly the same manner as though he had sold the property and given the cash to Mary. The reason for this is that the value of Mary's interest in the marital property (called a dower right) is presumed to be equal in value to what she receives.[1] Thus when Mary releases all her dower rights in exchange for property being conveyed to her, she is deemed to have paid a fair market price for the property.

> As part of a divorce settlement, John transfers title to their home, which was titled in John's name only, to Mary in exchange for Mary's release of her dower rights.
>
> If John originally paid $40,000 for the property and it has appreciated to $140,000, John will realize a long-term capital gain of $100,000. Mary has no tax consequences upon the transfer.

In the above situation, John has three options. First, if he is age fifty-five or over, he can make the one-time election to exclude the $100,000 gain from the sale of his principle residence (see Chapter 5).[2] Second, if he purchases a new residence of equal value within twenty-four months, he can elect to defer the gain.[3] Third, he can include the $100,000 gain in his income subject to the 60 percent exclusion for long-term capital gains.[4]

There are several circumstances in which a property settlement will not cause either spouse to incur any taxable income. Suppose, in the above example, title to the real estate had been in Mary's name. In a property settlement, John would have transferred all his interest in the property to her. But since his interest in the property was only a marital interest (in the case of a husband, called courtesy interest), his release of that interest would not have caused any tax consequences.

If John and Mary held all their property jointly (title in both their names) and they split the value of their property equally, the property split would be treated as a division of property and would be nontaxable to either one. In order for a division of property to occur, all property should be titled as tenants by the entirety (also called jointly with rights of survivorship; see Chapter 15).[5] If property is titled as tenants in common (joint interest but without the expression of survivorship rights), there is some question as to whether a true divison of property can occur. The reason for this is that title as tenants in common creates two distinct property interests that can be separately conveyed. This is not the case with title joint with rights of survivorship.[6]

If a property settlement is to be paid for a period of more than ten years, the payments, up to 10 percent of the amount to be paid, are deductible each year to the spouse making the payments and income to the spouse that receives them.[7]

Rick agrees to pay Charlene as a property settlement the total sum of $110,000, payable in the amount of $10,000 per year for eleven years.

For each of the first eleven years, Rick will be able to deduct $10,000 from his gross income and Charlene will be required to include a like amount in her gross income.

In order for a property settlement to be deductible, it must be made over a period of time that is *more than* ten years from the date of the divorce decree or separation agreement pursuant to which the payments are made. If the period of time is for ten years or less, the payments will be treated simply as a nondeductible property settlement unless they qualify as periodic payments described below.

Even if the more-than-ten-year rule is satisfied, if the payments are truly for the release of property rights (as opposed to being for the support of the recipient), the payments will not be deductible to the person making them or income to the person receiving them.[8]

Alimony

Alimony is the periodic payment of money or other property when such payments are imposed on the spouse making the payments pursuant to (a) a decree of divorce or of separate maintenance; (b) a written instrument that is incident to a decree of divorce or separate maintenance; or (c) a written separation agreement.[9] *Periodic* here means that the payments are made over a period of time and that the total amount of payments to be paid cannot be determined. Generally the easiest way to make certain that payments will qualify as alimony is to make the payments contingent on the nonhappening of some event. For example, payments that terminate in the event of the remarriage, death or change in economic condition will qualify as alimony.

In some states, the obligation to pay alimony automatically terminates in the event of the recipient's remarriage. In such a situation, the IRS has contested the deductibility of periodic payments that survive the remarriage of the recipient (such as when the payments are contingent only on the death of such spouse). This is something that must be noted if alimony payments are meant to be a disguised property settlement, as is discussed next.

When Alimony Makes Sense

Suppose your wife makes a fair and reasonable demand on you of $120,000 as a property settlement. She does not want any part of your

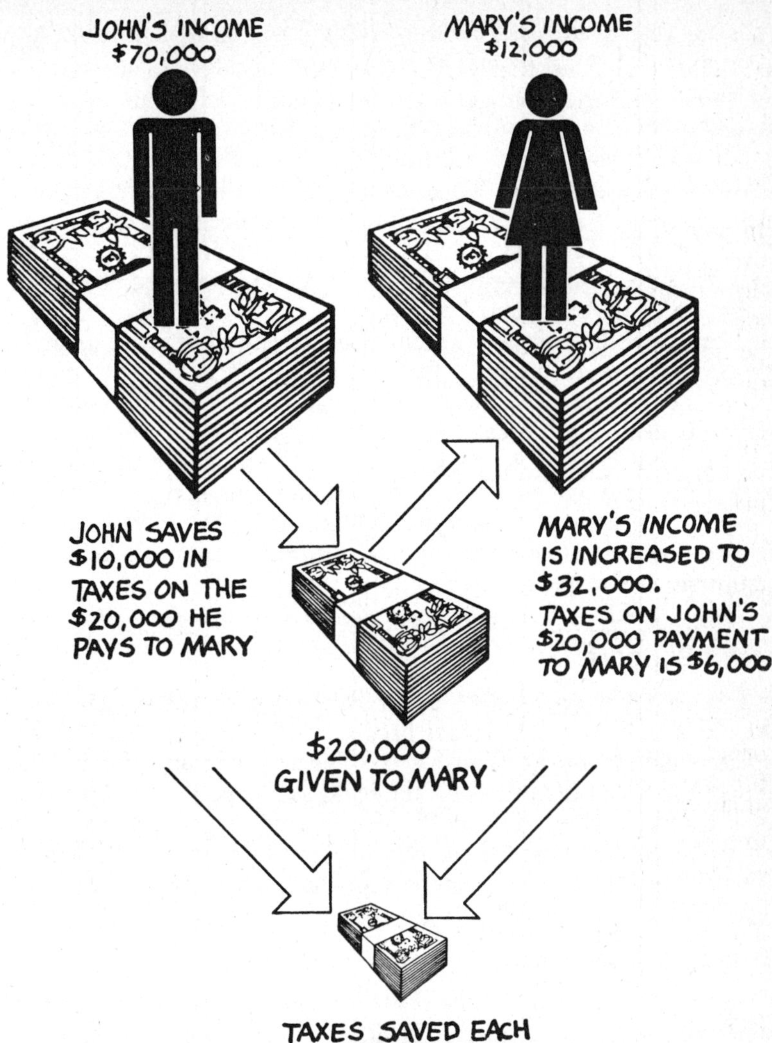

$70,000 a year income because she can go back to work as a receptionist and make $14,000 a year. Instead of your paying her the $120,000, you will both be better off if you give her a modest amount of cash as a property settlement (say $20,000) and give her the rest of what she wants *and more* as deductible alimony. If you promise to pay her $20,-000 a year for eight years (such payments to terminate in the event of her death), your net payment (after a 50% savings for the tax deductibility) is only $10,000 per year. This means that your total after-tax dollar obligation to her is only $100,000 instead of the $120,000 you were originally asked to pay. And this does not take into account the time value of money (obviously you would like to defer your obligation to pay for as long as possible).

Meanwhile your spouse will have to pay tax on the $20,000 she receives at an approximate 30 percent rate, taking into account her $14,000 of income as a receptionist. Her total after-tax benefit has now been increased from $100,000 to $132,000 ($20,000 property settlement plus alimony payments—after-tax of $14,000 ($20,000 less $6,000 for taxes × 8). You both gain!

The greater the difference in your taxable income from your spouse's, the more it makes sense for dollars to exchange hands through deductible alimony payments rather than through the mechanism of a property settlement. Each situation has to be analyzed, taking into account expected incomes and respective tax tables. But in most cases, the payment of alimony, which in reality can be nothing more than a disguised property settlement, can result in substantial tax savings. These tax savings can be divided between the spouses so that both will benefit economically in the long run.

Child Support

Child-support payments are not deductible to the noncustodial spouse or income to the custodial spouse.[10] If the noncustodial spouse makes child-support payments of $1,200 per year or more for a child, that spouse is entitled to claim the child as a dependency exemption (worth a $1,000 deduction until 1985, when indexing for inflation takes effect) unless the custodial spouse can prove he or she paid for more than one-half of the child's support for the taxable year in question.[11]

Deductible Child Support

In order for payments to be treated as child support, the payments must be clearly designated as such. If child-support payments are lumped together with alimony and called family maintenance, the entire payment will be treated as alimony. This result is based on a Supreme Court decision that stated that payments are presumed to be alimony unless they are specifically identified as child support.[12] Occasionally spouses will inadvertently label the payments family maintenance when a portion of the payment was intended to be child support. But in most cases, the styling of payments as family maintenance is done with the express purpose of saving taxes within the former family setting.

Ronald and Jane Padgett have five children ranging in age from 7 to 15. Jane is a homemaker and Ronald makes $90,000 per year. Ronald is willing to pay $3,000 per child per year for child support and $20,000 per year for alimony. These payments would cost him $35,000, of which he would recoup $12,500 (he is in the 50% tax bracket and $5,000 is deductible for claiming the children as dependents and $20,000 is deductible for the alimony) in tax savings, for a net cost of $22,500.

If instead Ronald pays a total of $40,000 as family maintenance, all deductible as alimony, his net cost after the tax savings is only $20,000. Meanwhile, Jane's after-tax dollars have increased by nearly $1,000, so that they both benefit.

If Ronald and Jane agree that child support will be paid as family maintenance, the document setting forth the payments should contain two special provisions: (a) the family maintenance will cease in the event of Jane's remarriage and genuine child support will commence; and (b) as each child reaches age eighteen, the family maintenance payments will be reduced by $3,000 per year. Also, Ronald should be covered by enough life insurance to pay Jane the remainder of this obligation at his death.

In most divorce cases in which dependent children are involved, the settlement is structured in such a way that all payments made by one spouse to the other are deductible as family maintenance or alimony. Both spouses generally are better off with this type of planning, and the only loser is the keeper of the federal government's tax coffers.

The Joy of Giving

If you are involved in the emotional upheaval caused by a failing marriage, probably the last thing you want to think about is making a gift to your spouse. However, giving can be painless when you realize the tax savings that may be involved.

Suppose you have $600,000 of assets in your name, and your spouse has $50,000. If your marriage is not doing well, you might expect to make a very sizable transfer of property to your spouse as a property settlement in the event of the demise of your marital relationship. If the property settlement consists of the conveyance of your Florida condominium, which you purchased for $50,000 eight years ago and which is now worth $220,000, your tax liability could be as high as $34,000. However, if you gave the property outright to your spouse, you would avoid taxes altogether. The unlimited marital deduction (see Chapter 10) enables you to give as much property as you want to your spouse, gift-tax free.[13] The drawback of the gift approach to your spouse is that he or she would have a basis in the property of only $50,000, versus $220,000 if the property were received via a property settlement. The gift approach can also help your estate planning. Note, however, that the gift in this situation should be made prior to the commencement of the divorce proceedings. Otherwise, the IRS might argue that it was a property settlement and attempt to collect taxes from you. Also, making the gift might have an adverse effect on your ability to negotiate a fair and equitable settlement with your spouse.

Estate-Planning Opportunities

When you lose your spouse, you also lose the marital deduction possibility from your estate settlement (unless you remarry), which is discussed in Chapter 10. Consequently, if you are elderly when divorce hits and you and your spouse have accumulated substantial wealth, you should consider a division of property (in a manner that causes the least amount of income taxes possible) so that neither spouse's estate for federal estate taxes is any greater than necessary. This will enable children to inherit much more of your property and Uncle Sam much less.

part II
Estate-Tax Planning

chapter 9

Introduction to Estate-Tax Planning

Now that you have learned some of the basics of income-tax planning, you will now get a sense of how to protect your accumulation of wealth from the IRS at the end of the road. Much of your effort to reduce your income-tax liability will be for naught if you do not take the necessary steps to minimize your estate-tax liability.

The 1981 Economic Recovery Tax Act of 1981 significantly changed the rules regarding the payment of estate taxes. The vast majority of taxpayers will pay no estate taxes when the unified credit is fully phased in in 1987 (see Chapter 10 for a discussion of the unified credit and how it affects your estates taxes)—unless inflation dramatically causes the size of estates to swell.

Nevertheless, our estate-tax structure can have a devastating impact on the taxpayers who must pay estate taxes. Plus there are scores of people who will not make it until 1987 and may generate a very large estate-tax liability for their heirs.

The only way you can be certain that the federal government gets little or none of the assets you have accumulated during your lifetime is to take the proper planning steps.

Rough Computation of Your Estate Tax

Your estate for estate-tax purposes will consist of your present financial statement (all assets minus liabilities) plus (if these items are not already included):

1. the face value of life insurance (less cash value) that you own or in which you have an incident of ownership (see Chapter 14)
2. gifts of life insurance policies made within the last three years
3. any gift taxes you have paid during your lifetime plus the value of gifts in excess of the exclusion allowance ($3,000 per beneficiary prior to 1982, $10,000 per beneficiary after 1981)

4. one-half of real estate or other assets you own jointly with your spouse with survivorship rights or as tenants in common
5. property you have transferred with "strings attached," such as a retained life interest or a transfer to take effect only on your death

Once you have totaled your estate, subtract an approximate 2 to 8 percent for funeral and administration expenses. The larger your estate, the less this percent should be. If you are married and are not on the outs with your spouse, you could subtract up to 100 percent of your net estate for property left to your spouse under the unlimited marital deduction. If you are counting on using the unlimited marital deduction, you should calculate (a) what tax your spouse will have to pay if you leave all your property to him or her; and (b) what tax you will have to pay if your spouse predeceases you.

Figure your estate tax on the remaining amount from the table in Appendix E. From this amount, subtract your unified credit for the current year (see Chapter 10) plus whatever gift taxes you may have already paid. This will give you a rough idea of what your federal estate-tax liability will be.

NOTE: If there is a chance that you will inherit significant assets from a spouse or parents, you should do a dry run with these assets included in your estate so that you can see where you are headed.

Estate-Tax Planning

The process of reducing or minimizing your estate tax consists of several steps, the most basic of which is the preparation of proper documents (such as a will and a trust). If you are married, you should consider the use of a marital deduction trust, which is discussed in Chapter 10 along with the opportunity to make unlimited gifts to your spouse.

If you are not married or if you have already adopted a proper will and trust arrangement, you need to consider the ownership of property, such as life insurance (Chapter 11), real estate (Chapter 15) or disposition of your own closely held business interest (Chapter 12). Finally you might want to consider charitable bequests (Chapter 16) or a gifting program among family members and the avoidance of probate (Chapter 14). In any event, you want to begin your planning with those issues that mean the most to your estate. For example, you do a lot more for your estate planning by getting right the ownership of your $200,000 life insurance policy than you can by struggling with gifts to children in trust. In fact, getting right the ownership of your life insurance may take care of the gift-to-children questions if the life insurance is placed in a special trust as is discussed in Chapter 11.

A comprehensive estate plan does not happen overnight. You and your attorney must decide what is the best arrangement of ownership of property as well as how you should accumulate wealth in the future. Nevertheless, it is important to do your estate planning now, because estate taxes will never be higher than they are during the current year. Therefore, there is a tremendous incentive to get your estate planning in proper shape. Moreover, estate planning is a process; it is never truly over until you die. The sooner you begin the process, the better your chances that your estate will be in good shape before it is too late to do any more.

chapter 10

How to Split Your Estate with Your Spouse

You have reached the ripe old age of forty-seven when you decide you would rather take it with you than leave it to Uncle Sam. You devise a way to transfer effective ownership of your assets to your wife and kids at your death, but in such a way that not all the assets will be taxed at your wife's death. You reduce the taxes at your death to zero and help your wife with her subsequent estate planning so there are nominal taxes at her death.

Although you can't take it with you, you have provided for your wife and children to take it with them.

Once you have spent your lifetime building an estate for yourself and your family, you want to keep it in the family and pay the lowest amount of taxes possible. One way to do this is to split your estate with your spouse and thereby reduce the overall estate taxes that have to be paid when you die.

The Unified Credit and What It Means to You

Estate taxes are calculated on the first dollar of each person's taxable estate. However, there is a credit against estate taxes, called the unified credit, which permits an individual to have a sizable taxable estate without having to pay any estate taxes.

The Economic Recovery Tax Act of 1981 substantially increased the unified credit over the next five years, when in 1987 an individual can have a whopping $600,000 taxable estate without having to pay any estate taxes.[1] Because of inflation, it is difficult to determine what the $600,000 exemption means in terms of today's dollars. Nevertheless, it does represent a radical change in the thinking of Congress. This is how the unified credit is phased in:

Year of Gift or Death	Credit	Exemption Equivalent
1982	62,800	225,000
1983	79,300	275,000
1984	96,300	325,000
1985	121,000	400,000
1986	155,800	500,000
1987	192,800	600,000

Because the unified credit is phased in over a period of time, it is important that you and your spouse take the proper planning steps to minimize estate taxes if your combined estates approach or exceed the *present* exemption equivalent. Otherwise, you could cause unnecessary estate taxes for your heirs if something were to happen to both of you in the near future. In an inflationary economy, the value of your assets will appreciate markedly. Thus it is important for you to do the proper planning even if your present asset holdings are less than the present exemption equivalent.

The Unlimited Marital Deduction

The 1981 legislation now enables one spouse to pass an unlimited amount of property during his or her lifetime, or at death, to the surviving spouse without generating any estate or gift taxes on the transfer.[2] The unlimited marital deduction creates the opportunity for a zero estate tax liability at the first death of you or your spouse. However, this technique must be combined with other estate-planning techniques in order for estate taxes to be minimized at the second death.

NOTE: If your estate plan consists of a marital deduction trust (see below) that was signed prior to September 13, 1981, your trust must be amended in order to qualify for the unlimited marital deduction. If the trust is not amended, your marital deduction will be limited to the greater of $250,000 or one-half of your adjusted gross estate.

Any property that passes outright to the surviving spouse qualifies for the marital deduction. Also, any property that provides income to the surviving spouse and over which he or she has a general power of appointment at death (the ability to direct whom the property will pass to) qualifies for the marital deduction.

A *qualified terminable interest* will be allowable for the marital deduction as well.[3] A terminable interest is a life estate or an income interest for lifetime in certain property, such as can be granted in the family trust discussed later in this chapter. In order for a terminable interest to be qualified, the executor of the estate (or the donor if the transfer is made during his or her lifetime) must make an election to have the terminable interest property pass as part of the unlimited marital deduction.

The qualified terminable interest approach makes sense when one spouse wants to provide for the other but does not want to give that spouse unfettered control over the assets that comprise the terminable interest. For example, an individual with a $1,200,000 estate could make a gift during lifetime to his spouse of $600,000 in a terminable-interest trust. Assuming he elects the marital deduction with respect to this gift, the $600,000 will not be included in his estate, even if his wife predeceases him. Also, the $600,000 can be used for the benefit of the husband if he survives his wife. In order for this to occur, the wife must elect to appoint an income interest back to her husband at her death. In this way the $600,000 can benefit the husband during his lifetime without being included in his estate. This type of planning only makes sense if (a) the donee spouse does not have substantial assets in his or her name; and (b) the donor spouse wants to exercise some control over the assets given to his or her spouse.

How Estate Splitting Works

Suppose Frank has an estate of $450,000 and his wife, June, has an estate of $250,000. If Frank dies and leaves everything to June, there will be no federal estate taxes at his death. However, even if June survives until 1987 or after, there will be at least $34,000 of estate tax at her death that could have been avoided.[4] And this calculation does not include appreciation of the assets left to June.

Suppose that in this case, Frank places as much property as is covered by the exemption equivalent ($225,000 in 1982) in trust for the benefit of June and his children and leaves the remainder of his estate to June in a manner that will qualify for the marital deduction.

> A trust is simply a contract between Frank and another person, usually a bank, that requires the trustee to hold, invest and distribute property according to the directions Frank has given it in the written contract.

If the trust is written to restrict June's rights to govern the disposition of the property in the trust, the trust assets will *not* be included in her estate.[5] However, the trust can provide for June and other family members to receive all the income generated by the trust assets and for June

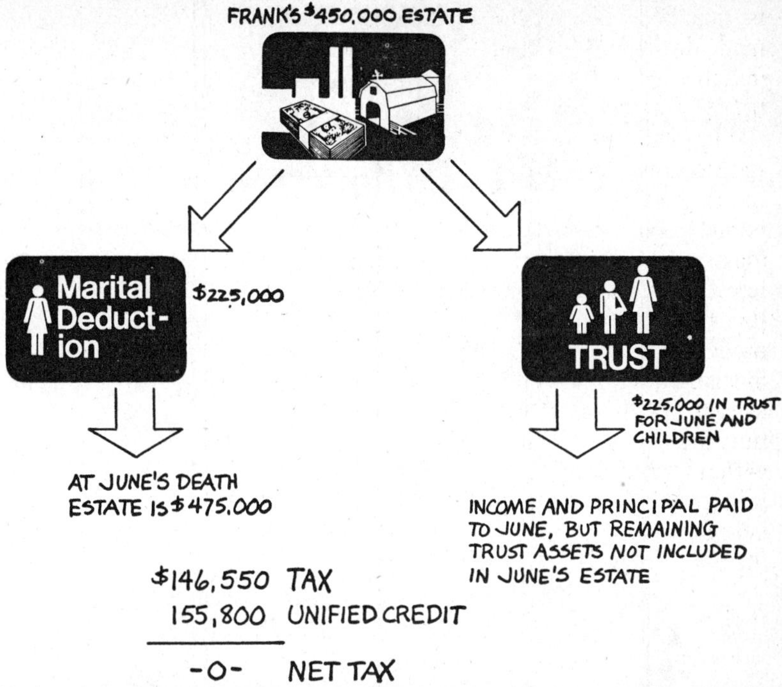

to receive additional trust property if she needs it. The trust can enable June to demand from the trustee each year the greater of $5,000 or 5 percent of the trust assets, without changing the nature of the remaining trust assets vis-à-vis inclusion in June's estate at her death.

At June's subsequent death, only the $225,000 that passed to her under Frank's marital deduction plus her own $250,000 will be subject to federal estate taxes. The remaining $225,000 in Frank's trust will pass outright to their children and will not be part of June's estate. The federal estate taxes on June's estate of $475,000 will be completely offset by the unified credit if she lives until 1986. If she does not, Frank and June will have done what they can to minimize estate taxes.

The family trust can also provide for significant income tax savings. The trust can be designed to provide for a *sprinkling* of income among family members. Sprinkling means that income dollars can be paid out to children, according to their needs determined by the trustee, and taxed at their lower tax bracket.

The money can be used by the children to pay for college, private-school education, camp or any other expenditure their mother does not have a legal obligation to make.

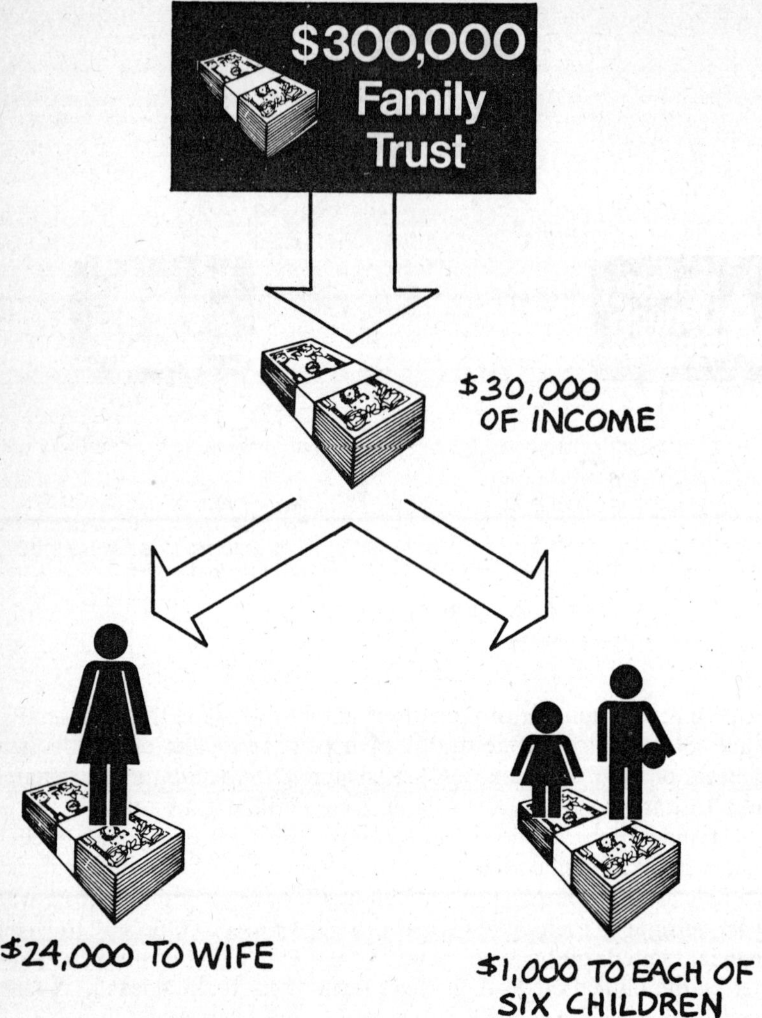

The Marital Deduction Trust

In the previous example, Frank could have created the same favorable result by leaving his entire $450,000 estate to a trust that would have split up his estate into a marital share (here $225,000) and a family share (here $225,000). The marital share would be held in a trust—the *marital trust*—and the family share would be held in the family trust. The family share then would not be included in his wife's estate at her subsequent death.

The marital trust either must be a qualified terminable interest (discussed on p. 117) or it must otherwise qualify for the marital deduction by giving June at least an income interest coupled with a general power of appointment over the assets held in trust. The family trust, on the other hand, must restrict the rights June has in the assets held in that trust. The document that creates the marital trust and the family trust is commonly called the *marital deduction trust.* Typically the marital deduction trust provides for the funding of the family trust first to the extent of the exemption equivalent (the maximum extent possible without generating any net federal estate taxes) and for the remainder of the estate to pass into the marital trust. As the years pass, the size of the family trust will increase to $600,000 by 1987. Thus, at some point, Frank may want to specify that only a limited amount of property will pass into the family trust and that the remainder will pass to June. This approach enables June to have complete control over a larger share of assets than would otherwise be the case unless the qualified terminable interest trust is used for the marital share. (See Funding the Family Share later in this chapter.) See Appendix F for a model marital deduction trust.

When You Should Be Interested

If you and your spouse have combined assets that exceed the exemption equivalent, you should each consider a marital deduction trust to minimize estate taxes at the second of your deaths. The larger your combined estates, the more important the adoption of a marital deduction trust becomes.

The only thing you should think twice about is that if you select an independent trustee, you are giving the power to someone other than your spouse to invest your money and to make decisions as to how much money your spouse needs to live on. For this reason, the trustee of your marital deduction trust should be carefully chosen. In addition, the trust should give you during your lifetime and your spouse after your death the ability to change independent trustees at any time.

If your trust is drafted to provide that principal will be distributed from the family trust only for identifiable circumstances, such as health, support, maintenance or education, it is possible to make your spouse the sole trustee of the trust. In such a situation, you will still avoid inclusion of the family trust assets in your spouse's estate. Check with a qualified attorney (see Chapter 25) to determine if your family trust is drafted in a way that permits your spouse to be sole trustee with no adverse tax consequences. Also, be mindful that you sacrifice investment and administration expertise by not using a bank as a trustee.

Because a bank can be hired as an agent to assist in the administration of trust property, it may be desirable for your spouse to be the sole trustee of your marital deduction trust. A bank or trust company can then be used to help administer only the property or assets with which your spouse needs help. This will enable your spouse to minimize trust fees at your death. The background of your spouse plus the complexity of your estate are factors to take into account in making this decision.

Other Reasons to Have a Trust

Even if estate taxes are not a problem for you, there are still important reasons you may want to have a trust.

1. When minor children are involved:
    (a) A trust that takes effect at your death can enable your spouse to save income taxes by paying income to or for the benefit of children. The trust must be a sprinkling trust, discussed on p. 119, to create the favorable income tax results.
    (b) If a trust is not established at your death, it should be established at your spouse's death to protect the assets you leave for your children.
2. The establishment of a trust can provide an investment vehicle for your assets, and the trustee can assist your spouse in financial planning.
3. If you leave everything outright to your spouse, he or she may remarry and the assets you thought would pass on to children or other family members may wind up in someone else's family instead.
4. The assets in the trust can be protected from the reach of creditors.

When to Pay Estate Taxes at the First Death

In almost every case, it is good planning to provide for zero estate taxes to be paid at the death of the first spouse to die. The reason for this is that the surviving spouse can make gifts of $10,000 per year on a tax-free basis to family members.[6] Thus if your surviving spouse is faced with a large estate, he or she can give away a significant portion of it. Also, Congress seems intent on eliminating estate taxes for most people. Thus if your surviving spouse lives past 1987, the exemption equivalent may be raised even above the $600,000.

There are some situations, however, in which estate taxes should be paid at the first death. Suppose you and your spouse are elderly or in poor health. In such a situation, it may make sense for some estate taxes to be paid at the first death to eliminate the problem of "estate tax bracket creep." Our estate taxes are based on a progressive tax system, with the maximum tax being 50 percent for 1984 and after (down from 70% for 1981 and before), so that assets will be taxed at a higher rate if they are included in an estate that already is large.

Suppose Joe has an estate of $2,500,000 and his wife has an estate of $600,000. If Joe leaves everything outright to his wife (except what can be placed in a family trust without generating any estate taxes), he will cause some assets to be taxed at his wife's death at a 50% tax rate, instead of a 37% tax rate, which would be available at his death.

Joe's decision as to how much to leave outright to his wife must be based on his wife's life expectancy. If she is in good health, Joe may want to take his chances that his wife can give away substantial assets before she dies and that perhaps the tax laws will change again.

When to Make a Gift to Your Spouse

If your estate and your spouse's estate substantially exceed the exemption equivalent, it is important that each of you has enough in assets to pass into a family trust, so that if something happens to one of you, the other's assets will be covered by the exemption equivalent.

It is 1985 and Rick has $800,000 in assets and his wife, Julie, $100,000. Rick should make a gift to Julie, assuming their marital relationship is excellent, of $300,000, so that if anything happens to Julie, Rick's estate would only be $500,000 for estate-tax purposes. This arrangement also gives Rick's estate a chance to grow to the $600,000 exemption equivalent for 1987 without generating any estate taxes.

Funding the Family Share
of the Marital Deduction Trust

Once you have decided to have a marital deduction trust, you must decide what portion of your assets will be allocated to the family share (the share that is taxed at your death) but not included in the estate of your spouse.

If you and your spouse are elderly or in poor health, you may want to use a formula that would equalize the size of your estates. This type of planning may cause some estate taxes to be paid at your death but would avoid "estate tax bracket creep" at your spouse's death. This is the so-called *equalization formula.*

If you and your spouse expect to live for quite a while, you should consider using the unlimited marital deduction to avoid estate taxes completely at the first death. The taxes saved may have to be paid at the surviving spouse's death, but the following are reasons to take a chance:

1. The surviving spouse will have the use of the money during his or her lifetime.
2. The surviving spouse can make gifts of $10,000 per year to each chosen beneficiary to reduce estate-tax liability.
3. Federal estate taxes may continue to be reduced by Congress before the surviving spouse's death.

Assuming you are committed to avoiding estate taxes completely at the first spouse's death and to minimizing estate taxes at the surviving spouse's death, you have two choices. First, you could fund the family share to the extent of the exemption equivalent (this is the method commonly used since the Tax Reform Act of 1976). This works fine for minimizing estate taxes but may take more property away from the control of the surviving spouse than is necessary (such as when the assets in the surviving spouse's estate are less than the exemption equivalent). Your second choice is to fund the family share to the extent necessary to reduce the assets that would be included in the surviving spouse's estate to the then-applicable amount of the exemption equivalent. If your assets plus your spouse's assets are less than the exemption equivalent, the family share would not be funded.

Let's examine how these two choices work:

In 1986, J.R. dies owning assets of $600,000, all of which pass into his marital deduction trust. His wife, Ellen, has assets in her name of $200,000. Under the first option discussed on p. 120, funding the family share to the extent of the exemption equivalent, the family share of J.R.'s trust would be funded to the extent of $500,000, leaving $100,000 to pass outright to Ellen, giving her unfettered control of $300,000 of assets. Under option two, reducing the assets that would be included in the surviving spouse's estate, only $200,000 would pass into the family share so that Ellen would have $500,000 of assets subject to her control. In both cases, no estate taxes would be paid upon either J.R.'s death or Ellen's death, since the exemption equivalent for each is at least $500,000.

The disadvantage of the second option is that if Ellen is a poor money manager, she may waste the additional assets left outright to her. Also, if she remarries, another family may eventually own J.R.'s assets. Nevertheless, we predict that the second option may soon become the more favorable method of funding the family share of the marital deduction trust.

If, in the previous example, J.R.'s estate was $1,600,000, the family share of his marital deduction would be funded to the extent of $500,-000 regardless of which option was chosen. The unlimited marital deduction would permit the remaining $1,100,000 to pass estate-tax free to Ellen, who would then have a total taxable estate of $1,300,000. She would be well advised then to make gifts to reduce the size of her estate.

Use of a Private Annuity After the Death of One Spouse

The private annuity is discussed in Chapter 12 as one means of transferring ownership of a closely held business or interest in real estate during one's lifetime. The private annuity is simply a sale of property from one person to another in which the purchase price is an unsecured promise of the purchaser to make periodic payments to the seller for the lifetime of the seller. Since the payments terminate at the death of the seller, there is no residual value included in the estate of the seller.

The private annuity can be used to great benefit after the death of one spouse and the formation of a marital trust and family trust. The surviving spouse simply sells his or her interest in the marital trust to the family trust, thus eliminating a significant portion of assets from the surviving spouse's estate while creating a flow of income for the surviving spouse's lifetime.

George dies in 1985, leaving a $2 million estate to Marge in a marital deduction trust. The family trust is funded to the extent of $400,000, and the remaining $1,600,000 is held by Marge. Marge sells the $1,600,000 of assets to the family trust for a private annuity. At her death, none of the $1,600,000 of assets is included in her estate (except what she has saved out of the annuity payments) but it passes to her children under the dispositive provisions of the family trust.

One Final Example

Rich has an estate of $400,000 and his wife has an estate of $150,-000. Assume Rich's estate plan includes a marital deduction trust, so that if he died in 1982, approximately $225,000 would be placed in a trust that would not be taxed at his wife's death (Trust B) and the balance (approximately $175,000) would be distributed outright to his wife or in a trust taxable at her death (Trust A), qualifying for the marital deduction. No tax would be due at Rich's death (the unified credit covers the tax on the Trust B assets), but about $33,500 of tax would be due at his wife's death with an estate of about $325,000 (Trust A plus her own assets) if she were to die in 1982. If she were to die in 1983, the estate tax would be $17,000, and for years after 1983, there would be no estate taxes at her death.

In 1987, no tax would be due at either death, whether or not a trust were used. However, it would not be wise for Rich and his wife to revoke their trust until their combined estates were covered by the exemption equivalent. Also, they should provide for inheritance and estate growth in their planning. Thus Rich and his wife should not make any dramatic changes in their estate plan for several years. However, Rich might consider a sizable gift to his wife to minimize his estate-tax exposure if his wife were to predecease him. Also, Rich's trust should be amended to provide for an unlimited marital deduction if it was signed prior to September 13, 1981.

chapter 11

How to Own Life Insurance

John Paul has a taxable estate of $600,000. His wife divorced him two years ago, so he has no marital deduction. He is responsible for four young children, and he wants to make certain they will be able to afford the cost of a college education.

John Paul decides to purchase $200,000 of insurance to cover his children in the event of his premature death. If he is the owner of the policy, the insurance will cause his estate to pay an additional $66,000 in federal estate taxes.

To avoid the estate-tax problem, John Paul sets up a trust that he cannot amend or revoke. He transfers the insurance to the trust and contributes cash each year to the trust for the payment of premiums.

When he dies four years later, the $200,000 life insurance proceeds are paid to John Paul's trust for the benefit of his children but are not included in his estate for federal estate-tax purposes. He has effectively given $66,000 more to his children.

If you are like most of us, life insurance will be the biggest part of your estate if you die before retirement. Consequently the manner in which you own life insurance is a tremendously important consideration when you are putting together an estate plan. Like John Paul, you do not want a portion of your expense of purchasing insurance to be for the benefit of the federal government.

When Life Insurance Is Taxed in Your Estate

Any life insurance that is payable to or for the benefit of your estate or in which you have an incident of ownership will be taxed as part of your estate. An *incident of ownership* entitles you to, among other things, any of the following rights:

1. to assign ownership of the policy
2. to change beneficiary
3. to obtain a policy loan
4. to pledge the policy for a loan
5. to surrender or cancel the policy

In order to keep life insurance out of your estate, you must give up *all* incidents of ownership of the policy.[1] Also, you must live for at least three years after transferring ownership of a life insurance policy in order for it to be excluded from your estate.[2] This rigid three year requirement for the gift of a policy is independent of the value of the policy you transfer.

When You Should Own Your Own Life Insurance

Generally you should own a policy of life insurance on your life if the ownership *will not* create any additional federal estate tax.

Suppose your estimated estate is $500,000, $300,000 of which is life insurance. If you are married, you can own the life insurance without creating any federal estate taxes at your death because of the unlimited marital deduction. However, it only makes sense for you personally to own the policy (as opposed to putting it into a trust, which we will talk about later) if you establish a marital deduction trust, as discussed in the previous chapter. The marital deduction trust permits you to split your estate with your spouse and to avoid excessive taxation at your spouse's death if he or she survives you.

NOTE: If you do not take advantage of the estate-tax savings available under a marital deduction trust, there is no federal estate-tax advantage to owning your own policy. The only advantages would be that you would have the right to elect settlement options and would control the policy in the event of a breakup in your marriage.

When Your Spouse Should Own the Life Insurance on Your Life

Because of the unlimited marital deduction, there is not an overwhelming advantage to your spouse owning life insurance on your life. The primary advantage is that if your spouse predeceases you, the life insurance policy can pass in a way that will not be included in your estate.

Suppose assets in your name total $600,000, and assets in your spouse's name, consisting of your home, total $180,000. Let us consider what should happen if your spouse, who owns $200,000 of life insurance on your life, should predecease you. In this situation, your spouse's assets, including the life insurance policy, should pass into a family trust (see previous chapter) so they will not be included in your estate. Your estate is already so large that significant estate taxes may have to be paid at your death, unless you remarry. The family trust will have to continue to pay premiums on the policy to keep it in full force and effect.

You might ask where the family trust will get the cash to pay the premiums. One way is for you to buy your home from the trust for interest only for a fixed period of time, say for twenty years. This gives you an interest deduction, transfers ownership of your home to you subject to a $180,000 liability and creates income for your spouse's family trust. A portion of the trust income can be used to pay the life insurance premium, and the remainder can be spread among yourself and your children, thus effecting income tax savings among family members (the beneficiaries of the income are the ones who must pay tax on it, but at their respective tax rates).[3]

NOTE: A special provision must be added to your trust to provide for the purchase of your home for interest only. Also, the trust should state what the interest rate is that you have to pay (such as, in today's climate, 12%–14%).

The beauty of keeping the life insurance in your spouse's family trust is that at your death, the proceeds will not be taxed in your estate; thus the life insurance proceeds pass for the benefit of your children both income-tax free and estate-tax free.

In summary, the ownership of life insurance on your life by your spouse can work best if your spouse predeceases you. But what can you do about the possibility that you will predecease your spouse?

The Super Trust

If you transfer ownership of your life insurance policy to a trust that contains special provisions (a so-called *super trust* because it is so wonderful),[4] the proceeds of the life insurance can be kept out of your and your spouse's estates, as long as you live for at least three years after making the transfer.

The life insurance trust must be irrevocable[5]—this means you cannot amend or revoke it once it has been established. Also, the trust must be designed so that you have no incidents of ownership in the policy, and neither you nor your spouse should be trustee of the trust. Other provisions you should consider having in the trust and that make it truly "super" are:

1. Income of the trust will be used to pay premiums on your life insurance. This will cause income (and losses) of the trust to be taxed to you. Thus if the trust borrows from a policy's cash value to pay future premiums, the interest on the borrowings will pass through to you as long as you contribute the amount of interest payment to the trust. This creates a favorable income tax benefit for you.[6]

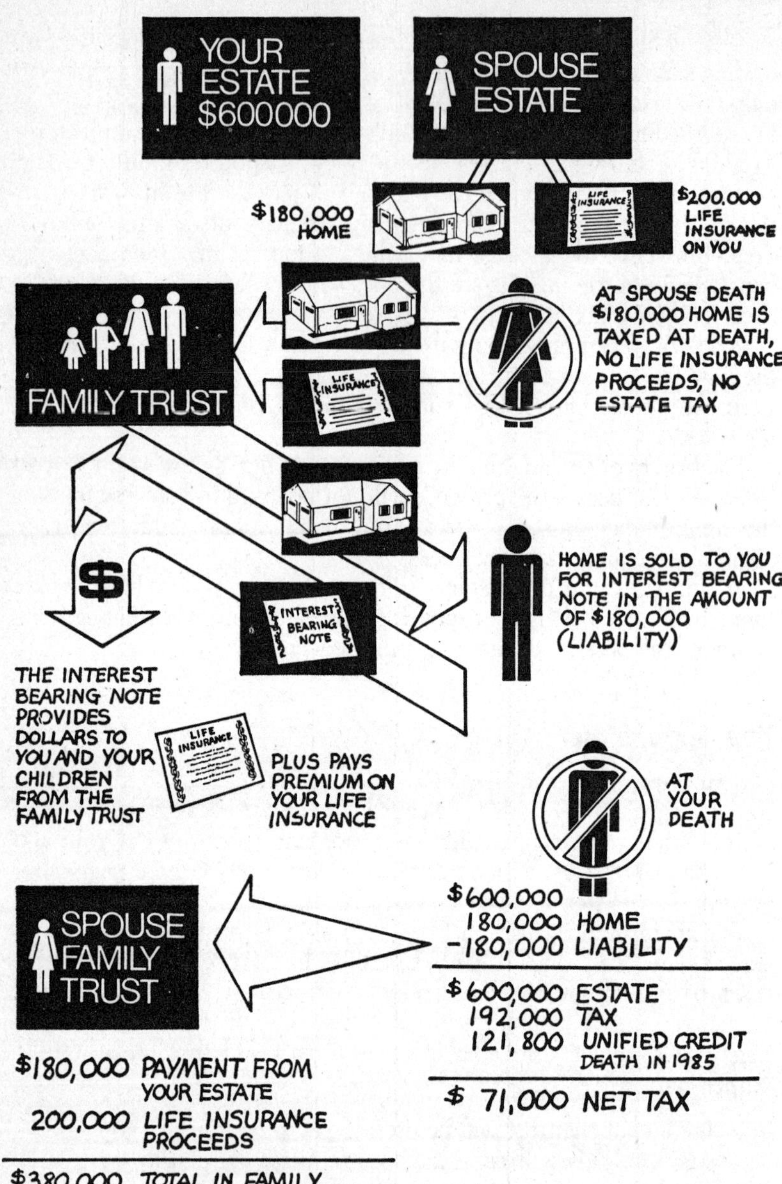
YOUR ESTATE $600000
SPOUSE ESTATE
$180,000 HOME
$200,000 LIFE INSURANCE ON YOU
LIFE INSURANCE
FAMILY TRUST
LIFE INSURANCE
AT SPOUSE DEATH $180,000 HOME IS TAXED AT DEATH, NO LIFE INSURANCE PROCEEDS, NO ESTATE TAX
$
INTEREST BEARING NOTE
HOME IS SOLD TO YOU FOR INTEREST BEARING NOTE IN THE AMOUNT OF $180,000 (LIABILITY)
THE INTEREST BEARING NOTE PROVIDES DOLLARS TO YOU AND YOUR CHILDREN FROM THE FAMILY TRUST
LIFE INSURANCE
PLUS PAYS PREMIUM ON YOUR LIFE INSURANCE
AT YOUR DEATH
SPOUSE FAMILY TRUST
$600,000
180,000 HOME
-180,000 LIABILITY
$600,000 ESTATE
192,000 TAX
121,800 UNIFIED CREDIT
DEATH IN 1985
$71,000 NET TAX
$180,000 PAYMENT FROM YOUR ESTATE
200,000 LIFE INSURANCE PROCEEDS
$380,000 TOTAL IN FAMILY TRUST AT YOUR DEATH NO ADDITIONAL TAX
TOTAL BENEFIT FOR CHILDREN $980,000 LESS TAX OF ONLY $71,000

2. Contributions to the trust will be subject to withdrawal by your named beneficiaries. This will permit contributions, up to a certain amount, to be treated as present gifts for estate-tax purposes and thus enable you to avoid any gift-tax consequences.
3. Your spouse will have the power to appoint trust property (including a life insurance policy) to you or to your children. This creates some flexibility for this otherwise unchangeable and inflexible instrument.
4. At your death, the trustee will be able to use trust assets (such as cash from the life insurance proceeds) either to purchase assets from your estate or to loan money to your estate. This enables the trust to provide liquidity to your estate for the payment of estate taxes and administrative expenses.
5. As with all trust documents, the trust should state what happens to the assets at your death, what the powers of the trustees are and under what circumstances, if any, the trustee can be replaced.

The super trust can work wonders in keeping life insurance proceeds out of both your and your spouse's estates. But remember—you must live for three years after making the transfer of the life insurance to the trust. Thus this estate-planning technique will not be of much use to you if you are in failing health. See Appendix G for a model super trust.

Generally the super trust is an essential part of estate-tax planning for very large estates. It maximizes the benefits to you of owning life insurance and enables you to control what happens to your property until death.

Life Insurance Owned by a Qualified Plan

Chapter 13 presents information on how assets in a qualified plan can be paid out in a manner that will bypass your and your spouse's estates. If you own life insurance and are covered by a qualified plan that permits life insurance to be held for your benefit, you should consider transferring the life insurance to your qualified plan. This technique can keep the life insurance proceeds out of your and your spouse's estates creating the same result as the super trust.

Generally, you are not permitted to sell assets to a qualified plan because of the potential for abuse. However, an exception exists for the sale of life insurance both to and from a qualified plan as long as the policy is transferred for a price equal to its then-existing cash value.[7]

The transfer of life insurance to a qualified plan has the following advantages over the transfer of life insurance to a super trust:

1. You do not have to live for three years after the transfer in order for the proceeds to be kept out of your estate. The transfer is treated as a sale, not a gift.[8]
2. If the qualified plan is already in existence, you do not have any significant expense in making the transfer. A super trust is an expensive document for your attorney to prepare because of its complexity.
3. You have much more flexibility with a qualified plan. Ownership can easily be transferred back to you. This is not always the case with a super trust.
4. The qualified plan will already have money in it; thus you do not have to come up with your own bucks for the payment of premiums.

There are, however, several disadvantages of choosing a qualified plan over a super trust for the ownership of your life insurance. First, the term coverage portion of your life insurance is taxed to you—at rates that get very high for individuals over sixty years of age.[9] The income charges, however, will be recaptured if the policy is distributed back to you. Second, you may outlive your participation in the qualified plan. If this happens, the qualified plan proceeds, including the life insurance policy on your life owned by the plan, will be distributed to you. You will then be faced with the following options:

1. Terminate the life insurance coverage.
2. Keep the life insurance and suffer the additional estate taxes that will be generated by having the life insurance proceeds included in your estate.
3. Keep the life insurance and transfer it to a super trust. In this case, you will then have to live for three years after making the transfer to keep the proceeds out of your estate.

You are never faced with these options, of course, if you control the qualified plan and intend to keep working until death does part you from your business. In this case, the qualified plan assets do not have to be distributed during your lifetime.

Ownership by Children

A final option for the ownership of life insurance is to have your adult children own the policy on your life. This will result in the insurance proceeds being excluded from your estate.[10] Perhaps equally beneficial is that if your adult children are in a higher income tax bracket than you, the payment of interest by them on borrowings on the policy to pay premiums will result in a greater tax savings to them than it would to you.

How to Transfer Control of a Closely Held Business

Ralph Bosken, age 56, owns a plastics business conservatively valued at $600,000. His son, Mark, is a rising star in the development of new plastics and is ready to take over his father's business at any time.

Ralph wants his business interest converted into cash at his death for the benefit of all his children. He wants his son to be the successor owner, but he does not want to give up control of the business until he is ready to retire.

Ralph enters into a buy-sell agreement with Mark and his plastics corporation, whereby the plastics corporation will buy enough stock at his death to pay for his estate taxes and funeral and administrative expenses, and Mark will purchase the remainder of Ralph's stock. Mark then will become the sole shareholder of the business, and Ralph's estate will get its cash.

If Ralph had wanted to limit the value of his stock, he could have sold one share of common stock to Mark, traded his remaining common stock for preferred stock (which has a fixed value), and thereby transferred control of the corporation (and future appreciation) to Mark.

As a business owner, you have to come to grips with the question of who will be your successor and how that successor will acquire your business interest. No one will ever quite be able to run your business as well as you have, but you want to find someone who will do nearly as good a job, or your business might die with you.

Also, you need to consider how much you want to receive for your business and when you want to sell it. You might consider transferring ownership of your business during your lifetime, if you have something else you want to do, or you can plan to hold onto it until death do you part.

Buy-Sell Agreement

If you want to wait until death to transfer your business interest, a reliable way to transfer it to a key employee or family member is by means of a buy-sell agreement. A buy-sell agreement contains a commitment to buy (by the purchaser) as well as a commitment to sell (by your estate) and limits your ability to transfer your business ownership during your lifetime to anyone other than the prospective purchaser. Because buy-sell agreements are a very common—yet very important—agreement, we will spend some time looking at them in depth. They can accomplish the following objectives:

1. Transfer money into your estate in the event of your death.
2. Fix the value of your business in your estate for estate-tax purposes.
3. Enable your successor to have the security of knowing that he or she eventually will be able to take over your business.

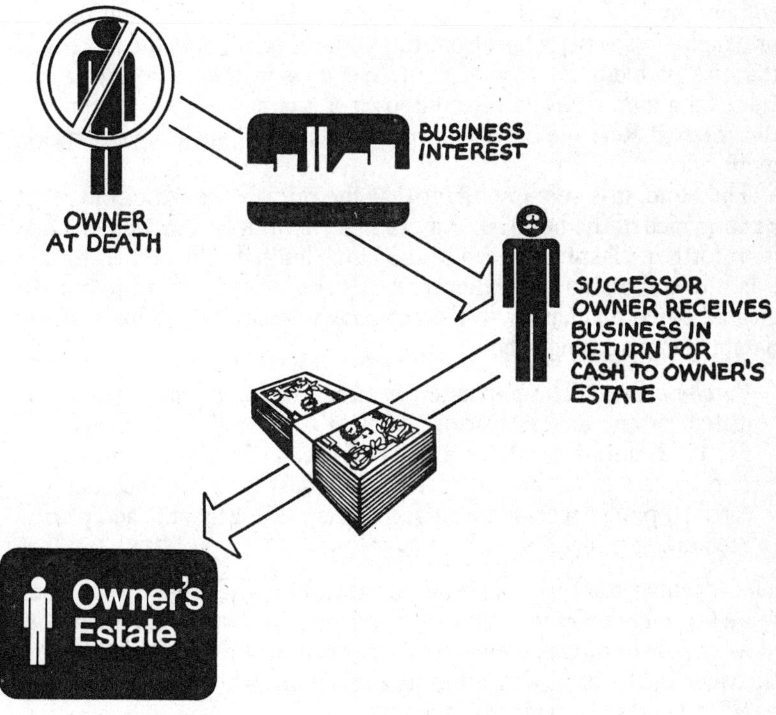

Note that in order to obtain these results, however, a buy-sell agreement must contain the following requirements:

1. a commitment to buy and a commitment to sell
2. a determinable purchase price to be paid for the business that is fair and adequate when the agreement is made
3. a right of first refusal—if the business is to be sold to an outside person, it must be first offered to the prospective buyer at a price not greater than that spelled out in the buy-sell agreement.[1]

Purchase Price

In a family setting (for example, one in which a father wants to sell his business to his son or daughter at his death), the purchase price for the business is a very sensitive item. In such a case, there is a significant advantage to the father's estate in setting the price artificially low: if the price is acceptable to the IRS, the estate will show a reduced value for the stock, the size of the gross estate will be reduced and estate taxes will be saved. Meanwhile, the business stays in the family, and the son or daughter can use dollars from the business to support the mother, if that is a problem. Because of the tremendous incentive to place a low value on a family business for purposes of a family buy-sell agreement, the Internal Revenue Service is very suspicious of such buy-sell agreement prices.

Therefore, it is very important that the price be linked to the profit performance of the business. For example, a formula valuation (such as is set forth in Chapter 13) can be used for a limited valuation of stock in a family corporation, and then that valuation can be increased or decreased based on changes in the net book value of the company stock. Sample language might be:

Purchase Price: The purchase price shall be $2,000 per share adjusted for any increases or decreases in book value from October 31, 1982, until the date of the shareholder's death, such increases or decreases in book value to be determined by the corporation's certified public accountant in accordance with generally accepted accounting principles.

The advantages of this technique are that (a) the IRS will probably look more favorably upon the purchase price; and (b) if the corporation does grow rapidly in profits, the buy-sell agreement will markedly hold down the value of the stock over a formula valuation (which is what the IRS might otherwise be tempted to apply).

Suppose a $500,000 book value company that was making modest profits makes $100,000 in after-tax profits over a three-year period. Based on a formula valuation that takes into account a capitalization factor, the price would increase by $450,000 over that three-year period.

If a formula price were initially used and allowed to fluctuate only with changes in book value, the price would only increase $300,000.

Cross Purchase vs. Entity

A cross purchase buy-sell agreement is an agreement between the business owner and an individual, such as a key employee or co-shareholder, for the purchase of the owner's business at death. An "entity" buy-sell is an agreement between the business owner and the business she or he owns (such as the partnership or corporation) for the purchase of her or his business interest at death.

In the case of a corporation, an entity buy-sell is very attractive because it permits the use of corporate dollars to fund the purchase price. A buy-sell agreement is usually funded with life insurance on the business owner (the dollars for the purchase price become available at a very convenient time). It is desirable to use corporate dollars to pay for the life insurance premiums, since these after-tax corporate dollars have usually been taxed at a lower rate than the dollars available to individuals. Also, the dollars in the corporate till are more accessible than those from an individual's pocket.

Family Business Owners Beware*

An entity buy-sell agreement for a family corporation can create severe tax problems because of *attribution* rules. *Attribution* means stock owned by one person is deemed to be owned by another because of the family connection.[2] This attribution can cause dollars paid from the corporation at death for stock to be treated as payments of dividends subject to hefty income taxes.[3] Suffice it to say that in the parent-child corporate setting, it is good to avoid a straight-entity type buy-sell agreement. Rather, consider a combination agreement whereby the corporation purchases as much stock as it can without generating any dividend treatment (a so-called 303 redemption requires that the value

---

* Because of the 1982 Tax Act, stock redemptions can now also be made in the family setting in the event of death.

IN ENTITY BUY-SELL, THE CORPORATION OWNS LIFE INSURANCE ON A & B

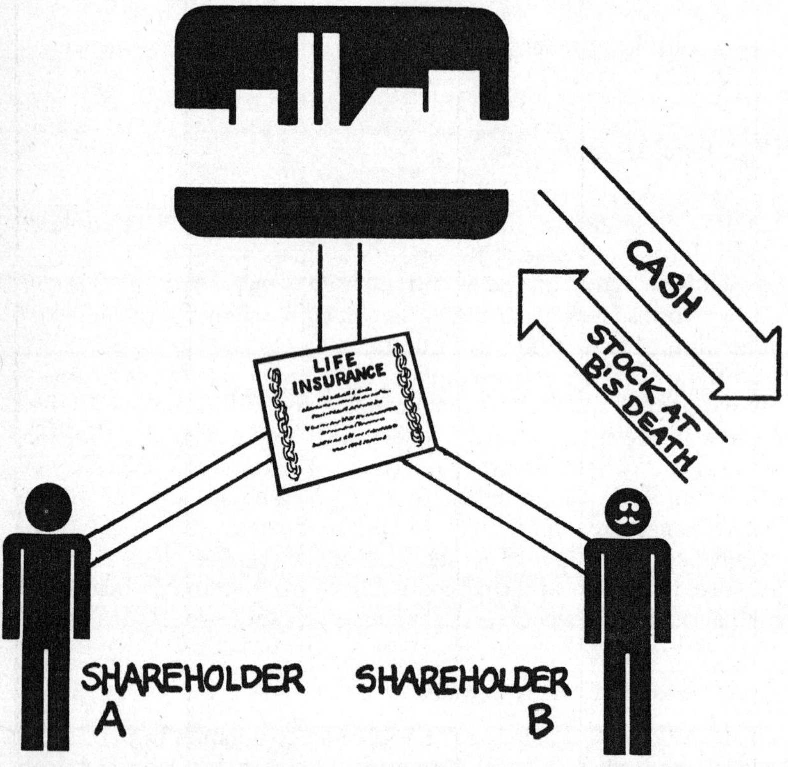

of stock be at least 35% of the adjusted gross estate and the amount of stock purchased be not greater than the value of estate taxes, funeral bills and administrative expenses) and the remainder of stock is purchased by the offspring who will take over the business.[4]

NOTE: When the son or daughter has a large monetary commitment at the parent's death, life insurance can usually be purchased least expensively on a split-dollar basis, in which the corporation shares in the payment of the premium. (See Chapter 23 for a discussion of split dollar.) *Important*—the split dollar setup should be of the collateral assignment variety.

In a nonfamily setting, the sole shareholder has tremendous flexibility as to where his estate gets dollars for his stock. He can sell the stock directly to a key employee, or he can sell one share at his death to his key employee and redeem the remaining shares with the corporation. The latter technique works extremely well when the corporation is in a very strong cash or profit position and can easily afford to purchase nearly all the owner's stock.

Recapitalization

Recapitalization is a technique of restructuring stock ownership (preferred stock with a fixed value is issued in exchange for common stock) to keep future appreciation of the business out of an individual's estate. After the restructuring, the preferred stock can be subject to a buy-sell agreement or can be given to other family members as income-producing property.

Preferred stock is stock that is generally dividend bearing, has a fixed call price and is treated preferentially on liquidation of the corporation.

Recapitalization occurs most frequently in the family business setting because it definitely means one shareholder giving up something in favor of another shareholder. If recapitalization occurs in a nonfamily setting, the "giving up" shareholder must get something back from the corporation in exchange for fixing his or her stock ownership interest. What the person gets back might be in the form of qualified-plan benefits, which can be kept out of his or her estate (see Chapter 13), or life insurance benefits.

Typically, a parent will transfer all his or her common stock in exchange for preferred stock, which has a fixed value (not in excess of the book value of the company) and is usually dividend bearing. This trans-

FUTURE APPRECIATION PASSES
ONTO OTHER SHAREHOLDERS

fers all future appreciation of the corporation to the other shareholders, who in this case would be family members.

Schmitt, age 58, owns all the outstanding common stock of Target Corp. The present value of Target Corp. is $4 million, and the value is expected to increase to $5 million in five years. Schmitt makes a tax-free gift of a few shares of common stock to his son and then, pursuant to a plan of recapitalization, Schmitt exchanges all this common stock for newly authorized preferred stock paying a fixed annual dividend (in a nontaxable reorganization).[5]

The advantages of a recapitalization are as follows:

1. It fixes the value of stock in the owner's estate and passes appreciation to family members.
2. It creates a source of income for the surviving spouse.
3. All future increases in value of business inure to the benefit of common stock owners.

The disadvantages:

1. Dividend dollars that are paid on preferred stock are taxed twice.
2. A business owner who recapitalizes loses control of the corporation, since preferred stock should be nonvoting.
3. Sale of the preferred stock may be taxed as a dividend.[6]

Preferred stock can also be issued on the initial formation of a corporation, such as when real estate is incorporated. If a real-estate owner transfers the real estate to a corporation for preferred stock and gives the common stock to his or her children, any future appreciation of the real estate will pass to the benefit of the children and not be included in the original owner's estate. Thus this is a way for the real-estate owner to "freeze" or fix the value of that real estate in his or her estate. Nevertheless, in addition to the other disadvantages, the incorporation of real estate raises two additional problems: (a) the corporation may be treated as a personal holding company subject to additional taxes on profits not paid out as dividends; and (b) most states' franchise taxes are based on the value of the corporation's assets—and the transfer of substantial real estate to a corporation can thus generate significant franchise taxes.

Personal Holding Company

A personal holding company is a corporation that receives a large share of income from dividends, rents or personal services. Such a corporation pays penalty taxes on any after-tax income that is not distributed as dividends to shareholders. The purpose of the penalty tax on personal holding company undistributed income is to prevent individuals from using the corporate structure to avoid the payment of tax on passive income. This penalty tax is now up to 50 percent (down from 70%).[7]

However, in the family-owned corporate setting, the formation of a personal holding company can be advantageous. Suppose Mr. Schmitt in the previous example transfers all his stock in Target Corp. to a new corporation in exchange for common stock and preferred stock. He can then give the common stock to his son and shield his estate from any appreciation of the Target Corp. stock. The new corporation will be a personal holding company, because it receives all its income from the ownership of the Target Corp. stock; yet there are several advantages that the Schmitt family receives:

1. If Target Corp. is worth more than its book value (most corporations are), Mr. Schmitt can take preferred stock in the new corporation, which has a greater value than he would be permitted on a straight recapitalization.
2. The new corporation's preferred stock *will not* give rise to dividend treatment upon its sale.

Family Partnership

An alternative to the recapitalization or personal holding company methods to freeze the value of a business or real estate is the formation of a family partnership. A family partnership has two classes of partners: (a) frozen or fixed partners, who have a fixed interest and who have a first call on partnership profits up to a predetermined amount (such as 14% of their fixed interest in the partnership); and (b) regular partners, who take what is left of the partnership and its profits after the frozen partners take what they are entitled to. Typically parents are frozen partners and children are the regular partners. This results in a very similar situation to the preferred stock—common stock relationship available through a recapitalization or formation of a personal holding company.

The family partnership is an excellent vehicle for freezing an interest in real estate without generating any of the problems caused by incorporating real estate.

The *family partnership freeze* has the following advantages over the

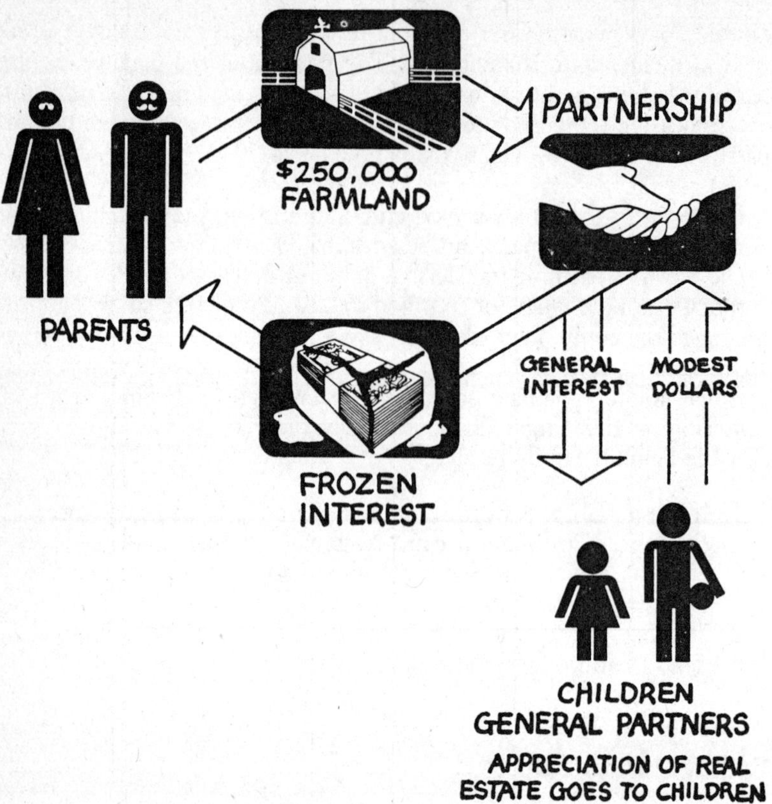

freeze through the corporate recapitalization or formation of a personal holding company:

1. Whereas dividend dollars distributed to a shareholder of a corporation are subject to double taxation, all income and losses pass through the partnership and are taxed only once—to the partners.[8]

2. Distributions from a partnership will generally not cause gain until the cash received exceeds the partner's basis in the partnership interest. If this gain occurs, it will be treated as a capital gain.[9] In the family corporate setting, a shareholder will have to satisfy certain rules in order to be eligible to receive capital gains treatment on the receipt of distributions that are in exchange for this stock.[10]

The disadvantages of the family partnership freeze are the following:

1. Capital must be a material income-producing factor in the family partnership. This means a substantial portion of the gross income of the family partnership must be attributable to the use of capital in the partnership business.[11] A corporate freeze does not have this requirement.
2. The valuation of a partner's interest in a partnership is more difficult than in a corporate setting, and it may be more difficult to qualify for the installment payment of estate taxes (see Estate Tax Deferral for Closely Held Business Interest later in this chapter) in the partnership setting.[12]

In the most basic type of family-partnership setting, the parents would contribute property for a partnership interest that would have a fixed liquidation value and carry a preferred income position. By agreement, the parent's interest would have a ceiling on its capital rights. The children's partnership interest, on the other hand, would have income and capital distribution rights that are secondary. The children's position is highly leveraged and stands to benefit the most if the partnership business proves successful.[13]

The family partnership is an idea whose time has come. Tremendous flexibility is available to you, and you can retain control of the "frozen" property with much more certainty than in a preferred-stock recapitalization.

Installment Sales

Property, including a business ownership, can be sold to take future appreciation out of the owner's estate. Since the property is transferred, the only value that is included in the previous owner's estate is the cash and promissory note that was given for the property. Typically in an installment sale, the promissory note will provide for payments over a period of time—like a home mortgage—at a modest interest rate. An installment sale is valuable because (a) generally the property transferred will appreciate more rapidly than the rate of interest on the unpaid balance of the purchase price; and (b) the sale of the property is not subject to the same levels of IRS scrutiny as if it were included in the estate. To protect yourself on the valuation question, appraisals should be obtained and careful records maintained of the installment-sale transaction.

The installment concept has one major drawback—it creates current income taxation to the previous owner on every payment received.[14] That tax, which is based on his gain at the time of sale, would not be present if he held the property until death, because the basis in property is stepped up to its date-of-death value.[15] Also, at death, the residual gain that is contained in the unpaid installments will be taxed. Thus there is a tradeoff of income taxes for estate-tax savings. The installment sale can work very well in the family corporate setting, where a parent desires to cease being connected actively with the business. In this case, the parent shareholder can redeem all his stock with the corporation and have the redemption treated as a sale for tax purposes. This transfers the ownership and control of the corporation to the remaining common shareholders. Note that in a family redemption, a special filing with the IRS is required.

Private Annuity

Instead of payments being made for property on an installment obligation basis in which the obligation survives death, consider a private annuity. The private annuity, briefly discussed in Chapter 10, is an unsecured promise of the purchaser to make periodic payments to the seller in return for the transfer of property. The payments generally terminate in the event of death of the seller. Because the payments are based on the life expectancy of the seller, the periodic payments may be considerably greater than those payments required on an installment basis for the same property if the seller is old. However, since the payments terminate on death, there is nothing left of value to include in the seller's estate. Thus, the private annuity can be an excellent estate freezing technique.

The annuity payments received by the seller are comprised of three elements for income tax purposes: (a) a nontaxable recovery of basis; (b) capital gain; (c) ordinary income.[16] The annuity payments made by the purchaser are treated as capital expenditures for the acquisition of property. Prior to the death of the seller, the purchaser's basis for depreciation purposes will be equal to the present value of the annuity at the time the annuity contract is made until the payments made actually exceed that value.[17] Upon the death of the seller, the purchaser's basis must be adjusted to reflect the payments actually made less the depreciation deductions actually taken.

When a Private Annuity Makes Sense

Suppose you are not in great health. A private annuity could result in substantial estate-tax savings for you.

Unless you are known to be afflicted with an incurable physical condition and death therefrom is imminent, you are *required* to use standard IRS actuarial tables, which are based on your age assuming good health.[18] Thus even though you may know your life expectancy is not what it should be, you can assume it is standard for private annuity purposes. This may be as valuable to you as buying life insurance at standard rates when you think for one reason or another you should be rated.

Pluses and Minuses

The primary advantages of the private annuity are the following:

1. The transferred property is permanently removed from the seller's estate without any gift or estate-tax consequences.
2. The seller receives payments over his or her life expectancy, which (a) creates a source of income for retirement and (b) enables the seller to spread the tax consequences of the sale over a number of years.
3. It creates less ill will in the family setting than an outright gift of a business interest to "active" family members.

The disadvantages of a private annuity include the following:

1. If the seller outlives his or her life expectancy, the cost to the purchaser could be prohibitively high. Also, unless the seller consumes the payments, the payments could add to the value of the

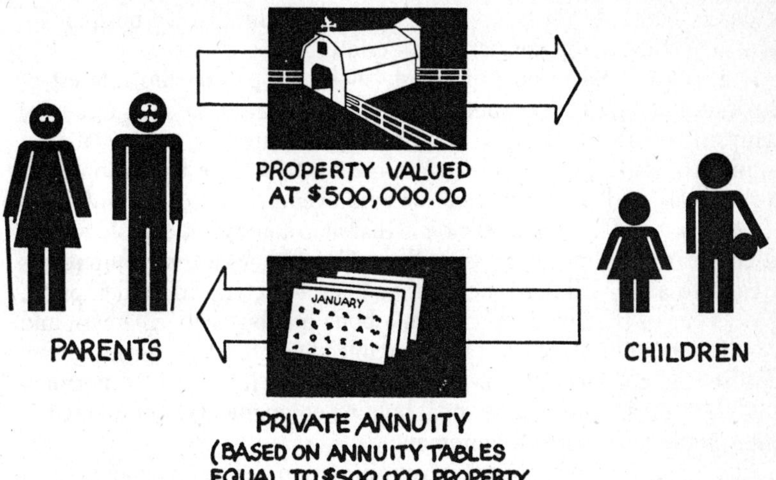

seller's estate. Finally the capital-gain portion of the annuity payments will be taxed as ordinary income if the seller outlives his or her life expectancy.

2. The seller has no guarantee that the annuity payments will be made according to the time of the agreement. This can be a problem if the property is not income producing. In order to protect the seller, the purchaser should own life insurance on the purchaser's life for the benefit of the seller. Then if the purchaser predeceases the seller, the seller can still receive his or her annuity payments in full.

3. The purchaser is not allowed any interest deduction on the payments made to the seller.

4. If the seller dies shortly after the purchase, the following occurs:

    a. The seller's estate sustains an economic loss that may be resented by other family members who are not part of the annuity purchase.

    b. The transferee has a low basis in the property.

NOTE: With both the installment sale and the private annuity, be certain that you transfer the property at its fair market value—otherwise the IRS might scream *gift* and cause additional taxes to be paid at your death.

Estate-Tax Deferral for Closely Held Business

Generally estate taxes have to be paid within nine months of the date of death. However, an exception exists when a closely held business interest constitutes a major part of an estate.

If a closely held business interest (such as a partnership interest or stock in a closely held corporation or a combination of such interests) comprises at least 35% of the adjusted gross estate (the gross estate less administration expenses), the estate taxes attributable to this business interest can, with one exception, be paid over a period of time of up to fifteen years.[19] The one exception is that an estate is not eligible for the fifteen-year installment provision if the closely held business interest is subject to a buy-sell agreement other than a Section 303 redemption. This is one of the few drawbacks to a bona fide buy-sell agreement and should not outweigh a buy-sell's favorable characteristics. Also, the special installment election may not apply to an interest in a personal holding company, since a personal holding company may not satisfy the active trade or business requirement.[20]

The fifteen-year installment payout provision permits payments to be completely deferred (with a nominal 4% interest on the first $1,000,-000 of business value and interest at the current interest rate—20% in 1982—on the excess) until the sixth year. Then for years six to fifteen, payments can be made at the rate of one tenth of the tax attributable to the business interest per year with an interest rate at the current rate (20% in 1982) on the unpaid balance.

A gross estate is worth $1,000,000. The family business interest is $600,000, and total estate taxes are $280,000. Sixty percent of the $280,000 of federal estate taxes can be paid over a ten-year period beginning five years after the decedent's death.

The policy behind this provision is to permit successor owners by inheritance to continue the closely held business rather than having to sell it to pay estate taxes.

In spite of the apparent attractiveness of the deferral of the payment of estate taxes, the use of estate-tax deferral should be a secondary or tertiary planning device and not be given too much importance. Remember—deferral of estate taxes is not nearly as important as the minimization or complete elimination of estate taxes.

Transfer of Business Ownership for Modest Estates

The advent of the unlimited marital deduction and the increasing exemption equivalent discussed in Chapter 10 create a new opportunity for individuals who have modest-size estates to be involved in creative planning for the transfer of their business interest. Since in these cases, the concern no longer has to be focused only on avoiding excessive estate taxes, the business owner can plan the transfer of a business along the lines of being more income-tax conscious.

Instead of the business owner owning significant insurance on his or her own life, paying for that insurance with after-tax dollars, and attempting to minimize the value of the stock that would be purchased by the successor owner, whether a relative or not, the business owner can essentially create a large purchase price for the business ownership and arrange for the life insurance to be paid to his or her estate from the business in exchange for the business ownership. This method works best in the corporate setting, where the sale of stock will occur income-tax free. (The purchase of a partnership interest can create some income to the extent that it represents a price paid for unrealized receivables.) In this setting, it is very desirable to shift thinking from being estate-tax conscious to income-tax conscious. The advantage, of course, to the corporate setting, is that the corporate dollars are taxed at a rate of only 16 percent (15% after 1982) up to the first $25,000, which enables a significant amount of insurance to be purchased with cheap after-tax corporate dollars. However, this approach does not work well in a family setting unless a family member will directly purchase the deceased's business interest.

Dr. Sara M. owns $250,000 of life insurance and is a 50% shareholder of M & N, M.D., Inc. The other shareholder is not related to Dr. Sara M. Dr. Sara M. is presently paying a premium of $8,000 per year, for which she has to make $16,000 of income. She enters into a stock-redemption buy-sell agreement whereby the corporation will purchase her stock interest for $250,000 at her death, and transfers her life insurance policy to the corporation. The corporation now has to make only $9,524 to make the insurance-premium payments of $8,000 per year.

Also, if your business interest will not be sold at your death, you may want a high value to be placed on it so that your heirs will have a higher cost basis in the business interest they receive.

Gloria J. owns a corporation that specializes in computer software. Her daughter, Julie, has worked with her in the business and would like to become the owner at her mother's death. Julie also would like to sell some stock to one of the key employees, Ralph.

Gloria's 100 shares of stock are bequeathed to Julie, who values it in the estate at $160,000. Only nominal state estate taxes have to be paid, and Julie takes the stock with a stepped-up basis of $160,000. She is then able to sell 40% or 40 shares to Ralph for $64,000 with no income-tax consequences.

If other children were involved who would be equal heirs of her estate, Gloria J. might insist that her daughter Julie pay a fair price for the stock so that all her children would be treated equally at her death. If this were the case, this would be a good situation for Julie to own life insurance on her mother's life to fund the purchase price.

chapter 13

How to Reduce Estate Taxes with the Use of a Qualified Plan

Paul Slonaker, D.D.S., has worked twenty years to acquire an estate of $600,000. He dislikes income taxes—he dislikes even more the fact that every additional dollar he makes will also be subject to estate taxes either at his death or at his wife's subsequent death.

Dr. Slonaker installs a defined benefit plan in his corporation that requires a yearly contribution of $35,000. Dr. Slonaker calculates that in ten years, the plan assets will grow to a total of $500,-000—all of which will be kept out of his estate if he dies and also out of his wife's estate. The estate-tax savings could be very large (over $100,000) if his wife predeceases him or if she has significant assets in her own name.

If you have accumulated a sizable estate, you should be sensitive to the fact that every dollar you earn may be taxed twice—once by income taxes and then again by estate taxes at your death or your spouse's subsequent death. The buildup of wealth in qualified plans (plans qualified under the Internal Revenue Code) enables you to avoid this double liability. Qualified plans are especially important to you for the next few years if you have a moderate-size estate, since they can make up for the loss of not having the full $600,000 exemption equivalent (see Chapter 10) available to you.

Exclusion of Qualified Plan Assets from Your Estate*

The assets you accumulate in a qualified plan will bypass your estate if they are paid out from the plan at your death to someone other than your estate and if certain conditions are met, including the condition

---

* The 1982 Tax Act has limited the estate-tax exclusion for qualified-plan assets to $100,000. This may make the super trust discussed in Chapter 11 the proper place for your life insurance. (IRC §2039(g))

that you do not receive the favorable income-tax treatment available for lump-sum distributions.[1] The logic behind these rules is that you cannot have both favorable income tax consequences and at the same time estate-tax exclusion.

The buildup of wealth in a qualified plan can be a very important part of what you have to pass on to your family at your death.

In addition, the qualified-plan assets can be kept out of not only your estate but your wife's estate if you make your family trust the beneficiary of the qualified-plan assets. Your family trust (see Chapter 10) should provide that none of the qualified-plan assets will be used for the payment of death taxes. In this way, the qualified-plan assets can be made available for the benefit of your spouse but not be subject to taxation upon her death.[2]

Suppose you already have a taxable estate of $600,000. Let's look at the savings created by the buildup of substantial wealth in a qualified plan.

Value of Qualified Plan Assets	Savings if Marital Deduction Available	Savings if No Marital Deduction Available
$ 400,000	0	$151,000
$1,000,000	0	$400,000

Although the estate-tax savings at your death can be diminished to zero if your spouse survives you (because your estate can now make use of the unlimited marital deduction; see Chapter 10), the total taxes saved at your spouse's subsequent death will in most cases be very significant, especially if the qualified-plan assets would otherwise cause her estate to increase above the amount covered by the unified credit (see Chapter 10). This is because your spouse will not have the marital deduction available.

NOTE: The estate-tax exclusion of qualified-plan assets makes a qualified plan an excellent place for life insurance to be owned. (See Chapter 11.)

If you are not married, you have all the more reason to be concerned about the accumulation of wealth in your estate.

Cutting into Corporate Profits with Qualified Plans

One of the bugaboos of successful closely held corporations is the accumulated-earnings tax, which is a penalty tax on corporate profits

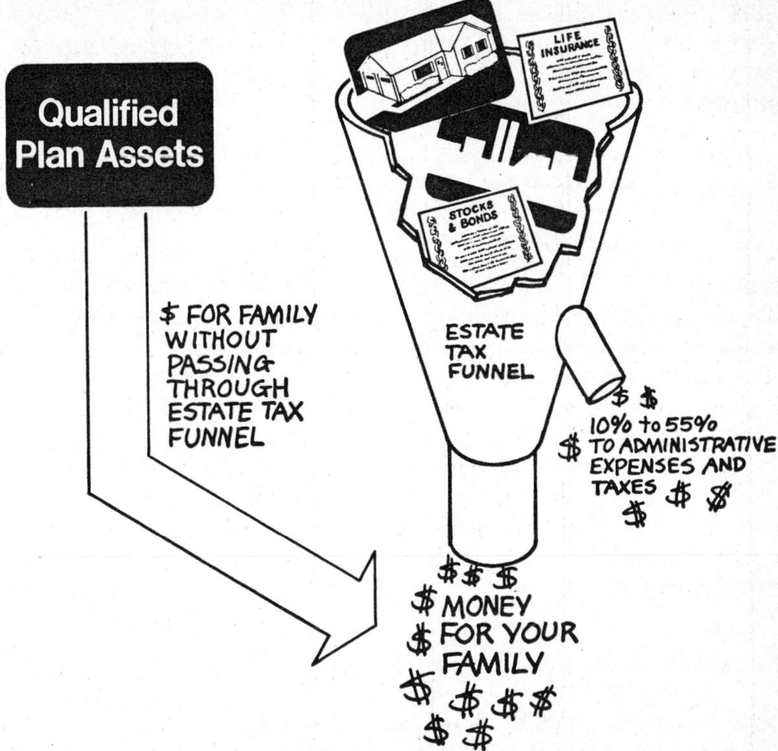

in excess of $250,000 ($150,000 for professional-service corporations) that have been permitted to accumulate beyond the reasonable needs of the business.[3] If profits accumulate beyond the $250,000 benchmark, the burden falls on the taxpayer to prove that the accumulation was for the reasonable needs of the business.[4] Rather than take a risk with this problem, it makes sense for a good share of those profits to be shifted to qualified plans. This will reduce the risk of an accumulated-earnings tax problem while producing additional benefits for employees.

In addition to bucking the accumulated-earnings tax problem, contributions to qualified plans can have a healthy effect on the price of the corporation's stock. By soaking up corporate profits, contributions to qualified plans can hold down the estate-tax valuation of stock.

Estate-Tax Valuation of Stock

Without a valid buy-sell agreement (see Chapter 12), the IRS will insist on a valuation of stock at its fair market value at date of death.[5] In determining fair market value, the IRS will look at a number of factors, not the least of which is corporate profits.[6] One of the formulas used for computing fair market value of closely held corporate stock is the following:

$$BV = \text{Book Value}$$
$$ABV = \text{Average Book Value over last 3 years}$$
$$AP = \text{Average after-tax profits of corporation over last 3 years}$$
$$\text{Value} = BV + 3(AP - .1ABV)$$

The 3(AP−.1ABV) is a capitalization factor that reflects the value of the company based on its ability to generate profits. This is one way of valuing goodwill. Any company that cannot generate much more than a 10 percent return on average book value does not have much goodwill.

As you can see, profits have a very significant effect on the value of stock in this formula. Suppose a $1,000,000 book value company expects $200,000 before-tax profits for the next three years. If it makes no contribution to qualified plans, its after-tax profits each year will be approximately $125,000 (assuming a modest dividend payout of $3,700 each year). At the end of three years, this is what the factors in the IRS formula look like:

$$BV = \$1,375,000$$
$$ABV = \$1,187,000$$
$$AP = \$200,000$$
$$\text{Formula: } \$1,375,000 + 3(200,000 - 118,750)$$
$$\text{Value} = \$1,375,000 + 243,750 = 1,618,750$$

If, instead, this corporation contributed $80,000 each year to a qualified plan, after three years (assuming dividends of $2,000 per year), the factors in the IRS formula look like this:

$$BV = \$1,249,000$$
$$ABV = \$1,124,500$$
$$AP = \$120,000$$
$$\text{Formula: } \$1,249,000 + 3(120,000 - 112,450)$$
$$\text{Value} = \$1,249,000 + 22,650 = 1,271,650$$

The reduction in stock valuation is over $345,000 through making large contributions to a qualified plan. If your estate is in the 40 percent estate-tax bracket, the estate-tax savings from this planning would be in excess of $130,000! Plus your estate would get the benefit of the qualified-plan assets allocated for your benefit.

The following situations should raise concerns about the valuation of stock when a sizable estate is involved:

1. A buy-sell agreement exists, but between father and son or mother and daughter, etc. (the IRS is not very accepting of agreed-upon share valuations in a family setting).
2. There is no buy-sell—either the stock will be passed on to a family member or the stock will be sold to some nonfamily member for the best price available.

In the latter situation, a Section 303 redemption should be contemplated (a redemption by the corporation of enough stock to pay estate taxes, funeral and administrative expenses), so that there is at least some purchase of stock at death to establish a benchmark for fair market value. A Section 303 redemption is available only if the value of the stock is at least 35 percent of the deceased's adjusted gross estate (gross estate less funeral and administrative expenses).[7]

Summary

Qualified plans may be an extremely important part of estate planning for the large estate. The nonbusiness owner has the opportunity, with them, to accumulate substantial wealth in a way that will bypass both his or her own estate and a spousal estate at death. The business owner can use the qualified plan both to bypass estate taxes as well as to help control the value of stock in his or her estate. The latter situation is especially important when the business owner has made no plans for a successor owner or for fixing the value of the business in his or her estate by means of one of the methods discussed in Chapter 12.

chapter 14

How to Avoid Probate–Making Gifts and Setting Up Your Own Trust

You have had it with government red tape and want the administration of your estate to be as simple a task as possible. What you do is create a lifetime trust to which you transfer all your assets and which you name as beneficiary of all your life insurance. At your death, the trust acts like a will and provides for the disposition of all your property—without the property going through the expensive and time-consuming process of probate.

You are about to learn the basic steps you need to go through to avoid probate. This can result in a very significant savings for your heirs—at the expense of your attorney and friendly probate court. But before you get too excited about saving probate costs, keep these three things in mind:

1. For large estates (estates in excess of the exemption equivalent discussed in Chapter 10), the most significant cost to be concerned about at death is federal estate taxes, not probate.
2. Even if federal estate taxes are not a problem, probate fees can be overrated—in fact, the state you own your assets in is a much more important consideration because of state estate taxes. (If you have your choice of states, pick Florida or Nevada, which effectively have no state estate taxes.)
3. Reorganizing your ownership of assets to avoid probate may create more trouble and expense than it is worth.

What Is Probate?

Probate is the process of settling an individual's estate. The mechanism of estate settlement involves ascertaining the net assets of the estate and distributing the assets to the heirs. More specifically, probate consists of:

1. Identifying, appraising and reporting all assets of the deceased.
2. Identifying and paying all estate debts.
3. Filing tax returns.
4. Paying attorney fees, probate court fees and executor fees.
5. Distributing property according to the terms of the deceased's will, or if there is no will, according to state statute.

Assets that (a) are given away during one's lifetime, (b) pass according to contract (such as joint bank accounts or life insurance proceeds) or (c) are placed in a lifetime trust are *not* subject to probate.

When to Make Gifts

If you are well off, it makes sense for you to make gifts to those people you care about. First, it is much more fun to give property away during your lifetime than to hold onto it until death. You have the pleasure of seeing people enjoy your gifts. Second, there can be a real tax savings in making gifts.

There are favorable federal estate-tax consequences that come from making gifts. The first is that future appreciation of this property, as mentioned earlier, will not be included in your estate. Second, as discussed in Chapter 10, a gift to a spouse can be a principal part of marital estate-tax planning. In addition, annual gifts of $10,000 or under are now excluded from your estate regardless of how long you live.[1] (There is an exception here for gifts of life insurance; see Chapter 11.) These $10,000 gifts can mean significant estate-tax savings if (a) you are in a high estate-tax bracket; and (b) you live many years after commencing an annual gift program—or you have lots and lots of beneficiaries.

NOTE: If you choose to make gifts to an irrevocable trust, the amount of your gift should be limited to the amount a beneficiary has the right to decline to withdraw—$5,000 as of the end of 1981.

George Winkler, age 68 and now single, has $740,000, in assets. He also has five children and eighteen grandchildren. He makes a gift of $115,000 to an irrevocable trust for all his offspring. Each beneficiary has the right to withdraw $5,000, so the money contributed to the trust qualifies as a personal gift. Even if George dies within three years of his act of beneficence, his estate for federal estate-tax purposes (and for probate purposes) will be reduced by the full $115,000 amount. More than $40,000 of federal estate taxes will be saved.

If George had made the gift direct to each offspring, he could have made a $10,000 gift. However, when he makes a gift to a trust, he must limit his gift per beneficiary to $5,000 or else a portion of his gift will not qualify as a present gift.[2]

Finally, there can be an advantage to making very large gifts and paying the gift tax on them—because appreciation of the property transferred will not be added back into your estate.

The only disadvantage is that the recipient of a gift does not get a stepped-up basis in the property at death (a basis equal to the fair market value), as would be true if the transfer were made at death.[3] The donee gets the same basis in the property as the donor had at the time of making the gift.

Interest-Free Loan

The interest-free loan was discussed in Chapter 2 as a means of transferring income from one taxpayer to another. The interest-free loan can also be used to transfer wealth from one estate to another estate-tax-free.

> Grammie, a widow, has $3 million in assets and takes great delight in her two children and four grandchildren. Even if she makes a $10,000 gift each year to each of her loved ones, her estate will still continue to grow rapidly. Grammie's attorney suggests to her that she lend $1 million interest free to each of her children, so that appreciation on that money will not be included in her estate. In this way, Grammie still has use of one million in cash if she needs it and is able to pass a very substantial benefit to her children estate-tax-free during her lifetime.

In this example, if Grammie's children were in a high tax bracket, they could reinvest the money in a way that would not generate any additional income taxes, such as in a single-premium whole life policy (discussed in Chapter 5), municipal bonds or a single-premium deferred annuity (also discussed in Chapter 5).

Bank Accounts

To avoid probate on bank accounts, the account should be titled "Richard or Mary." The "or" gives either party access to the assets and, for probate purposes, means that the assets pass pursuant to contract at death and are not part of the estate.

Putting Property in Trust

A lifetime trust (a trust established during one's lifetime—also called an inter vivos trust) can be used to keep assets that can easily be placed in trust, such as stocks and bonds, cash and real estate, out of your probate estate. You and your spouse can be trustees of the trust and, as trustees, invest all the trust assets. Or you can use a bank or other individual as trustee. The formation of the trust will not change your net worth or disposable income. In fact, income generated by the trust should be paid to you, since (unless you have created a very special type of trust—an irrevocable trust—see Chapter 3) it will all be taxed to you.[4] Avoid charlatans who tell you this kind of trust can be set up to enable income and taxes thereon to be distributed to family members. This simply is not the case for this type of trust. See Chapter 24 on Tax Shams.

Your trust document should specify the following:

1. the trust corpus or assets
2. your rights to amend or revoke the trust
3. what will happen to trust income during your lifetime
4. what will happen to trust assets—undistributed income and principal, life insurance proceeds, etc.—at your death
5. powers of the trustees
6. who is the trustee, how he or she will be paid, who will be the successor trustee

If you do transfer stocks and bonds to such a trust, generally it is easier to deal with such assets if they are held in the name of a nominee.

Make certain that a qualified attorney prepares your trust. The document determines what happens to your assets at your death and has the same force and effect as your will; thus it should be given the same care and consideration as your will.

Note that any life insurance you own should name your trust (or spouse) as beneficiary to keep the proceeds out of your probate estate. See Chapter 11 for a discussion of the ownership of life insurance.

Owning Real Estate

Real estate that is in your lifetime trust will not be subject to probate. However, real estate that is in your name will be included in your probate estate *unless* the real estate is held jointly with right of survivorship. The survivorship rights cause the real estate to pass according to the terms of the real-estate deed; therefore, there is no need for the probate court (or attorney for the estate) to have jurisdiction over the real-estate transfer. (See Chapter 15 for a discussion on the ownership of real estate, including ideas on how to freeze the value of real estate in your estate.)

Recap and Checklist

The steps to take to keep your assets out of your probate estate are:

1. Make gifts of surplus wealth.
2. Put bank accounts—checking and savings—in joint names—Robert or Marie.
3. Put real estate in joint names with survivorship rights.
4. Establish your own lifetime trust to own the remainder of your assets.
5. If you want your estate to avoid probate completely, transfer all your personal property, such as furniture, cars, silver and golf clubs, to your lifetime trust.

But be careful: you do not want to jeopardize your ability to minimize federal and state estate taxes for the sake of avoiding probate. Also, you do not want to restrict your investment flexibility.

When to Take Avoiding Probate Seriously

If you ever feel you are on death's doorstep, it makes good sense for you to take the steps discussed herein to avoid probate. Fees and expenses will be saved and the whole process of settling your estate will be simplified for your loved ones. While you are at it, ask your attorney about the purchase of flower bonds. These are bonds that are purchased at a discount and mature to full value at death if the bonds are used to pay federal estate taxes.[5] Imagine an $8,500 investment maturing to $10,000 at death—it takes some of the pain out of leaving this world to pass on to the next.

One Final Thought on Avoiding Probate

There is one drawback to avoiding probate that you should consider if your estate (or your trust) will either receive income at your death or you will possess significant income-producing assets. By avoiding probate, you will prevent your heirs from using your estate as a separate taxpayer for purposes of reducing income taxes. For example, suppose an individual dies on February 1, 1983, and has a $25,000 bonus paid to his estate on March 15, where the bonus was earned prior to his death. His estate can elect a taxable year that ends on March 30, thus trapping the $25,000 bonus in a short tax year and reducing the tax that would have to be paid on that income. (Of course, this only makes sense if the tax bracket for his estate is less than the tax bracket of the eventual recipient of the bonus.) Future income of the estate (such as rents, interest or cash) would then be subject to the estate-tax year ending March 30, 1984, or, if distributed, would be taxed to the recipient (which could be his trust). In such a situation, the income-tax advantages may far outweigh the cost of probate. Thus, in your planning, you must be certain that by avoiding probate, you are not also avoiding the ability for needed income-tax planning after your death.

chapter 15

How to Own Real Estate

Suppose all the assets you have accumulated during your marriage are either held jointly with survivorship rights or are in your name. After reading Chapter 10, you and your wife have decided that you should take advantage of the unlimited gift to a spouse, so that she can have enough assets in her name to create a family trust for her estate if she predeceases you.

As you examine your financial statement, you note that the fair market value of your house (which is held jointly with survivorship rights) is $260,000, but that the mortgage is only $68,000. You give your interest in the house to your wife and have her adopt a family trust that will hold the real estate if she predeceases you. She pays all future mortgage payments, utilities and taxes from her own checking account, so you cut down on your time of writing out checks each month.

The tax rules governing the treatment of real estate in your estate have been made a great deal simpler by the 1981 act. Yet there are some complexities in determining the best manner in which real estate should be owned.

The degree to which real estate will be included in your estate depends on how the property is titled at your death. Since real estate is an appreciating item and either is or probably will be a very significant part of your estate, it is important that you understand how the real estate in your estate will be treated and whether or not the title to the real estate should be changed for more favorable tax treatment. Also, you should learn how the value of your real estate can be fixed so that inflation will not continue to cause its value in your estate to bulge.

Two Types of Joint Ownership

If you are married, chances are the title to your home is in a joint name, such as "Bob and Marie Smith." If it is held in two names, the title can either be held as tenants by the entirety (also referred to as jointly with right of survivorship where the property is held jointly by a couple who are not husband and wife) or as tenants in common.

For estate tax purposes, there is no longer any difference between holding title as tenants by the entirety or as tenants in common. In each case, one-half of the value of the property will be included in the estate of the first to die, regardless of who has paid for the property.[1]

If your property is titled "Bob and Marie with rights of survivorship" or similar language, the property is titled as tenants by the entirety. This means that complete ownership of the property will pass automatically to the survivor at the death of one of the title owners. Ownership by this title also means that either all of the property must be conveyed or none of it—there is no undivided one-half interest that can be transferred.

The main advantage of ownership as tenants by the entirety is that the title to the property at your death passes directly to your spouse without going through the probate process (see Chapter 14). Ownership of the real estate is governed by the language on the deed and is not governed by anything in your will. The automatic transfer of title at death makes tenants by the entirety a popular means of holding title to the property.

If, on the other hand, you hold title to your property as tenants in common (such as simply "Bob and Marie"), each of you now owns a distinct one-half interest in the property. This one-half interest can be sold, given away or transferred at death without the other share similarly passing. Now you have to plan for what happens to this interest in real estate in your will, since your one-half interest in the real estate will only pass to the person you designate.

When Tenants by the Entirety Makes Sense

If you and your spouse have a modest amount of assets (if your combined estates, including life insurance, are less than the current exemption equivalent), it makes sense for you to own your house as tenants by the entirety. This will create an automatic transfer of the ownership of property at death and keep your home out of the probate process.

If title to real estate is held as mother and daughter, with rights of survivorship, title to the property will pass automatically to the daughter at her mother's death. This is a preferred means of holding title to property if a mother wants her home to pass to her daughter at her death, since it enables the real estate to bypass probate.

Property owned out of state should be owned as tenants by the entirety to facilitate estate administration. Otherwise, an out-of-state attorney will have to be retained and additional probate costs will have to be insured. However, do not sacrifice estate taxes just for ease of administration. If it makes sense from a federal estate-tax planning viewpoint for property to be owned other than as tenants by the entirety, *do it!*

When Tenants in Common Makes Sense

You should consider holding property as tenants in common when you need to prevent your spouse's interest from coming back to you if your spouse predeceases you.

> John owns $400,000 of stocks, bonds and life insurance. He and his wife own a $300,000 home, which is titled as tenants in common. Mary provides in her estate plan that if she dies, her one-half interest in the home will pass into a family trust for John's benefit but will not become part of John's estate, which is already large enough.

In this example, Mary's trust could be set up to permit John to buy the one-half interest in real estate for interest payments only. This is to give John the ability to control fully what happens to the real estate as well as to permit John's family to use the family trust as an income-distributing device. This technique also works well when the entire estate interest is transferred to a family trust. John obtains an interest deduction for the payment of interest to the trust. The interest payments constitute income, which can be distributed to John or sprinkled among his children.

Title in One Spouse's Name Only

In many situations, title to real estate preferably should be in the name of one spouse only. This enables the real estate to be transferred at death in a manner that enables it to be kept out of the surviving spouse's estate. Suppose Dan is a business executive who has accumulated $380,000 in various investments plus $200,000 of life insurance. His wife, Liz, owns some jewelry, a small savings account and their $220,000 home. By keeping the house in Liz's name, Liz and Dan can prevent the $220,000 home from adding to Dan's estate if Liz predeceases him. In order for this to occur, Liz should have her own trust, to which she would transfer the real estate in the event of her death. The trustee would then hold the real estate for Dan's benefit in such a manner that it would not become part of Dan's taxable estate. This approach ties in with what was discussed in Chapter 10 on splitting one's estate with one's spouse.

The Real Estate Freeze

If you own a farm or have a large investment in an office building or residential property, one of your concerns should be that future appreciation of your real estate will increase the size of your estate. Thus if your estate is such a size that estate taxes will be paid at your death, it would be helpful for you to freeze or fix the value of the real estate you own in your estate. The methods available to you of fixing the value of real estate in your estate are much the same as the methods available to an owner of a closely held business to fix the value of his or her business in his or her estate. Accordingly, review Chapter 12, especially the sections on family partnerships, installment sales and private annuities.

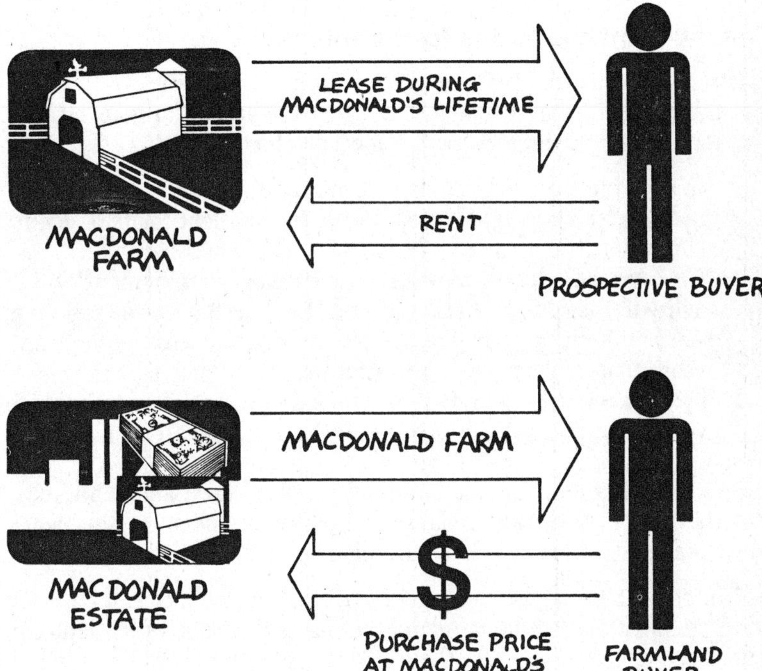

If you desire to retain valuable real estate instead of selling it to family members, the method you should consider to freeze its value is the formation of a family partnership. This lets you retain ownership of the real estate while passing appreciation to your children.

Also, if you are not in good health, do not sell your farm or valuable office building to a nonfamily member. The sale during your lifetime will create long-term capital-gains taxes that could be avoided by holding onto the real estate until death. Consider instead a lease agreement with a mandatory buy-sell at your death. This will enable your heirs to avoid the long-term capital-gains taxes, because your estate will get a basis in the real estate at your death equal to its then fair market value.

Consider also the possibility of a private annuity (discussed in Chapter 12) if you are in failing health. This can be of great benefit to your heirs.

Special Considerations for Farmland

If you own farmland that you or your family have been actively farming, the farmland may be subject to special valuation in your estate.[2] The tests that must be met for the special valuation are:

1. You or your family must have been actively farming the property for five of the last eight years prior to the decedent's date of death. This requirement can also be satisfied if it would have been satisfied if the decedent has died on the date of his retirement or disability if one of these events preceded his death. (In the case of a spouse inheriting property, the test is an active management test rather than a material participation test.)
2. The fair market value of the farmland—its appraised value if it were to be sold on the open market—must be at least 25% of your estate.
3. Your children, grandchildren (or even great-grandchildren), spouse or other blood relative must become the successor owner and must continue actively farming the property.

Assuming that the above conditions are met, your estate can elect an alternate valuation for the farmland that bases the value of the land for federal estate-tax purposes on the *use* of the property as farmland rather than on its fair market value. This can have a considerable impact on your estate tax situation.

Suppose the fair market value of farmland at your death is $600,000 but the alternate valuation is $200,000. By electing the alternate valuation, your estate can reduce its asset value for federal estate-tax purposes by $400,000.

The alternate valuation can be calculated several different ways, including (a) dividing the net cash rentals for comparable land (rentals less real-estate taxes) by the annual effective interest rate for all new Federal Land Bank loans; (b) capitalization of the fair rental value of the land; or (c) a value based on sales of a comparable farm significantly removed from a metropolitan or resort area so that nonagricultural use is not a significant factor in the sales price.

NOTE: The maximum reduction permitted for an estate is $700,000 in 1982 and $750,000 for subsequent years.

The only drawback to electing alternate valuation is that if the property is sold or if the immediate family ceases to farm the property actively, the estate taxes that had been saved will be recaptured. The recapture is 100 percent if an event triggering recapture occurs in the first year following the owner's death. After the initial first year period elapses, the amount of recapture decreases 10 percent each year.[3]

> Farmland with a fair market value of $600,000 an an alternate valuation of $200,000 is sold for use as a shopping center five years after the death of the owner. Fifty percent of the federal estate taxes that had been saved are recaptured on its sale.

In any event, the recapture is never as bad as the initial payment of the federal estate tax would be because of the time value of money.

chapter 16

Charitable Contributions in Estate Planning

Jeff Marcel, seventy, has an estate of over $2 million, which he primarily wants to leave to his daughter and two young grandchildren. However, he has made modest contributions to his alma mater, University of Michigan, during his lifetime and would like to do something special for this fine university at his death.

Jeff provides in his estate plan that $250,000 of assets will pass into a charitable lead trust that will pay Michigan $15,000 per year for twenty-four years and at the end of that time revert to his grandchildren, who will by then be starting their own homes and families. By making the charitable gift at death, Jeff will have reduced his taxable estate by over $185,000 dollars, thus saving his estate more than $90,000 in federal estate taxes.

Also, he calculates that the $250,000 will grow to over $1,000,000 in twenty-four years if the trust averages a 13% rate of return over that period of time before each annual payment of $15,000 to Michigan. If estate taxes had been paid on the $250,000 of approximately $90,000 and the remainder invested at 12%, the amount of money that Jeff projects would have been available for his grandchildren in twenty-four years would be $1,280,000, only 28% more.

Tying your gifts to charity into your overall tax plan is one way to ease the tax burden you and your family must shoulder. Chapter 3 discussed how charitable giving can benefit you from an income-tax standpoint. Now we take a look at how estate-tax savings arise from the charitable gifts you make.

Charitable Giving and the Marital Deduction

Before the 1981 act, it was advantageous for a married taxpayer to make a charitable gift at death as part of his total estate. The gift would increase his total estate, increase his marital deduction and lessen the estate taxes that would have to be paid by his family.

In 1980, Peter had an $800,000 estate and purchased $200,000 of life insurance that he assigned to his favorite charity, retaining an incident of ownership. When Peter died in 1981, his adjusted gross estate was $1,000,000, his marital deduction (which was then the greater of $250,000 or half of his adjusted gross estate) was increased to $500,000 and his taxable estate was $300,000 ($500,000 less $200,000 for the charitable gift). Estate taxes saved: over $30,000.

Now, however, with the unlimited marital deduction, there is no reason for an individual to make a charitable gift in such a way that it will be included in his or her estate.[1] Thus if you previously set up a charitable gift of life insurance to take effect at your death but retained an incident of ownership in that life insurance, there is no reason for you to continue to retain that incident of ownership.

The advantage of waiting until death to make a charitable gift is that you receive the benefit of that asset during your lifetime. The charitable gift, in such a case, will be included in your estate but then deducted from the taxable portion of your estate so that it will not generate any estate taxes.[2] If you have a marital deduction trust (see Chapter 10) and wish to make a charitable bequest during your lifetime, the language used for allocating assets to the marital share and the family share of your trust should take into account the charitable gift (see Appendix D).

Charitable Remainder Trusts

One way to get a current income-tax benefit and an estate-tax deduction is through the transfer of money or other property to a charitable remainder trust. A charitable remainder trust is a trust that pays income to the donor or her or his designated beneficiary for a stated period of time or for life and the remainder to a charitable organization.[3] The income-tax deduction is based on the contribution less the value of payments to be made based on annuity tables. The estate-tax deduction is based on the value of the property passing to the charity upon your death. As in the case of the life insurance policy discussed above, the remainder interest is part of the gross estate but deductible from the taxable estate.

There are three basic types of charitable remainder trusts.

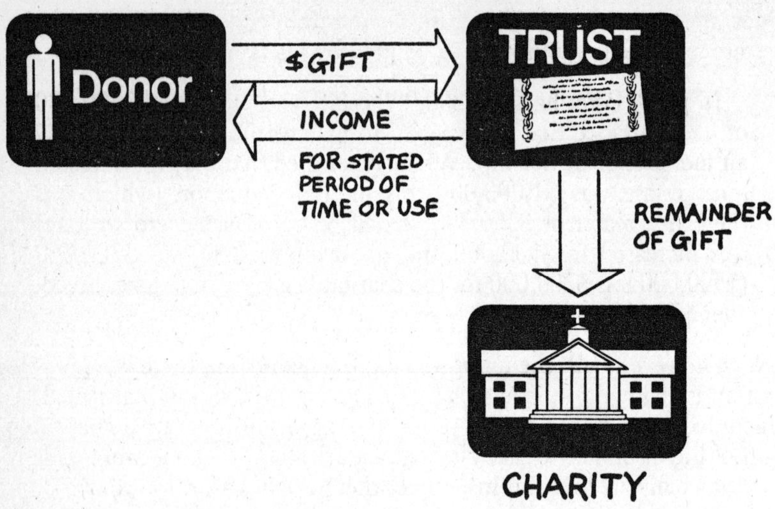

Charitable Remainder Annuity Trust

The charitable remainder annuity trust (which consists of assets contributed by the donor) provides for the payment of a fixed income each year (not less than 5% of the value of the property initially placed in trust) to the donor or the donor's designated beneficiary. If the income from the assets is not sufficient to make the payments, the difference is paid from capital gains or principal. Upon the death of the beneficiary or the lapse of a stated term (not exceeding 20 years), the remainder income passes to a charitable beneficiary.[4]

Frank, age fifty-five, wants to be charitable to his church but cannot afford to give up any income. He transfers $100,000 of appreciated securities held for more than one year into trust. The securities return income to Frank of only $3,000 per year, but the trust is designed to pay him $5,000 per year for the rest of his life with the remainder to a charitable beneficiary. In the year of the contribution, Frank will receive a $48,520 income-tax deduction and is not taxed on any appreciation of the securities.

If Frank had been age sixty-five, he would have been entitled to a greater income-tax deduction ($59,823) because of his shorter life expectancy.

NOTE: An annuity trust must prohibit contributions after the first year of valuation purposes.

Charitable Remainder Unitrust

This trust is essentially the same as the charitable remainder annuity trust except that the sum that is paid each year to the donor or the designated beneficiary is a *stated* percentage of the assets (not less than 5% of the annual value). The payments, unlike the annuity trust, can be limited to the actual income earned. Because payments from this trust increase as the value of the trust assets increase, the charitable remainder unitrust will be the more beneficial trust, provided the trust assets are invested profitably. Also, unlike the annuity trust, the unitrust does permit additional contributions in future years.[5]

Pooled Income Fund

A pooled income fund is a fund maintained by a public charity, which pays out to the donors each year a pro-rated portion of the income earned by the fund. The pooled income fund cannot invest in tax-exempt securities. At the death of a donor, the assets inure to the benefit of charity.[6]

An individual can establish a charitable remainder (either an annuity trust or unitrust), which can create a very favorable tax result when the surviving spouse is named as the only noncharitable beneficiary. In such a case, the entire trust will be deductible from the estate of the person who establishes the trust, part as a marital deduction and the remainder as a charitable deduction. Moreover, upon the death of the surviving spouse, no part of the remainder of the trust fund will be included in the surviving spouse's estate.

The ability to make a large charitable gift now that takes effect after the surviving spouse has received an income interest for his or her life makes this a very attractive estate planning idea.

> Ray, who has an $800,000 estate, would like to make a sizable gift to the Boy Scouts of America upon his death but is concerned about whether his wife will have sufficient income to take care of her needs after his death. To satisfy both concerns, Ray establishes a $300,000 charitable remainder trust in his estate plan, which will distribute $25,000 of income each year to his wife, with the remainder at her death to the Boy Scouts. None of the $300,000 will be taxed in either Ray's estate or his wife's estate.

The Charitable Remainder Trust After the 1981 Act

The use of the charitable remainder trust as a combination gift to spouse and gift to charity seems very beneficial in concept, but it can be improved upon by the use of a qualified terminable interest trust, which is discussed in Chapter 10. Under the qualified terminable interst trust, you can leave a portion of your estate in a trust for the benefit of your spouse, which will pass to the individuals or charity you name at your spouse's death. If your spouse elects to have the property treated as subject to the marital deduction, it will be excluded from your estate at your death but then included in your spouse's estate at his or her death.[7] If the remainder interest is a charity, then the remainder that is included in your spouse's estate will be subject to the charitable deduction, and there would be no net increase in his or her estate.[8]

The advantage of the qualified terminable interest trust is that your surviving spouse will have much more flexibility and protection as compared to a charitable trust interest. Thus if you like the idea of naming a charity as a remainder beneficiary, it would make more sense for you to use a qualified terminable interest trust than a charitable remainder trust. The only exception to this would be if you wanted to limit the amount of income that your spouse were to receive from property that you were to set aside, in which case you might choose the charitable trust arrangement.

Charitable Lead Trust

The charitable lead trust is an income-tax-savings device that works just the opposite of the way in which a charitable remainder trust does. With a charitable lead trust, the income (either a fixed amount or a percentage of the assets) is paid to a charity and the remainder to a noncharitable beneficiary. The donor gets an income-tax deduction in the year of setting up the trust equal to the value of the income interest but is taxable on the income earned each year in the trust.[9] If the trust is designed to last more than ten years, the donor is not taxed on the income generated but also does not get the large income-tax deduction in the year of the gift.

The charitable lead trust is a popular device for the taxpayer who has an unusually high income year and is willing to accept some income in future years to gain the benefit of a large income-tax deduction in the current year. Under a five-year trust that distributes 9% each year of the contribution, the donor is entitled to an income-tax deduction equal to about 46% of the contribution. The reversion of the principal to the donor (or to his or her designated noncharitable beneficiary) upon the termination of the trust makes the charitable lead trust similar to the Clifford Trust discussed in Chapter 2.

If the donor dies before the expiration of the trust, the estate will partially recapture some of the income previously deducted. The estate-tax consequences depend on who is the beneficiary of the reversion interest. If the reversion beneficiary is the donor, the full value of the remainder will be included in the donor's estate at her or his death. If the reversion beneficiary is someone other than the donor, the donor will be deemed to have made a gift to the reversion beneficiary at the time of setting up the trust. For example, if the trust is a five-year trust paying out 9% each year of the contribution, the gift to the reversion beneficiary would be 54 percent of the principal (and 46% of the principal will be deductible as a charitable contribution).

Estate-Tax Savings of a Charitable Lead Trust

The estate-tax savings of the charitable lead trust occur if you set up a charitable lead trust at your death. An estate-tax deduction is allowed for the actuarial interest of the income interest provided by the trust.[10] For example, if you leave $500,000 in trust to pay $30,000 to Princeton University for twenty-four years (remainder to your children), your estate will be entitled to an estate-tax deduction of over $375,000. By setting the annuity payment at a high enough level or making the payments for a sufficient duration, you could entirely eliminate the tax on your bequest to the charitable lead trust.

NOTE: The annuity assumptions in the IRS tables are based on the old days, when a 10 percent return on money was considered extraordinarily high. Until the IRS revises its assumptions (and this may take a great amount of work and time), the charitable lead trust is an excellent estate-tax-savings device that can result in very significant benefits for your family. Be sure to consider this mechanism of making a gift at death if you are inclined to make a charitable bequest of some sort.

Limitations on Income-Tax Deductions
for Both Charitable Remainder Trusts
and Charitable Lead Trusts

Very large contributions to a charitable remainder trust may create an income-tax deduction that is in excess of that permitted during a calendar year. Generally you are limited to a deduction of up to 50 percent of your adjusted gross income, with the excess carried over to future years.[11] If you contribute appreciated property held for more than one year, your contribution will either be reduced by half of the appreciation or your contribution will be limited to 30 percent of your adjusted gross income.[12]

The deduction for your contribution to a charitable lead trust for the benefit of your charity will be limited to only 20 percent of your adjusted gross income. Plus you will *not* be permitted to carry forward the excess contribution. Thus make certain you will be permitted the full income-tax deduction for your contribution to a charitable lead trust in the year of your contribution.

chapter 17

Estate Planning in Community-Property States

Much of what you read in the previous eight chapters will have to be reconsidered if you are married and presently reside or formerly resided in one of the following eight community-property states: Arizona, California, Idaho, Louisiana, Nevada, New Mexico, Texas or Washington. These states base ownership of property on the general theory that husband and wife form a partnership and the property acquired during their marriage is the equal property of the spouses unless there is some specific agreement to the contrary.

Although the laws of each of the eight community-property states are different, emphasis will be placed on the community-property laws of California. Community property (property that is deemed to be owned equally by the spouses) is generally defined as all real property situated in California and all personal property acquired during the marriage while a person is married and resides in California.[1] There are exceptions to the general rule for certain property that is deemed to be owned solely by the spouse who originally acquired it, called *separate property*. Separate property is deemed to be owned by only the spouse in whose name it is titled.

Separate property in California is defined as (a) property owned by a person prior to marriage; (b) property acquired after marriage by gift or from an estate; (c) income of separate property or property acquired with the income or proceeds from the separate property.[2]

One final twist to the California law pertains to spouses who move to California after having accumulated property in noncommunity-property states. In such a case, California characterizes this property as quasi-community property.

Quasi-Community Property

Quasi-community property is property that would have been community property had the spouses acquired the property while living in California.[3] For all purposes except divorce and death, quasi-community property is treated as separate property. In a divorce situation, quasi-community property, both real and personal, is treated as community property for purposes of California law. In the event of death of the acquiring spouse, only real property acquired in another state is treated as community property. This means that if during your marriage you acquired real property in Ohio in your name, move to California, and die, the Ohio property will be treated in California as community property for purposes of your estate settlement. However, if instead your wife had died and had no title interest in the real estate, she would not be deemed to own any interest in the property. If the real property had been acquired in California, one half of its value would have been included in the estate of the first to die, regardless of which spouse died first.

In order to put the principles of community-property ownership into focus, we will briefly discuss the impact of community-property laws on the basic principles discussed in the rest of this section on Estate-Tax Planning.

Spousal Estate Splitting

The key to spousal estate splitting discussed in Chapter 10 is that when the first spouse dies, this act alone transfers a significant portion of the property into a family trust. The result of this is to reduce estate taxes at the surviving spouse's subsequent death by virtue of the fact that the family trust assets are excluded from the surviving spouse's estate. In community-property states, the surviving spouse is deemed to own a one-half interest of whatever property is owned by the deceased. However, the marital deduction in community-property states permits essentially the same result for married couples as in separate property estates—that is, an unlimited amount of property can pass to the surviving spouse free of estate taxes.

> In 1982, suppose you and your wife own property of $850,000 subject to community-property laws, and all the property is in your name. Automatically $425,000 would be subject to tax *unless* the property was left to your spouse in a manner that would qualify for the unlimited marital deduction. Estate taxes saved: approximately $60,000.

In this situation, the best estate-planning result is for the $225,000 included in your estate to pass into a family trust rather than for your entire estate to pass outright to your wife.

In order to achieve the result of having property pass into trust at death, the following must occur:

1. The deceased specifically indicates his or her desire to effect distribution of the entire interest of the community.
2. The surviving spouse acquiesces in that distribution.

In this way, the property can be placed in trust, where it can be split to effect the advantages discussed here and in Chapter 10.

Ownership of Life Insurance

When life insurance is purchased in a community-property state, the policy is deemed to be owned equally by the spouses. This has several implications. First, if your wife owns life insurance on your life and you die, even though your wife is the owner, one half of the proceeds will be included in your estate for federal estate-tax purposes. Second, if someone other than your spouse is the beneficiary of the policy, your spouse would be deemed to have made a gift to the beneficiary at death equal to her one-half interest in the policy. This can have a significant impact on her subsequent estate taxes.

If insurance is owned in a noncommunity-property state (as discussed in Chapter 11) and then you and your wife move to a community-property state, the insurance proceeds will be apportioned as between separate property and community property, based on the time that the policies were paid for in the noncommunity-property state vs. the community-property state.

> You live in New York for four years after acquiring a life insurance policy. You move to California and live there for six more years before your death. Forty percent of the proceeds will be treated as separate property and 60 percent will be treated as community property.

In order to sidestep the community-property problems of life-insurance proceeds and the dual-ownership concept, it is possible for the spouse to waive his or her community-property rights. The waiver should include a statement of the following:

1. The spouse waives any community interest in the life-insurance policy, and the policy will be the separate property of the other spouse.
2. The spouse consents to the use of community property for the payment of premiums and declares that premium payments constitute a gift to the spouse who is making the payments.

3. The waiver is executed for good and valuable consideration, and any interested party may act in reliance thereon.

This form of waiver is usually available through insurance companies in community-property states and should be reviewed with your attorney before it is signed. This waiver is especially important in the super trust setting, to enable the spouses to keep the life-insurance proceeds out of both their estates.

Transfer of Closely Held Business Interest

Buy-Sell Agreements

Care must be taken in the area of buy-sell agreements to make certain the following does not happen:

1. The stockholder's spouse predeceases the stockholder and disposes of his or her property interest (including the community-property interest in the stock) at death to some third party who is not a party to the agreement.
2. The stockholder dies, and the stockholder's spouse seeks to claim his or her community-property interest in the stock outside of the agreement.

The best way to avoid these problems is for the spouse to waive his or her rights in the stock or even to be a party to the buy-sell agreement. Note that if the property is quasi-community property under California law, the death of the nonowner spouse will not have any effect at all on the stock held pursuant to the agreement.

Recapitalizations, Personal Holding Companies, Installment Sales and Private Annuities

In any situation in which there is a transfer of shares of stock during a lifetime, there should be an agreement in writing that defines the ownership rights of the respective spouses. For example, it would defeat the purpose of a recapitalization and the desire to transfer future appreciation to younger generations if the nonowner spouse did not release his or her community-property interest and thus could effectively be deemed still to own part of the one-half interest of the stock that was originally recapitalized. Also, in the event of the sale of property, the nonowner spouse should enter into the sale to transfer his or her interest or the sale may be invalid as to the one-half interest of the nonowner spouse.

Qualified Plans

The community-property laws provide that each spouse is deemed to own a one-half interest in a participant's qualified-plan benefits. Accordingly, upon the death of the participant, only one half of the assets in the qualified plan would be included in the participant's estate if it were paid out as a lump-sum distribution subject to the special ten-year income averaging. If it is desirable for the qualified-plan proceeds to be kept out of the estate of both spouses, the nonparticipating spouse should execute a waiver of all rights and qualified plan assets as part of the estate-planning process. However, there is a fairly popular view that the interest a person has in a qualified plan cannot be transferred. Thus it may not be possible for the nonparticipating spouse to waive his or her interest in a qualified plan.

Avoiding Probate and Gifts

The general rules regarding the avoidance of probate applies as well in community-property states. Nevertheless, it is important that the ownership of property be reviewed to determine the extent to which joint ownership and ownership by a trust may have an adverse impact on estate tax in the community-property state.

In the case of gifts, especially gifts to minor children under the Uniform Gift to Minors Act, it is important that the nonowner spouse *not* be the custodian, since custodianship could cause the inclusion of one half of the gift assets in the estate of the custodial spouse. Accordingly it makes more sense for a brother or sister of the parents to act as custodian for gifts that are made to minors. Also, as discussed before with regard to the sale of property, any gift should effectively be made by both husband and wife in community-property states, so that the property is completely conveyed and one half of the property cannot be treated as the property of the nonowner spouse.

Ownership of Real Estate

In community-property states, a husband and wife can own property as joint tenants, tenants in common or as community-property owners. In joint tenancy, husband and wife own equal half interests, and each has the power to convey his or her fractional interest. At the death of a joint tenant, the ownership of the property vests in the surviving spouse.

Interests in tenancy in common need not be equal; for example, the husband may own two thirds and the wife one third. Each has the power to convey his or her fractional interest both during lifetime and at death. This is the same as tenants in common in noncommunity-property states.

Ownership of community property means that husband and wife own equal interests during their marriage. At the death of either husband or wife, one half of the community property belongs to the surviving spouse; the other half is subject to transfer through the deceased's will.

If it is desirable for a fractional interest in real estate to be transferred to a person other than the surviving spouse, the property should be owned by tenants in common or as community property. Ownership by joint tenants will cause an automatic transfer of the property interest at death to the surviving spouse.

The federal estate-tax laws regarding farmland are such that it does not make any difference whether the land is owned in a community-property state or not, so there is no loss that can occur through the ownership of farmland.[4] Note, however, that only one half of the value of the land can be considered in determining whether the percentage test is satisfied.

Charitable Gifts

In nearly all cases, it is possible to get the same benefits from community property with regard to charitable giving as is true with separate property.

Summary

If you are in doubt as to whether you own any property as community property or whether you have ever owned any property as community property, it is important that you get your property rights clarified and that your estate planning take into account the manner in which your different property is owned. Some very significant estate-tax savings can be effected in community-property states with proper planning, and there is no reason the estate-tax savings in community-property states should be any less than is available in separate-property estates.

Business Tax Planning

chapter 18

Introduction to Business Tax Planning

If you have your own business, you have attractive tax planning opportunities that are not available to the typical high income employee. More important, the tax advantages that are available to you do not depend on the size of your business or the number of employees. In fact, the greatest opportunities for tax savings are in the very small, highly profitable businesses.

Key factors in ascertaining your ability to save taxes are (a) the extent to which your business can pay expenses for you in a way that is tax deductible to the business (and would otherwise not be to you); and (b) the extent to which you and your family do not need all the money your business makes for basic living expenses. These factors determine the amount of tax planning that is available for you in your business.

Typically small businesspeople are so caught up in running their business that they do not give sufficient attention to financial and tax planning. Yet it may be twice as valuable for them in terms of their overall income picture to spend time saving one dollar of taxes as it is to spend the same amount of time making an additional dollar of profit. Despite this, many small businesspeople spend more hours generating profits than they spend in planning. The following chapters show how one can remedy this disparity.

chapter 19

How to Make Your Business Work for You

Frank and Joe have comparable manufacturing-representative businesses. Each earns $80,000 per year total, but only Joe is incorporated.

Frank pays tax on his full $80,000 of income, resulting in a tax liability of over $25,000 per year. Joe, on the other hand, takes a salary of only $40,000 from his corporation and uses the remaining dollars in the corporation to provide tax-free health, disability and retirement-plan benefits. Through his tax planning, Joe saves $10,-800 more in taxes more than his friend Frank.

You want to get the maximum benefit out of the dollars your business makes. If you need every profit dollar from your business for living expenses, you are limited in your tax-planning opportunities. However, if your profits are being plowed back into your business or, better yet, being set aside into savings or investments, a glorious tax savings future may await you.

When to Incorporate

If you are an unincorporated business, such as a sole proprietorship or a partnership, should you incorporate? The answer depends on several factors:

1. a. Are substantial profits (more than $5,000) being plowed back into your business each year?
   b. Are you able to save significant dollars (more than $3,000) each year from the income you make?
2. Do you pay more than $1,500 each year for disability and health-insurance premiums?
3. a. Do you have a small number of employees (12 or less)?
   b. Is your income at least $20,000 more than that of your non-owner employees?

4. Is your highest taxed income dollar (effective tax rate for additional income) taxed at least at a 35% tax rate?

If your answer to these four questions is yes, you should in all likelihood incorporate. If your answer to all four questions is no, you should put this book down and start reading *The Wall Street Journal*. If you are somewhere in between, you ought to do an incorporation study, the basics of which are outlined at the end of this section.

The Tax Magic of Incorporating

The most obvious advantage of incorporating is that the corporation is a separate taxpayer from yourself and is faced with tax rates far lower than those you are paying.

Corporate Income	*1982 Tax Rate*
$0–$25,000	16% (15% for 1983 and later)
$25–$50,000	19% (18% for 1983 and later)
$50–$75,000	30%
$75–$100,000	40%
over $100,000	46%

If your corporation makes $100,000, it will pay federal income tax of only $26,250. Compare this with the tax you would pay personally on an additional $100,000 of income. Consequently it is beneficial to split your business profits between yourself and your corporation and lower your overall tax liability.

The following example illustrates the potential tax savings by putting part of your income in a corporation:

> In 1982, with $80,000 of self-employed net income for a married person filing a joint return with two dependent children, assuming $10,000 in itemized deductions, the total tax is $25,350.
>
> Suppose, instead, $40,000 of personal income and $40,000 of corporate income. The personal tax is now $7,629 and the corporate tax is $6,850. The total tax is $14,479.

In the second approach, over $10,800 of taxes are saved. Other advantages of incorporating include:

1. increased qualified plan benefits (see Chapter 21)
2. deductibility of health and disability premiums plus a portion of life insurance premiums (see Chapter 23)
3. limited liability for most types of corporate liability
4. ownership interests more easily transferred

The economic disadvantages of incorporating are: increased legal and accounting requirements, increased Social Security taxes and, in most states, increased unemployment and workers' compensation contributions. In addition, operating through a corporate structure requires additional recordkeeping, which can become cumbersome.

The best test of whether incorporating is the right thing for you to do is to run your business through the following incorporation analysis:

PERSONAL

Unincorporated Net Income	$94,100	
Less: Keogh Contribution (15%)	14,100	
Less: excess itemized deductions	6,600	(10,000–3,400 zero
Tax Table Income:	$73,400	bracket amount)
Calculated Tax:	$25,350	(including Social Security Tax at 9.35% of Social Security Taxable Wage Base)
Total Spendable Dollars	$48,050	($80,000–10,000–25,350)
Less: personal savings contribution	10,000	
Less: health & disability premiums	2,500	
Discretionary Dollars To Spend:	$35,550	

CORPORATE SETTING—All income distributed to you as salary:

Total Corporate Income—net of unincorporated business expenses	$94,100	(same as your unincorporated income)
Less: additional expenses for accountant, legal, Social Security	3,000	(this is strictly an estimate; it can vary)
Less: disability & health premiums	2,500	
Less: savings contribution	24,100	(make this the same as your personal savings & contribution to Keogh Plan)
Total available for income to you as salary	64,500	
Less: excess itemized deductions	6,600	(10,000–3,400 zero bracket amount)
Total Tax Table Income:	$57,900	
Tax:	$17,200	(calculate Social Security tax at 6.70%)
Discretionary Dollars:	$37,300	(64,500–10,000–17,200)

Compare the discretionary dollars left to you after taxes and similar expenses in a personal and a corporate setting. If there is a substantial difference, incorporating may be the solution for you. The next three chapters of this book will give you more ideas on how a corporation can save you taxes.

Interest-Free Demand Loans

Suppose you are incorporated and have built up some dollars of corporate wealth. Instead of paying these out as dividends or as compensation, you might consider an interest-free loan of money to yourself.

Interest-free demand loans in the family setting were discussed in Chapter 2. Interest-free demand loans in the corporate setting are almost the same. Like those among family members, interest-free demand loans here have been specifically approved by some court decisions and yet have not been accepted by the IRS, so there are some risks involved and you might have to go to tax court to prove your point.[1]

Because interest-free loans might be questioned by the IRS, you may be in a situation in which it makes no sense for your corporate loan to be interest free. Suppose you borrow $30,000 from your corporation at the start of the calendar year. If you control the corporation and have no minority shareholders who might dissent, you could bonus back to yourself at the end of the year any interest you would have to pay on the loan. The tax result for you will be the same as if the loan were interest free—as long as you are certain the following conditions exist:

1. You are not taking a deduction for medical expenses (which is based on your gross income less business expenses).
2. You do itemize expenses (so that you will get the deduction for the additional interest expense).
3. Your income is already in excess of the Social Security Taxable Wage Base (so that your bonus will not be subject to Social Security taxes).
4. The bonus paid to you will not be treated as unreasonable compensation. What this means is that you are not overpaid by the corporation.

Be Careful with Corporate Loans

Many states prohibit corporate loans to shareholders. This can be very troublesome if there are minority shareholders. Otherwise, this restriction is generally not fatal. Your lawyer can advise you about your state law.

The loan from the corporation to the shareholder should be as close to an arm's length transaction as possible. Consequently you should make sure there is a corporate resolution approving the loan, a promissory demand note that bears a reasonable rate of interest, regular repayments of interest plus principal and collateral (such as a second mortgage on a house) put up for the loan.

Many of my corporate clients use interest-free demand loans from time to time. Although I prefer my clients to use the safer interest-bearing loans, an interest-free demand loan is easy to administer and can be repaid by a year-end bonus in order to create a safety factor. In fact, I advise my clients to remove any interest-free loans from their books at the end of the corporate year by a bonus if this does not create an unmanageable tax liability.

Automobile Expenses

If you drive your Oldsmobile Cutlass for your work, remember to deduct the expenses associated with it. You can deduct either the maximum amount per business mile permitted by the IRS (20¢ for 1982) *or* your actual expense in operating the car for business.[2] Generally the actual expenses for your use of the car will be higher than the mileage allowance—as long as you take into account depreciation. You are allowed a pro-rated deduction for insurance, repairs, gasoline, oil and depreciation.[3]

Assume you purchased your car on February 12, 1982, for $9,000. Suppose, for example, you drove a total of twelve thousand miles in 1982, eight thousand of which were for business. If you took the $.20 per mile allowance, you would be entitled to a deduction of $1,600. On the other hand, assuming gasoline expenses of $600, repair expenses of $300, insurance of $300 and accelerated depreciation (ACRS) of $2,250, total expenses for the first-year operation of the car total $3,450. When this is allocated proportionately to business usage, you would still be entitled to a deduction of $2,300—one and one-half times as much as permitted by the mileage allowance! On top of this, there is also a first-year tax credit of $360 allowed for the purchase of a new car. Of course, in subsequent years, you will not be entitled to the same depreciation deduction or to any additional investment tax credit. You would also have the option to expense up to $5,000 of the business portion of the car in 1982.[4] This would leave only $1,000 to depreciate over three years, and the tax credit would be reduced to $60. However, the tax deduction in 1982 would be increased from $2,300 to $6,050.

Where Should Your Car Be Owned?

If you have a choice, make sure you personally buy the car, not your corporation. One of the "soft" issues on your tax return is how much your car was actually used for business versus how much it was actually used for pleasure. If the car is owned by you personally and you lose some of the deduction you claimed for business usage, you will have to pay an additional tax equal to a maximum of 50 percent of the disallowed deduction. However, if the car is owned by your corporation, the lost deduction will be taxed to the corporation as income *and* the personal use of the car will be passed through to you as a dividend. Thus in addition to the corporate tax, you may wind up with a personal income tax liability equal to the personal usage value passed to you, taxed at your maximum tax rate.

This is one of the hardest concepts for my clients to understand. Nearly everyone thinks there is some magical advantage to owning a car in a corporation. There is not.

Putting Family Members on the Payroll

Family members, even minor children, can be paid a fair wage for the work they do for your business. The payment to children generally shifts your income from a high-tax bracket to a low-tax bracket, saving overall family taxes.

If you do have family members on the payroll, be certain to document responsibilities, hours worked and tasks completed. Do not become too greedy with this concept, since the IRS tends to get excited about overpaid children of owners.

There is not much advantage to having a spouse on the payroll (except for the $2,000 IRA contribution; see Chapter 5) unless you want him or her or yourself to be eligible for health-insurance or life-insurance coverage. For example, in a sole proprietorship setting, health-insurance premiums for the sole proprietor and his family are not deductible. However, if health insurance is provided for employees and the sole proprietor's spouse happens to be an employee, then the health insurance premiums covering both the spouse and the sole proprietor (as employee and spouse)—and even the medical reimbursement plan (see Chapter 23)—can be paid for with tax-deductible dollars.

Working at Home

Congress has tightened the rules permitting a home-office deduction. Now you have to use a home office exclusively and regularly as your principal place of business or use it with customers or clients in dealing with them on a regular basis.[5] In any such event, the office space can be depreciated on a pro-rata basis, and other house expenses, such as utilities, can also be deducted on a pro-rata basis.

It is no longer possible to claim a home-office deduction if your employer provides office space and you simply have an office at home where you work after hours. However, if it is for the convenience of your employer for you to maintain a home office, such as for security reasons or for additional warehouse space, you will be permitted the home-office deduction. In any event, the use of an office at home may entitle you to deduct the cost of mileage from your employer's office to your office at home.

NOTE: If you have been taking a home-office deduction, the sale of your home will probably result in a capital gain on the portion of your home used as an office. You will have to pay some tax on this capital gain, since it is not subject to the same favorable income-tax treatment as the gain on your personal residence.

Entertainment Expenses

Since the IRS closely examines the deductibility of entertainment expenses, it is important that you do it right. The general rule is that entertainment expenses, to be deductible, must have been incurred in a setting where business was discussed, where there was some expectation of the development of a business relationship or, in the case of a pure entertainment setting (golf course or ball game as opposed to business lunch), where business is discussed before or after the event.[6] If you use a lodge, boat, airplane or sporting box for business entertainment (as opposed to an actual business meeting), the expenses of the property (such as operating cost, depreciation or repairs) that relate to the business may not be deducted.[7] However, if you can show that such an entertainment facility was used over 50 percent of the time for the actual conducting of business, then you may deduct the expenses that relate to such business use. Club dues are deductible if you can show that the club was used primarily for the furtherance of your trade or business and the dues were directly related to such business.[8] For all entertainment expenses, keep a detailed account of the amount spent, the time and place, the business purpose and the person or persons entertained.

Subchapter S Corporations

A Subchapter S corporation is a corporation that passes through its income (whether or not it is actually distributed) or losses on a pro-rata basis to its shareholders.[9] There are five situations in which the election of Sub S status makes sense:

1. You believe your corporation will incur losses and want to pass these losses through to the shareholders.
2. Children own stock in the company either outright or as beneficiaries of simple trusts, and the Sub S election is used to pass income through to your children so that it will be taxed at their lower tax rates. (This is yet another way of accumulating those college funds.)
3. Your corporation owns valuable real estate that you desire to sell to an unrelated party. The Sub S election permits you to pass through the gain from the sale to the shareholders on a favorable taxable basis. Otherwise the gain would be taxed twice—once to the corporation and again when it is distributed to the shareholders as a dividend.
4. You want to avoid the unreasonable compensation issue by passing through very large amounts of additional compensation to shareholder-employees. Also, you want the Sub S election to obviate the possibility of incurring an accumulated earnings tax problem.
5. Your corporation is purchasing new or used property, and you want to pass the investment tax credit through to yourself as a shareholder of the corporation.[10]

If your Sub S corporation is not achieving one of these five purposes, it probably should not be a Sub S corporation.

NOTE: A corporation must make a special election in order to be taxed as a Sub S corporation, and this election must be timely made. Also, once the Sub S election is made, there are specific requirements as to how it is revoked or terminated.[11]

Occasionally a Sub S corporation will be established to avoid Social Security taxes. For example, suppose your corporate income is $40,000 and you pay yourself $15,000 from the corporation as earned income. Social Security taxes will only have to be paid on the $15,000 of earned income, and the remaining $25,000 of income will pass through to you without Social Security taxes having to be paid on it. In abuse situations, the IRS will claim that you are not paying yourself enough compensation and charge you with penalties for the underpayment of Social Security taxes.

chapter 20

Deferred Compensation– Retirement Packages for Key Employees Only

Rockwell Enterprises, Inc., has ten key employees who are responsible for the tremendous volume of sales the company has experienced over the past five years. The directors of Rockwell Enterprises have been concerned about the loyalty of these employees, since similar employees have been enticed to switch jobs through lucrative offers from competitors.

Rockwell establishes a plan of deferred compensation for each of its key employees, which provides for payment to each key employee of $15,000 per year for ten years once the employee attains age sixty-five. If the employee dies prior to retirement, the payments will be made to the employee's spouse.

No payments will be made if the employee terminates employment prior to age sixty-five. Thus Rockwell feels it has created a powerful incentive to its key employees to remain with the company until retirement.

One way your incorporated business can provide important benefits is through the retirement packages it offers employees.

Retirement packages vary as much as vintages: you need to give some thought to what suits you best, for they are not all alike. In general, there are two basic types of plans: *qualified plans* (or, more formally, qualified deferred compensation plans; these are discussed in the next two chapters) and *nonqualified deferred compensation plans*, which are more commonly known as deferred compensation plans. Qualified plans entitle the employer to a current tax deduction and so are more seductive for those who are looking for immediate tax benefits. Both types of plans "defer" compensation until a subsequent period of time, for example, when the employee retires.

Deferred compensation plans are what this chapter is all about. These nonqualified plans typically require the corporation to make periodic payments to a key employee upon his or her retirement, or to make the same payments to the employee's spouse or other designated beneficiary if the employee dies prior to retirement. As long as the employee relies on only the mere promise of the employer to pay him or her later and is required to render future services in order to be eligible for the benefits, the employee is not required to include the deferred payments as income until he or she actually receives them.[1] Thus the employee will not pay tax upon them until he or she retires and is most likely in a lower tax bracket.[2] Correspondingly, the employer gets a deduction for the payments only when they are included in the employee's income.[3]

What's So Special About Deferred Compensation?

A deferred compensation plan can be set up for just one person or for several. Thus the plan can discriminate in favor of highly compensated employees. In fact, this is the primary advantage to a deferred compensation plan over qualified retirement plans, which can not be discriminatory.[4] Also, the plan can provide that payments will be made to the employee only if she or he continues employment with the company and until attainment of age 65, and renders consulting services after retirement.[5] Consequently deferred compensation can be an excellent way to supplement a key employee's retirement income while at the same time giving that employee an additional incentive to stay with the employer throughout her or his productive working years. Also, these plans have lower administrative costs than qualified plans and generally have less burdensome reporting and disclosure requirements.[6]

There are two types of deferred compensation plans: employer installed and employee directed. The difference in these plans is where the money comes from to fund the plan. In both situations, the employer must elect to provide the plan.

How to Go About Installing a Plan

For the employer-installed deferred compensation plan, the corporation, through its board of directors, adopts a plan of deferred compensation for the key employee(s). The key employee then enters into a contract with the employer that provides essentially the following:

WHEREAS, Jones has been a key employee of the Company and

WHEREAS, the Company wants him to remain until retirement and is willing to provide some additional benefits to him to encourage him to stay.

IT IS AGREED:

1. If Jones stays with the Company until age sixty-five, the Company will pay him $20,000 a year for ten years.
2. If Jones dies before retirement, his benefit passes to his spouse, or if she dies, to her designated beneficiary or estate.
3. In consideration of the money he receives, Jones must be available for consulting and must not enter into competition with the Company.
4. If Jones terminates employment prior to retirement, there is no benefit.

The cost of this plan is paid for by the employer. It may be funded by the purchase of a life-insurance policy or an annuity, or it may be unfunded, meaning that the employer will pay for the benefits from its general assets. If a plan provides a death benefit for the employee, the death benefit is usually provided by a life insurance policy on the employee but owned by the employer.[7]

What Makes Life Insurance Funding a Good Deal

The beauty of using life insurance to fund a deferred-compensation plan is that the life-insurance proceeds are received income-tax free by the employer yet are tax deductible when paid out as a deferred-compensation death benefit to the employee's spouse.[8,9] Consequently this can benefit the cash flow of a company that carries a life-insurance-funded deferred-compensation plan.

Suppose $100,000 of life insurance is purchased to provide a death benefit of $20,000 a year for ten years.

At Jones's death, the company receives $100,000. Suppose this $100,000 is invested in preferred stock that brings a return of 10 percent per year (85% of which is income-tax free to a corporation).[10] Thus, $100,000 of life insurance proceeds can produce an after-tax benefit of over $9,250.[11]

If the company is in the 50% tax bracket, the after-tax cost to it of a $20,000 deductible payment is $10,000.

Net cash flow is only a negative $750 per year, *plus* the company still has $100,000 principal. The life insurance provides a benefit to both Jones and the company upon Jones's death and thus serves in part as key-employee insurance.

Employee-Directed Deferred Compensation

A deferred-compensation plan can also be established by employees if doing so is permitted by the employer. All eligible employees can elect to defer income—that is, they take a cut in salary, only to receive the reduction plus interest in a later year, when their tax bracket is lower.[12, 13] The corporation gets no deduction for the income deferred by the employee until such income is actually paid.[14]

An age-fifty-five employee with an income of $80,000—50% tax rate on top $20,000 of income—elects to defer $10,000 per year for ten years in an employer-initiated plan.

Assuming modest interest, the fund grows to $160,000 in ten years.

The $160,000 will buy an annuity of $16,000 per year for the employee at age sixty-five, taxed at a rate well below 50 percent, depending on the employee's other sources of income at age sixty-five.

If the employee dies, his beneficiary receives all the deferred income plus interest.

The plan must provide for the employee to have a substantial risk of forfeiture in income deferred; otherwise the employee will be taxed currently on deferred income.

Warning

The IRS does not like employee-directed deferred-compensation plans.[15] In the past, it has been reluctant to approve them. However, Congress has temporarily thwarted the IRS's attempt to nix the unfavorable tax consequences of those plans.[16] In the future, Congress will have to make a final decision of whether to permit employee-directed deferred compensation. From a policy standpoint, Congress has in the past been very supportive of plans and techniques to help individuals with retirement planning. Employee-directed deferred compensation is just one more technique, which Congress should continue to support. In any event, the employee must elect to defer the receipt of income *before* he or she actually earns the income in order for the deferral to be valid.

When Should a Deferred Compensation Plan Be Used?

Not every corporation is ripe for a deferred-compensation plan. Here are the characteristics to look for in evaluating whether an employer-installed plan or an employee-directed deferred-compensation plan is best for you:

Employer-Installed Plan:
1. The company has many employees but comparatively few key employees.
2. Competition is keen for employer's key employees.
3. The company desires to give additional benefits to a select group of employees as an inducement to them to continue employment.
4. Profitability and cash flow are good enough to justify an additional corporate expense.

Employee-Directed Deferred Compensation Plan:
1. At least one of the characteristics above is lacking.
2. The company wants to give employees an opportunity to plan for retirement *and* is willing to undertake the necessary recordkeeping and reporting requirements (employees and government agencies generally need to be given information about the plans).[17]
3. The employee should participate only if:
    a. The company will promise a reasonable rate of return on money deferred.
    b. The company is in a solid economic situation and will not "use up" money the employee defers.
    c. The employee is in a high tax bracket and expects to be in a lower tax bracket at retirement.
    d. The employee does not need additional income to meet current living expenses.

Potential Tax Problems

If the death and disability benefits of a deferred-compensation agreement parallel those of a life-insurance contract bought by the corporation to provide the benefits, such benefits may be held to be taxable as a currently received economic benefit. The determination as to the taxability of the benefits would be made on whether the employee receives a current measurable benefit.[18] Consequently the benefits of a deferred-compensation plan should not specifically refer to the benefits provided by a life insurance contract that may be purchased by the employer.

Also, one federal court decision has determined that the purchase of life insurance to fund a death-benefit-only plan made the plan "funded" for purposes of the vesting and funding requirements common generally only to qualified plans (see Chapter 21).[19] A death-benefit-only plan is similar to a plan of deferred compensation except that it provides a benefit only in the event of the employee's death. This case has been severely criticized and will probably not be followed in future decisions.[20] The concept of *funding* has been understood to turn on whether an employee had an identifiable interest in any assets of the employer and not on whether the employer made any investments to hedge its promise to pay the employee at some future time. For example, under the more reasonable approach, a plan would be considered to be funded if the employee had some ownership interest in the life insurance policy, such as the right to change the beneficiary.

In order to avoid the possibility of corporate-owned life insurance being determined to constitute funding of a plan, design your deferred-compensation plan to follow these guidelines:

1. The life insurance is payable only to the employer, and the policies are subject to the rights of creditors of the employer.
2. The plan benefits are not based on the life insurance policies.
3. The plan participants and beneficiaries are not told that life insurance will be used to provide the plan benefits.
4. Neither plan participants nor beneficiaries have any interest in the policies.
5. The plan does not require or permit employee contributions.[21]

These guidelines should provide a safe harbor for avoidance of the funding issue.

Deferred Compensation As an Aid to the Sale of a Business

Under most circumstances, the purchase of a business requires the payment of significant after-tax dollars. The installation of a deferred-compensation plan in a corporation can enable the purchaser to pay for a portion of the purchase price with before-tax dollars. This can benefit both the seller and the purchaser.

Jackie K., age sixty, has been trying to sell her tin plating corporation for twenty-eight months for a minimum of $400,000. High interest rates have scared away prospective purchasers.

To help solve her problem, Jackie installs in her corporation a deferred-compensation plan to provide benefits for herself and her family of $20,000 per year for fifteen years upon her attainment of age sixty-five or, if earlier, upon her involuntary termination of employment.

Since she will be receiving significant benefits at age sixty-five (or earlier if the new owner terminates her employment), Jackie is willing to drop her asking price for her corporation to $250,000. The reduction in purchase price revives the interest of several qualified purchasers, who like the idea of paying some monies to Jackie that will be tax deductible to the corporation.

Qualified Plans–Basic Information

John Q. was a practicing attorney for eight years. Although he had increased his income to $60,000 a year, he had not been able to save enough money to make a down payment on an inexpensive condo in Ft. Lauderdale.

John Q. incorporated his practice and installed a profit-sharing plan to which he contributed 15 percent of his compensation each year. After three years, he borrowed $18,000 from the plan at 5 percent interest to make a down payment on the condo of his dreams.

A qualified plan can make your dreams come true. With inflation and high taxes, it has been difficult, if not impossible, for you to save a buck. Yet with qualified plans, you not only are able to save your own money, you are able to save a portion of Uncle Sam's. In fact, understanding and using qualified plans may be your most important step in successful tax planning.

What Is a Qualified Plan?

A qualified plan is a written formal agreement between an employer and a trustee or trustees that states:[1]

1. the basis on which contributions will be made[2]
2. for whose benefit the trustee holds the employer's contribution
3. how and when distributions will be made to the plan participants

Because a qualified plan is a legal document, be certain to consult your attorney before adopting a qualified plan.

The plan must contain specific provisions regarding participation, vesting,[3] how and when distributions are made, investments, and the like in order to receive IRS approval. IRS approval is an assurance but not a guarantee that the employer will get a current tax deduction for

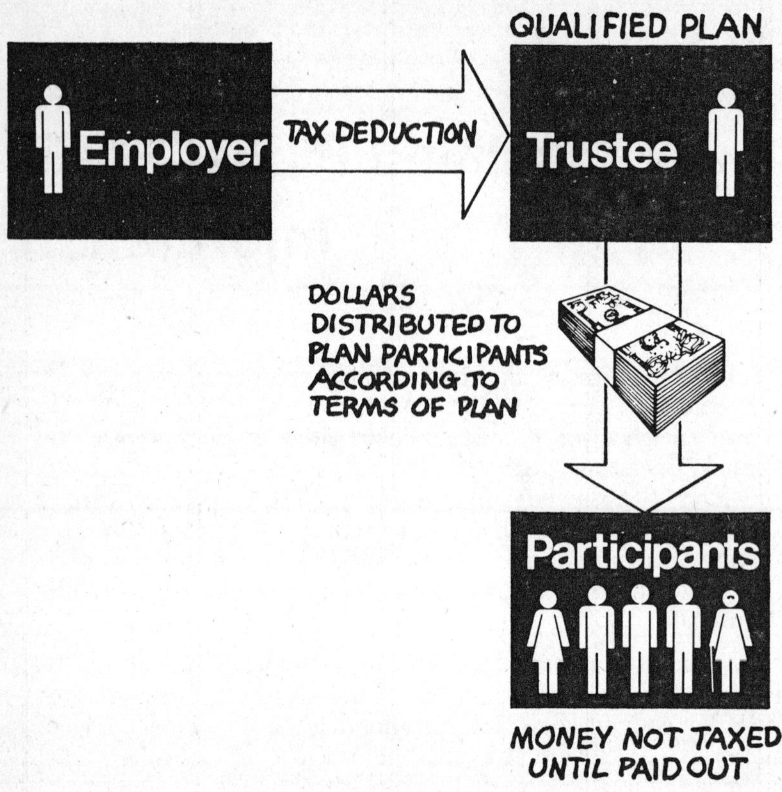

his or her contributions, the contributions will earn income on a tax-free basis and employees will not be taxed on the money held in trust for them until later, when a distribution occurs. However, the employer is not required to obtain a determination letter.

Why Qualified Plans Are Such a Deal

There are two general reasons the use of qualified plans is such an excellent tax-planning strategy.

First, unlike other tax shelters, a qualified plan can receive preapproval by the IRS. This means that its tax effects are virtually guaranteed, which simply is not the case with other tax shelters.

Second, the money contributed to a qualified plan can go into almost any investment you desire. Other types of tax shelters do not permit such investment flexibility. (Equipment leases, for example, require the investor to invest in equipment with the hope of making a profit.)

There are also four specific advantages of qualified plans:

1. *Glorified savings account.* In essence, a qualified plan is little more than a glorified savings account. Before-tax dollars are contributed to the plan and permitted to accumulate on a tax-free basis.[4] These dollars are then available to plan participants on a tax-free basis (through loans) or on a taxable basis (through such events as termination of employment or attainment of retirement age).

2. *Favorable income-tax treatment.* In addition to the savings feature,

distributions from a qualified plan are not subject to some of the disadvantages other income is. First, distributions are never subject to Social Security taxes. Also, a qualified lump sum distribution is taxed at very favorable rates.[5]

A lump sum distribution is a distribution from a corporate plan after at least five years of plan participation that is made on account of (a) termination of employment, (b) death, or (c) attainment of at least age 59½. The five-year-participation requirement does not apply for a distribution made in the event of death. For example, a lump-sum distribution of $100,000 is taxed at a rate of under 18 percent. This rate is independent of the tax rates on a participant's other taxed income. After 1983, the tax on a lump-sum distribution of $500,000 will be under 30 percent.

The favorable tax treatment of lump-sum distributions makes qualified plans a more desirable wealth accumulation vehicle than IRAs, which provide no income tax advantages on distribution—thus they are simply vehicles of tax deferral. Other advantages of qualified plans over IRAs are (a) premature distributions are not subject to a penalty tax; and (b) the assets of a qualified plan can be borrowed by plan participants.

Periodic payments from a qualified plan are treated as earned income (if tax rates ever increase above 50% again on unearned income) and are not subject to Social Security taxes.

3. *Favorable estate-tax treatment.* From an estate-tax standpoint, distributions from a qualified plan can be excluded from an employee's estate (see Chapter 13) as well as from the employee's spouse's estate.[6] This makes a qualified plan an exceptional vehicle for the buildup of wealth for an employee who already has a sizable estate. Moreover, the qualified plan can be an excellent place for life insurance to be owned so that it can be excluded from the participant's estate (see Chapter 11).

4. *Retention of employees.* Finally, a qualified plan can be an inducement for employees to remain with an employer. A plan generally provides for an employee to earn with each year of employment a vested interest in the plan benefit. Thus employees may give up substantial dollars if they terminate employment before becoming fully vested.[7] For many employees, their only significant savings will be in their qualified plan benefits.

Corporate Qualified Plans vs. Plans for the Unincorporated Entity

There are significant differences between corporate qualified plans and Keogh or HR 10 plans, which are the qualified plans for an unincorporated entity. The primary difference is in the level of contributions that is permitted. Keogh plans are generally limited to the lesser of $15,-000 or 15 percent of compensation (which cannot exceed $200,000 for purposes of determining an individual's contribution). Corporate plans permit a significantly larger contribution. If compensation of over $100,000 is used for a Keogh plan, contributions must be made for the benefit of common-law employees of at least 7.5 percent of their compensation.[8]

The following are additional limitations of Keogh plans:

1. Keogh plans require a corporate trustee, such as a bank or an insurance company, to hold and invest plan assets,[9] whereas corporate plans permit individuals who may be the owners of the company to be trustees.
2. Keogh plans prohibit borrowing by plan participants.[10]
3. A severe limitation exists against Keogh plans being integrated with Social Security, which is a feature that enables more highly compensated employees to receive a greater share of the contribution.

Even if you are covered by a corporate qualified plan, you are allowed to establish a Keogh plan if you have self-employment income, such as from consulting or director's fees. Thus a Keogh plan can provide a very attractive savings vehicle for income dollars earned outside your normal employment.

Different Types of Corporate Qualified Plans

There are two basic categories of corporate qualified plans—*defined contribution plans* and *defined benefit plans*. A defined contribution plan derives its name from the fact that the plan dictates contributions, not benefits. It bases contributions on a percentage of each participant's compensation. The benefit for each participant is the money or other assets allocated to the participant's individual account plus investment income thereon. A defined benefit plan, on the other hand, takes its name from the fact that it promises a benefit for each participant. Contributions to the plan are mathematically determined. An individual's benefit under a defined benefit plan is what the plan promises.

Any plan that is integrated with Social Security is designed so that highly paid employees receive a proportionally greater benefit than lower-wage employees. The purpose of integration is to attempt to equalize retirement benefits among low- and high-income employees as a percentage of pay. Integration is discussed more fully in the following chapter on plan design. Social Security is discussed in more detail in Chapter 5.

What follows is a list of the main characteristics of the basic types of plans for corporations.

Defined Contribution Plans
Profit Sharing

Permits contributions between 1 percent and 15 percent of the total compensation of the participants in the plan. Primary advantages are (a) flexibility; (b) forfeitures are reallocated among accounts of remaining participants; and (c) participants can borrow from individual accounts at an interest rate that may be as low as 5 percent. (See the discussion of Borrowings beginning on p. 204 of this chapter.) This is an excellent first plan for the employer who has unstable profits or modest cash available for contributions.

Money Purchase

Requires contributions at the level set forth in the plan. Contributions can be as high as 25 percent of a participant's compensation. This is an excellent second plan: it is usually used in conjunction with either a profit-sharing plan or a defined-benefit plan. If it is used with a profit-sharing plan, each participant is limited to receiving a maximum of 25 percent of compensation in the allocation of contributions and forfeitures to his or her account in both plans.[11]

Target Benefit

A form of money-purchase plan, this plan requires contributions based on a formula to provide a promised benefit for employees at retirement age. Total contributions to a participant's account are limited to 25 percent of the participant's compensation.[12] Contributions under this plan are based on a participant's age and compensation; thus it is a very favorable plan for the older, highly compensated individual.

Stock Ownership

We include here stock bonus plans as well as the well-publicized employee stock ownership plan—ESOP.[13] Either stock plan creates a market for closely held corporate stock and can be a vehicle of corporate finance. Dollars contributed to the plan or borrowed by the plan (such as can be done with an ESOP, whereby the employer guarantees the loan) can be used to buy treasury stock, thus creating more dollars of operating capital for the corporation that has such a plan. The disadvantages are that there is dilution of stock ownership for the existing shareholders (although terminated employees do not have to be given their benefit in the form of stock) and that the ESOP participants must be given voting rights on the stock in their accounts in certain situations. The limitations on contributions in an ESOP has been increased to 25 percent of compensation of each participant.[14] In addition, repayment of interest and principal on borrowings made by an ESOP in certain circumstances are not treated as part of the employer's contribution to the plan. Finally, a tax credit may be available for contributions to an ESOP, based on a prescribed percentage of the compensation of all employees under the plan.[15]

Defined Benefit Plans

Unlike defined contribution plans, there is no limitation on the total dollars that are contributed to this plan. It is not unusual for a plan to provide for contributions of up to $100,000 per year for a key employee. The only limitation is that the plan cannot promise a benefit in excess of 100 percent of an employee's compensation (or, if less than 100%), a stated dollar amount, well over $120,000, which increases with cost of living).[16] This is an excellent plan for very large contributions. A defined benefit plan can provide flexibility in the age at which normal retirement benefits commence to cause larger contributions to be made on behalf of selected key employees.

Types of Keogh Plans

Keogh plans are similar to corporate qualified plans except that there is no Keogh plan comparable to the stock bonus or ESOP. As discussed on pages 200–201, Keogh contributions to a defined contribution plan are limited to the lesser of $15,000 or 15 percent of a participant's compensation. Also, the benefit that can be provided under a Keogh defined benefit plan is significantly less than that provided by a corporate defined benefit plan. The result of this decreased benefit is that in most cases, the contribution on behalf of a participant to a Keogh defined benefit plan can not be significantly increased above the $15,000 limitation.

The Simplified Employee Plan

This plan deserves separate mention because it can be easily established by either an incorporated or an unincorporated entity. This plan is like an expanded IRA account for each participant (see Chapter 5 for a discussion of IRA accounts) and does permit integration with Social Security for the unincorporated entity.[17] The maximum contribution that can be made to the plan is the lesser of $15,000 or 15 percent of compensation (up to $200,000). The primary attractiveness of the plan is the simplicity of setting it up. The government provides printed forms for adopting a simplified employee plan, but only for the unintegrated plan. Since this plan is an expanded IRA, distributions are restricted. Also, employees can easily make voluntary deductible contributions to this plan the same as to an IRA.

Borrowings—How to Get Present Benefits from a Qualified Plan

The ability of plan participants to borrow from their accounts is a great advantage of the *corporate* qualified plan. The basic requirements for borrowing are the following:[18]

1. Borrowing is limited to a participant's interest in the plan.[19]
2. Adequate collateral must be put up for the money borrowed.
3. A reasonable rate of interest must be paid.
4. There must be a repayment schedule.
5. Borrowing must be authorized by the plan document.
6. Borrowing must be available to all employees on an equivalent basis (such as a stated percentage of account balances).

There is an exception to the reasonable rate of interest requirement. It appears that a profit-sharing plan can enable a plan participant to borrow from his or her account at a 5 percent rate, as long as the participant repays the interest to his or her particular account. In such a case, the participant's account does not share in the general growth of the fund assets. The policy here is that the participant who borrows the money at a 5 percent interest rate cannot have the low interest rate and share in the plan's high investment return at the same time. *Note:* There has been no formal statement by Congress or the IRS permitting borrowing at 5 percent interest from a qualified plan. However, a plan provision permitting borrowing at such a rate has been approved by the IRS.

Borrowing from a plan does not work any great magic. Tax shelters or other investments that can be made with qualified-plan borrowed funds could also be made with other borrowed money. Yet the borrowing procedure can be simplified by using the assets of the qualified plan,

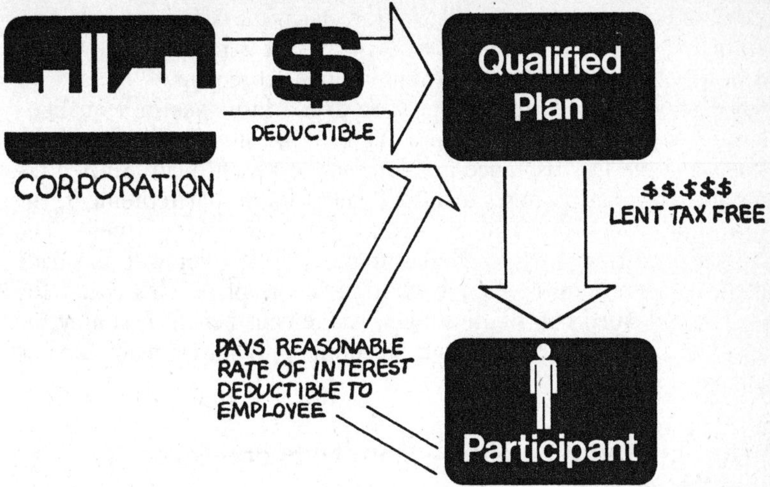

and interest rates may be lower than in the marketplace. Moreover, the plan assets are a wonderful source of funds for an emergency or for the down payment on that condominium in Florida. In fact, the ability to borrow makes true what we said earlier in this chapter: a qualified plan is a glorified savings account. The money, plus what you would have paid in taxes, is there when you need it.

Life Insurance in a Plan

Suppose you calculate that your qualified plan will provide you with $250,000 for your Florida retirement in fifteen years. If you check out early, your family will only get a portion of that benefit—unless you purchase life insurance in the plan. The purchase of life insurance in a plan can be viewed as simply a guarantee of the ultimate plan benefit. Live or die, your family will receive essentially the same plan benefits.

Estate planning can also provide a compelling reason for the purchase of life insurance in a qualified plan. If your estate is already subject to sizable estate taxes, an excellent place for you to accumulate additional wealth is in a qualified plan. Qualified plan assets, including the life insurance proceeds, can pass in a way that is kept out of your estate (see Chapter 13).[20] Since life insurance proceeds are already income-tax exempt, the purchase of life insurance in a manner that is estate-tax exempt creates the perfect tax result—none! The only cost is the income charged to the participant equal to the value of the pure life insurance coverage of the insurance (the face value of the policy less accumulated cash values). However, this tax cost is recaptured either at death or when the policy is distributed upon retirement.

The only drawback to the purchase of life insurance in a qualified plan is the poor investment return. You can get around this hurdle by purchasing the life insurance in your defined benefit plan. Since a defined benefit plan promises a stated benefit for you at retirement, the life insurance contract will not reduce your retirement benefit. The additional cost, if any, of the insurance in the plan will be made up through the employer's contribution to the plan. This is not the result in a defined contribution plan, where your benefit is simply the contributions allocated to your account plus investment income thereon.

Coverage Requirements—More Nuts and Bolts of Qualified Plans

Corporate Plans

Each employee who has attained the age of at least twenty-five and completed a full year of employment generally must be permitted to participate in a qualified plan. However, an employee can be required to wait for three years before he is eligible to participate in the plan if, when he becomes eligible to participate, he is immediately 100 percent vested in his account.[21]

Also, plans may impose additional requirements for participation to exclude otherwise eligible employees. As a means of curbing discrimination against rank-and-file employees, Congress requires that total participation in the plan either include 70 percent of eligible employees or that the definition of the group permitted to participate be determined not to be discriminatory *in favor of* employees who are officers, shareholders or highly compensated.[22] However, collective bargaining units,

Compensation	Number of employees	Number of employees eligible (based on age and service) to be in the plan	Number of employees in the plan
$25,000 & above	2	2	1
$20,000–25,000	3	3	0
$15,000–20,000	3	2	0
$10,000–15,000	6	4	3
under $10,000	4	3	2

nonresident aliens and employees who do not meet the already-mentioned age and service test need not be covered by the plan for purposes of meeting the percentage test or the nondiscrimination test. Suppose your company has fifteen employees, five of whom are under age twenty-five or who have completed less than one year of employment. Your plan, in order to satisfy the 70 percent test, need only cover seven of the ten eligible employees. Also, a plan can qualify if it covers a representative cross section of employees even though the percentage test is not satisfied.

This plan will probably satisfy the coverage requirements because it covers an adequate cross section of employees. If anything, the plan discriminates *against* highly compensated employees, whereas the prohibition is in discriminating in *favor* of highly compensated employees.

Plans for Unincorporated Business

Keogh coverage requirements are generally the same as for corporate plans except that all employees (excluding union employees and nonresident aliens) having three or more years of service and who have attained the age of at least twenty-five must be permitted to participate in the plan.[23]

Vesting—Who Owns What in a Plan

Vesting is the rate at which employees earn an ownership interest in the assets contributed to the plan.

The statutory requirements for vesting are much more liberal than what the IRS likes to see. The IRS will only give an unconditional qualification letter on vesting rates that follow what is permitted by statute when a plan was in effect before the change in the law in 1974 and had a vesting schedule that was as strict or stricter than that provided by statute. For such plans, the following vesting schedules are available:[24]

1. Cliff vesting. No vesting for the first nine years of service; 100% vesting after ten years.
2. Fifteen-year vesting. After five years, 25% vesting, increased by 5% after the next five years and 10% for the last eleven to fifteen years.
3. Rule of 45s. Combination of age and service requirement.

For new plans, the IRS used to be satisfied with a vesting schedule that was at least as favorable for employees as the following:

Years	Vesting
0–3	0
4	40
5	45
6	50
7	60
8	70
9	80
10	90
11	100

This so-called 4–40 vesting used to be a safe harbor (meaning the IRS would give an unconditional qualification letter), but the IRS has recently proposed more severe vesting for plans, such as 100 percent vesting after three years. Congress has not been pleased with the service's hard line on vesting and in December, 1980, passed legislation that temporarily locked the IRS into accepting 4–40 vesting.

In any event, a plan must not discriminate against lower-paid employees in operation. This means that you cannot summarily fire your employees just before they are about to earn a vested interest in the plan.

In a Keogh plan, which has owner-employees (employees who own 10% or more of the business), all employees must be fully vested.[25] This full and immediate vesting requirement for Keogh plans causes most employers to make employees wait for three years before participating in a Keogh plan.

Deductible Employee Contributions

The 1981 Economic Recovery Tax Act permits employees to make a voluntary deductible contribution to an employer's qualified plan, up to a maximum of the lesser of $2,000 or 100 percent of compensation. If the employees make such a contribution, the contribution will reduce their possible IRA contribution (discussed in Chapter 5).[26]

John, who makes $20,000 per year, contributes $1,500 to his employer's profit-sharing plan. The contribution qualifies as a deductible contribution. If John also wants to contribute to an IRA, he will be limited to $500 for himself plus $250 for his spouse if she is nonworking.

A qualified plan must contain the same restrictions as an IRA in order for employees to receive a deduction for their voluntary contributions. If a plan does not contain the special provisions, no deduction for employee contributions will be allowed.

Generally employees can receive the same benefit (and more if they want to contribute for a nonworking spouse) from contributing to an IRA as they can receive from contributing to their employer's qualified plan. The only reasons an owner-employer would want to amend his or her plan to permit such deductible contributions are (a) as a convenience to employees; (b) so that the owner could invest deductible contributions; and (c) so that the combined IRA contributions can earn a better investment yield collectively.

The 1982 Tax Act

The qualified-plan area has been changed dramatically by the 1982 Tax Act. Contributions and benefits have been cut back, cost of living increases postponed until 1986, Social Security integration changed for defined contribution plans, minimum benefits and contributions required for plans of small businesses, and parity created between corporate and Keogh plans. Also, borrowing has been restricted to the lesser of (i) $50,000 or (ii) one-half of your vested account, but not for loans of $10,000 or less. The payback period is five years unless the loan is for the improvement or purchase of a residence.

Beginning in 1984, the remaining tax advantages of incorporation are: lower tax rates within the corporation, the fringe benefits discussed in Chapter 23, and the ability to straddle your individual tax year.

If you own a small business, you will probably be required to amend your plan to provide for the borrowing changes discussed above, plus in 1984 to provide (i) a beefed-up vesting schedule, (ii) minimum benefits for lower-paid employees, and (iii) limitation on distributions to key employees before age 59½ (IRC §416).

Planning suggestions for a small business: Consider a cash or deferred profit sharing plan (IRC §401(k)) that contributes 10 percent of compensation for all employees and permits you to contribute on a deductible basis an additional 5 percent of your compensation. This plan can then be combined with an integrated money purchase plan that includes base contributions of 3 percent of all compensation. Alternatively, consider leasing your employees from your office manager's separate business so you will only have to provide for these former employees a benefit of 7½ percent for qualified plan purposes (IRC §414(n)). Finally, set up your plan to permit participation only after three years of service, at which time each participant will be 100% vested.

chapter 22

Qualified Plans–Design

Julius Duffy, M.D., Inc., an Ohio professional corporation, has a money-purchase plan and a profit-sharing plan, which together permit contributions for its key employee, Julius Duffy, M.D., of 25 percent of his $160,000 salary.[1]

Dr. Duffy would like to reduce his income to save on taxes but is willing to do so only if contributions to qualified plans for his benefit can be increased.

Dr. Duffy drops his salary to $100,000 (thereby saving $30,000 in income taxes) and combines his two qualified plans into one 25 percent money-purchase plan. In addition, he installs a defined benefit plan that will provide him a benefit of 40 percent of his compensation upon attainment of age sixty-five. Julius Duffy, M.D., Inc., contributes $25,000 to the money-purchase plan and $75,000 to the defined benefit plan for the good doctor's benefit.[2] The $30,000 of taxes saved by Duffy now work for his benefit in the qualified plans.

All things may be possible with qualified plans. A plan can be designed to benefit highly compensated employees over rank-and-file employees. Also, different plans can be used in combination to increase the contribution made by the company for its employees.

Qualified-plan design consists of two separate but related matters: what kind of plan or plans should be used and what specific provisions should be in the plan(s).

In the previous chapter, three aspects of plan design were presented—borrowing by participants, purchase of life insurance and deductible employee contributions—that should be considered in the design of every qualified plan. In this chapter, the specific plan provision of integration and the type of plan to use will be discussed within the context of (a) for whose benefit a plan is established and (b) how large a contribution the employer wants to make.

First, we will consider the design features that enable a plan to provide extraordinary benefits for the key employees of the company.

For Whose Benefit?

Most plans are designed to benefit primarily the individuals who are doing the most to enhance the profits of the company. These "key" employees are often owners of the company and are the risk takers. The specific design provision that can be used to give a greater benefit to key employees is integration with Social Security. Social Security integration means that the plan takes into account the fact that the employer is already making a significant contribution for retirement for each employee. For 1982, this is approximately 7 percent of pay up to $32,400.[3] The mandatory contribution by the employer produces some great inequities in Social Security retirement benefits as a percentage of pay.

Because of the inequity of Social Security benefits, plan design can

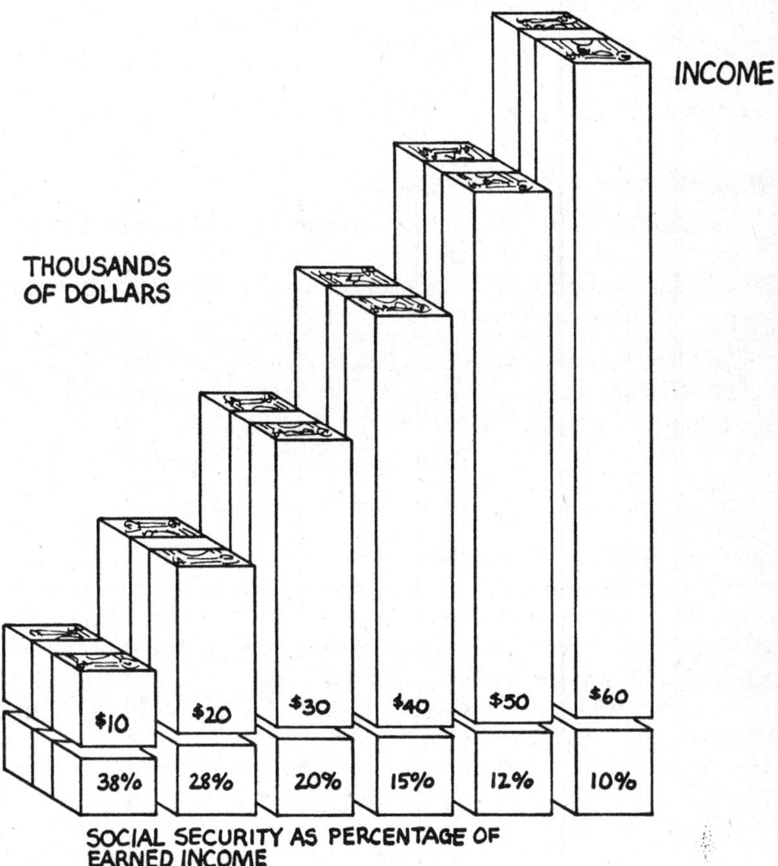

earmark greater contributions (in the case of defined-contribution plans) or greater benefits (in the case of a defined-benefit plan) for the higher paid employee.

Defined-Contribution Plan Integration

A defined-contribution plan (such as a money-purchase or profit-sharing plan) can provide an extra benefit of up to 7 percent of a participant's compensation in excess of the Social Security Taxable Wage Base (or any lesser amount). The Social Security Taxable Wage Base for 1982 in $32,400.[4] The amount that is chosen for an integration level (the level above which each participant's compensation receives a 7% additional benefit) is preferably set as low as possible without including the income of rank-and-file employees.

Key employees: $30,000–$60,000
Rank-and-file: $10,000–$14,000
Integration level would be set at $14,000.

Defined-Benefit Plan Integration

A defined-benefit plan can provide benefits for employees that are reduced by a percentage of what the employees will receive from Social Security.[5] Thus a defined-benefit plan can be established so that it will have no funding requirement for lower-paid employees.

Omnibus, Inc., adopts a defined-benefit plan that provides a benefit of 20 percent of pay for each participant less 74 percent of each participant's expected Social Security benefit. Ann, a secretary, makes $14,000 per year and will be entitled to $5,000 a year for Social Security. Her benefit of $2,800 under the plan is completely offset by the 74 percent of her Social Security benefit.[6]

Another way for defined-benefit plans to be integrated with Social Security is for the plan to provide for benefits of up to 37½ percent in excess of certain salaries set forth in a table provided by the IRS.[7] This table bases the salary level on the date of an employee's birth. This type of integration greatly favors older employees.

A target-benefit plan uses Social Security integration in the same manner as a defined-benefit plan.

Type of Plan

The type of plan that is used can have a very significant effect on getting a greater share of contributions to the highly compensated employees. Utilization of a target-benefit plan or a defined-benefit plan can be helpful in getting more benefits to *highly paid older employees.* The target-benefit plan and defined-benefit plan base contributions on benefits provided under the plan; thus older participants will require greater contributions than younger participants because there are fewer years to fund for their benefits.

Salary	Age	Required Contribution	Annual Benefit at Age 65
40,000	55	17,212	20,000
40,000	35	3,258	20,000
40,000	25	1,792	20,000

Dollars Available for Qualified Plans

Another factor that influences the type of plan used is the amount of dollars available for contribution to qualified plans. We will discuss plan design within this context by looking at dollars available for contributions as a percentage of the compensation of the participants in the plan. (Refer to coverage requirements discussed in Chapter 21 for a review of who must be covered.)

First, determine the compensation of those employees who will be covered by your qualified plan. Second, divide the amount of contribution you want to make by the compensation of plan participants. This will give you contributions as a percentage of payroll of participants.

Contributions up to 15% of Payroll of Participants

Suppose your total payroll for employees who would be eligible to participate in a qualified plan is $300,000. If you want to contribute up to $45,000, your contribution would be up to 15 percent of the compensation of the participants in the plan.[8] This is a modest contribution level.

At this level, you probably do not want to get locked into the same contribution amount each year; thus a profit-sharing plan would be best. As you desire to increase contributions, another plan can be added. The profit-sharing plan can be integrated with Social Security as discussed above to benefit more highly compensated employees.

The only other option that should be considered is a target-benefit plan. (See previous chapter.) This plan may provide for a greater proportion of dollars to be set aside for the accounts of the more highly compensated employees. The target-benefit plan works especially well if the highly compensated employees are also older. The only drawbacks are that the target plan requires yearly contributions and the employer does not have any contribution flexibility each year.

Contributions of 15%–25% of Payroll of Participants

Now a profit-sharing plan alone will not provide for a large enough contribution.[9] The solution is to add a money-purchase plan. This plan (with a contribution of 10% for each participant) can be combined with the profit-sharing plan to permit the employer to make the maximum contribution for each participant when only defined-contribution plans are used (25% of each participant's compensation), but with the advantage of flexibility.[10] In an economically depressed year, the employer only has to contribute the 10 percent required for the money-purchase plan. A target-benefit plan could also be used alone or with the profit-sharing plan—but the total contribution allocated to a participant's account cannot exceed 25 percent of his or her compensation.[11] If the target-benefit plan is used alone, the employer will have no flexibility as to contributions each year.

Another plan-design approach that may help get additional dollars into the plans for the benefit of you, the key employee, is to add a defined-benefit plan to the profit-sharing plan. The employer's total contribution will have to stay at or below 25 percent of the compensation of all participants, but the contribution may be allocated so that the combined benefits for you greatly exceed the 25 percent maximum available for a combination money-purchase plan (or target-benefit plan) and profit-sharing plan.[12] A defined-benefit plan is called for when (a) your salary is greatly in excess of that of other employees, or (b) you are significantly older than other employees.

> Ron Burrel, age forty-eight, makes $100,000 as the owner of his marble-making operation and has a total payroll for plan participants of $400,000. All his other employees are compensated in the $10,000 to $16,000 range.
>
> Ron's company contributes $60,000 to an integrated defined benefit plan, of which $45,000 is for Ron's benefit. Ron's company also contributes $40,000 to a profit-sharing plan in which $10,000 is allocated to Ron's account. Thus Ron essentially benefits from $55,000 of his company's contribution. A profit-sharing plan can be used because the total contribution here is limited to 25 percent of the compensation of the participants.[13]

If a money-purchase (or a target-benefit) plan plus a profit-sharing plan were used here, the maximum benefit that could have been allocated to Ron's account would have been 25 percent of his compensation or $25,000.[14]

NOTE: In many situations, it will be advantageous for the defined-benefit plan rather than the profit-sharing plan to be integrated.

When a profit-sharing plan is used in combination with a defined-benefit plan, the employer must be prepared to make the contribution to the defined-benefit plan each year. The flexibility in this arrangement is provided by the profit-sharing plan.

Contributions of Over 25% of Payroll of Participants

If a profit-sharing plan had been used previously, it *must* be dropped and its assets either held in trust or transferred to the corporation's money-purchase plan.[15] A defined-benefit plan now will have to be used either alone or in combination with a money-purchase or target-benefit plan.

In most cases, the defined-benefit plan alone can soak up all the employer's available contribution dollars. However, when a defined-benefit plan provides a maximum benefit (100% of compensation) and the employer desires to have additional dollars contributed to a qualifed plan, the employer can adopt a 10 percent money-purchase plan in addition to a defined-benefit plan.

NOTE: The rules on combining a defined-benefit plan and money-purchase plan or target-benefit plan are complex and depend on the types of plans the employer has had in the past. Contribution and benefit levels under IRC §415 *must* be checked out in every case.

For younger key employees, such as the twenty-four-year-old pro athlete, the maximum contribution for the key employee can sometimes be made by using a 25 percent money-purchase plan (or target-benefit plan that provides for the maximum 25% contribution for the key employee) and a defined-benefit plan that provides a benefit of 40 percent of final average compensation. There is no age cutoff when the 25 percent money-purchase plan should be used to maximize contributions; low retirement age defined-benefit plans (such as age 55 or under) can make a big difference in contributions required to the defined-benefit plan. Accordingly each case must be reviewed by an actuary to determine how contributions can be maximized.

Defined-Benefit Design

Maximum contributions to a defined-benefit plan can be achieved by making the date at which full benefits begin under the plan the key employee's age plus ten years. This in some cases may result in a normal retirement date in the plan of under age fifty-five or over age sixty-five. Your actuary must advise you on this specific aspect of plan design. However, the IRS through its regulations has not taken away the benefit of using unreal normal retirement dates. An over-age-sixty-five retirement date is particularly favored by the federal government, because this ties in with increasing the normal age at which employees can elect to be eligible for Social Security.

Flexibility in Defined-Benefit Plan Contributions

Everything we have said thus far indicates that the company must make its full contribution to its defined-benefit plan each year. However, there are two exceptions.

First, a plan can provide for a shareholder-participant to waive the accrual of his or her benefit for a plan year. The waiver of benefit means that the employee sacrifices part of the benefit the plan promises, but it also means that the employer does not have to make a contribution for the employee for that year. In a small plan, the employer's contribution will be primarily for the benefit of the shareholder-participant. Thus a waiver by the shareholder-participant will greatly reduce the obligation of the employer to make a contribution for the given plan year. The waiver can be made anytime before the expiration of the plan year.

Second, a plan can provide for the cessation of accrual of benefits for all employees.[16] In this case, the participants must continue to be given credit for vesting (their percentage of nonforfeitable interest in their benefits under the plan—see previous chapter), but they do not continue to accrue additional benefits under the plan.

The cessation of accrual of benefits can completely terminate the employer's obligation to make contributions to the plan. The only catch is that the employer must amend the plan before the start of the plan year to provide for the cessation of accrual of benefits. If the plan is amended during the plan year, the employees will have earned additional benefits, and the employer will be liable for the funding required for those benefits.

The advantage of cessation of accrual of benefits is that the employer can cease making contributions without going through the rigamarole of formally terminating the plan.

Relief, Inc., has a fiscal year ending October 31 and in 1979 installs a defined-benefit plan with a plan year beginning October 1 and ending September 30. Each year, the corporation funds the plan in October for the benefits to be accrued over the next twelve-month period. In 1984, Relief, Inc., has a rotten year and does not want to make the pension-plan contribution. By corporate resolution adopted September 30, 1984, it ceases the accrual of benefits under the plan for the next twelve months and removes its obligation to make a contribution for the fiscal year ending October 31, 1984. The next year, sales are up for Relief, Inc., and it reinstates its accrual of benefits under the plan.

Plans for Unincorporated Businesses

Contributions to a Keogh plan can be increased above the $15,000 limit in certain circumstances by using a defined-benefit Keogh plan.[17] However, in the long run (by making projections to retirement), the defined benefit Keogh plan generally will not add significantly to retirement income. The only situations where the defined benefit Keogh may make much sense are those in which the owner desires to provide a large insurance benefit in the plan.

If the unincorporated business owner feels too much of the contribution is for the low-paid employees, he should consider (a) a target benefit Keogh plan, which permits contributions to be slanted to the older, more highly compensated employees, or (b) a simplified employee pension plan (this is an expanded IRA), which permits Social Security to be taken into account in the contributions that are made to the plan.[18]

For most unincorporated businesses, significant study should be given to advantages of incorporating before a commitment is made to improve Keogh plan benefits.

Specific Plan Provisions

Once you have decided what type of plan you want, you must decide what optional plan provisions to include. Unless you have some valid reason against it, your qualified plan should provide for borrowings by plan participants in corporate plans. Also, your plan should provide for the purchase of life insurance at the option of the plan participant in the case of defined-contribution plans. The decision to purchase life insurance in a defined-benefit plan must be made by the company, not by each plan participant. In the defined-benefit plan, there should be a provision for waiver of accrual of benefits by shareholder-participants to protect the company from a portion of its contributions obligation in a rugged year. Finally you should provide for deductible voluntary contributions if you like the idea of having all your qualified-plan dollars within your control.

With regard to the plan provisions that must be in every plan, the following should be considered:

Participant—An Employee shall be eligible to participate on the Entry Date (usually the first day of the plan year) which is within six months of the Employee's completion of one Year of Service and the attainment of at least age 25.

Vesting—Vesting will be 40% after four Years of Service, increased by 5% for each of the next two Years of Service, increased by 10% for each of the next five Years of Service.

(Exception: If your company has a very high turnover of lower-paid employees, such as is true with many professional service corporations, you should use a vesting schedule of 10% per Year of Service so that lower-paid employees will receive some benefits from the plan.)

Year of Service—An Employee shall receive credit for a Year of Service for each twelve-month period beginning on the Employee's date of hire in which he or she completes at least 1,000 Hours of Service. Hours of Service shall be credited on the basis of 45 hours for each week in which a full-time Employee works at least one hour (this is to reduce the burden of record keeping).

Employee—Each Employee of Employer shall be considered an Employee for purposes of participating in the plan; except that an Employee who is a member of a collective bargaining unit which has negotiated with the Employer for retirement benefits [and nearly all of them do] shall not be eligible to participate in the plan.

A model profit sharing plan with the 5 percent loan provision discussed in the prior chapter is set forth in Appendix H.

chapter 23

How to Provide Certain Benefits Tax Free in a Corporate Setting

Your corporation is the closest thing to Santa Claus you will ever see outside of a December visit to Macy's. Whatever fringe benefits you want, your corporation should provide. The only catch is that your corporate dollar should be stretched to its maximum—that means using it in a tax-efficient way. The best way to use corporate dollars is to take advantage of the fringe benefits that are deductible to the corporation but not income to the recipient.

Qualified plans discussed in earlier chapters are an example of a fringe benefit. Believe it or not, the corporate contribution to Social Security is a fringe benefit. But most important, there are a number of fringe benefits that are necessities of life.

Health and Disability Coverage

Your corporation can provide health and disability insurance coverage for all employees on a favorable tax basis.[1] Generally disability benefits are provided for a more limited classification of employees than health insurance, which is a nearly universal benefit in today's climate. The cost of total and permanent disability insurance is tax deductible to the corporation and is not income to the employee, subject to certain limitations. The insurance must be purchased pursuant to a salary-continuation plan that has been adopted by the employer for employees (be certain not to mention shareholder-employees, since this will rile the IRS). This is the best way for disability insurance to be paid, since if the employee makes the payments, the premiums will not be fully deductible.

Adoption of a health-insurance plan for employees is also necessary for the employer to deduct the cost of the health-insurance premiums and the employee to exclude the benefits from income.[2] However, if health insurance is provided for all employees who satisfy minimum requirements (such as work for three months before coverage begins), the IRS will not get too excited about whether your corporation has a formally adopted plan. The reason—*public policy.*

In any event, do not pay for health and disability premiums with your own cherished after-tax dollars when your corporation can provide these benefits for you on an income-tax-free basis.

Medical Expense Reimbursement Plans*

Once you have yourself covered under a corporate health insurance program, most of your major medical expenses will be paid by insurance. But what can you do about the expenses that are not covered by insurance, such as the costs of routine checkups, dental expenses, new eyeglasses and the like?

Since medical expenses are deductible only to the extent that they exceed 3 percent of your adjusted gross income (see Chapter 1)[3]—and then only if you itemize deductions—it is desirable to have your corporation pay for uninsured medical expenses if this can be done in a manner that is deductible to the corporation and is not taxable to you. A medical expense reimbursement plan permits precisely this result. Unfortunately a self-insured medical expense reimbursement plan must be set up on a nondiscriminatory basis in order for it to qualify as a bona-fide fringe benefit and not be taxable to you.[4] It can be discriminatory only if the additional coverage is provided by an insurance company under a bona-fide insurance arrangement. It is very difficult to find a true insurance arrangement (as opposed to a self-funded plan) for a medical reimbursement plan.

Nondiscriminatory Coverage

If your corporation has ten full-time employees, all of whom are at least age twenty-five and have worked for you at least three years, seven out of the ten employees should be covered by the plan for it to be nondiscriminatory. On the other hand, if four of these employees are under twenty-five or have not been with you for three years, you only have to cover five employees. Why? Because, in general, you need to cover 70 percent of all employees who satisfy the minimum age and service test—are at least age twenty-five and have been employed for at least three years.[5]

---

* The 1982 Tax Act increased the 3% limitation for medical expenses to 5%. This makes medical reimbursement plans more valuable than ever. (IRC §213)

All employees   10
Less employees under 25
or not completed 3 years   <u>4</u>
Total   6
70% of Total = 5

You can get around the 70 percent test if you comply with the adequate cross representation test, which was discussed in Chapter 21. This test may enable you to exclude more employees than the pure 70 percent test. Even with the 70 percent test, at least 80 percent of those in the plan must submit a claim for benefits.

NOTE: Once the coverage requirement is satisfied, benefits under the plan are the *same* for all covered employees—such as reimbursement up to the extent of $1,500 for uninsured medical, dental and optical expenses. Reimbursement under a qualified medical reimbursement plan cannot be based on a percentage of compensation.

Diagnostic Procedure Reimbursement

There is one freebie in the medical reimbursement plan area—reimbursement of medical diagnostic procedure expenses.[6] This type of reimbursement plan can be on a discriminatory basis such as for officers (but not their dependents) only. Suppose $200 of your uninsured medical expenses are for general medical and dental checkups. If you paid these out of your own pocket and were in the 50 percent tax bracket, you would have to earn $400 to make the payments. If the corporation reimburses you, it only has to come up with the $200.

Do not miss this plan—Congress has made it favorable for you to adopt this plan because Congress wants you to have your health maintenance checkups regularly.

Model Corporate Resolution

The corporation hereby adopts a plan to reimburse all full-time officers of the corporation (but not dependents of such officers) for all uninsured medical diagnostic procedure expenses. Medical diagnostic procedures as used in this resolution shall mean any medical expense that is not for the specific treatment of a medical, dental or optical ailment or malady.

Life Insurance Benefits

Your corporation can provide several different opportunities for the purchase of life insurance on a tax-free or low-cost basis.

Group Term*

Group term insurance is an excellent vehicle for you to acquire substantial amounts of low-cost insurance. Group term insurance can be provided for employees on a pyramid basis, so that key employees receive substantially more insurance than rank-and-file employees. In order for the insurance premium to be deductible, the plan must qualify as group term insurance and the employer must not be a beneficiary under the policy.[7]

In order to qualify as group term insurance, the policy or policies must form part of a plan of group insurance. The requirements for what constitutes "a plan of insurance" are essentially as follows:

1. The plan must be established by an employer for employees.
2. The plan must make term insurance available to a group of lives. Such group must include all employees or a class or classes of such employees based on some factor that precludes individual selection.
3. The amounts of insurance protection provided under the plan must be based upon some formula that precludes individual selection of such amounts.
4. Generally the plan must cover at least ten full-time employees.[8]

NOTE: Plans that cover fewer than ten employees have special requirements that must be complied with in order for these plans to receive favorable tax treatment by the IRS.[9]

The cost of the first $50,000 of group term coverage provided for an employee is not included in the employee's gross income, making this amount of group term insurance an ideal fringe benefit for you. Any additional insurance coverage is taxed to the employee as income, based on the employee's age and amount of insurance coverage in excess of $50,000.[10]

There are several exceptions to the $50,000 ceiling. The cost of group term insurance is not included in an employee's income, even if it is in excess of $50,000, if (a) the employee has terminated employment with the employer and is disabled or has reached normal retirement age; (b) a charitable organization is designated as the sole beneficiary of the

---

* The 1982 Tax Act has tightened the qualification rules for group term plans (IRC §79). RLR plans will proliferate now that there are cutbacks in qualified-plan contributions. Consider giving yourself the option at age sixty-five of nonqualified deferred comp (Chapter 20) or paid-up life insurance under an RLR plan. An RLR fund can be used for other employee welfare costs such as health insurance and thus can indirectly be used as an offsetting cost to nonqualified deferred comp.

group term coverage; or (c) the employer is designated as beneficiary and the employer is not required to pay over the proceeds to the employee's estate.[11]

Group Permanent

Group permanent insurance or so-called Section 79 insurance is simply group insurance with a permanent (or whole life) insurance benefit that is added on to the term. The additional cost of the permanent coverage is fully taxed to the employee.[12] The permanent insurance may be provided for only one class of employees covered under the group term plan (such as for full-time officers only).

The advantage of group permanent coverage is that the cash value buildup passes through to the employee, so that he or she has access to additional dollars. More important, the premium for the whole life insurance is a level premium. This can be extremely important with older employees who may work well beyond the retirement age of sixty-five. Finally the permanent insurance gives the employee an insurance program that the employee can convert at a level premium upon termination of employment. This is desirable, since most group term programs offer no life insurance coverage for an employee's family when the employee retires from the company.

Retired Lives Reserve

A retired lives reserve program is another way your corporation can provide an insurance benefit for employees that will take effect after the typical group term coverage ceases. Retired Lives Reserve (RLR) is popular because it permits your corporation to set aside tax-deductible funds to provide insurance coverage at retirement for current employees. Your corporation obtains a current deduction for the cost of funding the plan, and its employees incur no tax liability.[13] There is no limit on the amount of nontaxable insurance coverage that can be provided for an employee under a RLR plan as long as coverage begins when the employee has terminated employment and has reached retirement age.[14] Within certain limits, the employer can select the classes of employees to cover and the amounts of coverage of such classes. The tax deductibility to your corporation and absence of income to its employees makes this a desirable method of providing insurance coverage after sixty-five. Importantly, the funds that are set aside for the RLR plan are credited with a reasonably high rate of interest (8%–11%) that is tax free.

Your corporation is entitled to a deduction for its contribution to the RLR plan as long as the amount of the contribution is based on an allocation of the cost over the working lives of the covered employees and the employer has no right to recapture any portion of the reserve while any active or inactive employee is covered by the plan.[15] The plan can be maintained with an insurance company, or your corporation can contribute nonrefundable dollars to an employees' trust. The RLR trust can also be used to provide other employee fringe benefits, such as health and disability insurance. If it is overfunded, such as might occur in the event of the early death of a key employee for whose benefit many dollars had been contributed to the RLR fund, these funds can be used for other benefits. Recapture of contributed funds will trigger tax liability for the employer.

During years of employment prior to age sixty-five, an employee is covered under the employer's group term plan. If an employee remains with the company past age sixty-five, any life insurance benefit provided by the employer will be taxable on the same basis as the group term cov-

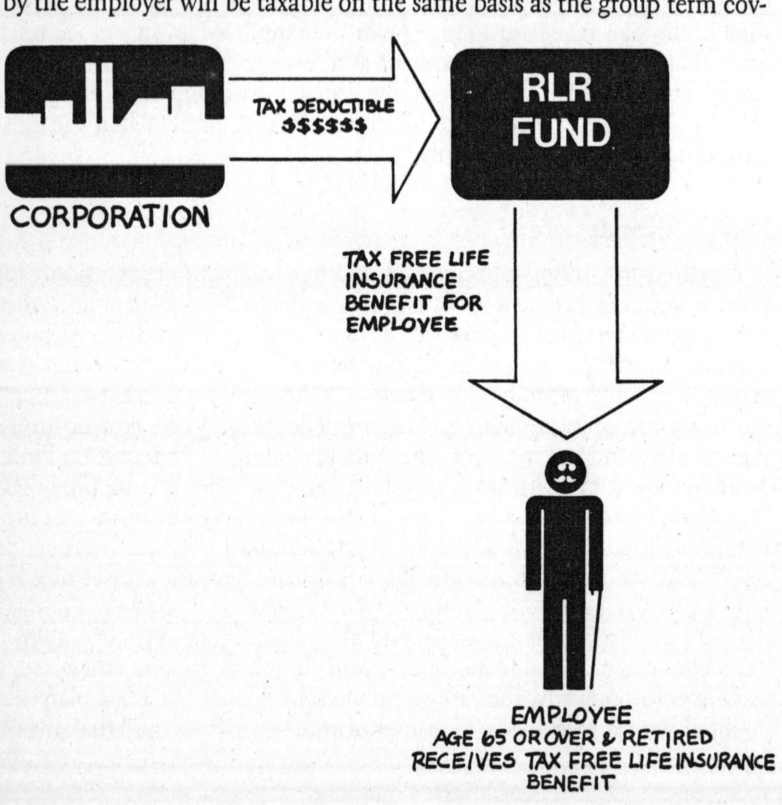

erage before age sixty-five.[16] However, upon retirement, there will be no tax consequences to the employee of insurance coverage provided under the RLR plan.

Split-Dollar Insurance

A split-dollar plan is a method of splitting the cost of permanent insurance to reduce the cost of the insurance coverage to yourself or another key employee.[17] Essentially corporate dollars are used to pay for the whole-life portion of an insurance policy, thereby reducing the outlay of cash that has to be made by the employee.

Under a split-dollar plan, the employer either owns the policy (the *endorsement method*) to the extent of the cash value or premium advanced (whichever is greater) or receives an assignment of the policy from the employee (a *collateral assignment*) to the extent of such figure. The employer is the beneficiary of the insurance proceeds to the extent of the cash value or premiums advanced, and the employee designates a beneficiary for the remainder of the proceeds. The employer generally pays the premium to the extent of the increase in the cash value of the policy, and the employee pays the remainder.

Since the employer is a direct or indirect beneficiary of the contract, the employer is not entitled to a deduction for its portion of the premium payment. The employee is taxed on the amount of economic benefit under the plan, and the employer gets no corresponding deduction.[18] If the employer pays the employee's share of the premium cost, the employee will be required to include such premium payment in his or her income, and the employer will be entitled to a corresponding deduction. Generally it is advantageous to have the employee's cost bonused to him or her, so that the employee can actually write out a check for his or her share. Otherwise, there is a possibility the employer will lose its tax deductions for the employee's share of the premium cost (which the employee *has* to include as income).

Key-Man Insurance

Key-man life insurance is purchased by a corporation to protect against the loss of a key employee. The insurance is designed to compensate the employer for any loss of profits attributable to the absence of the key man and to reimburse the employer for the expense of locating, hiring and training a replacement for the key man.

During the life of the key man, premiums are not deductible, since the employer is a direct or indirect beneficiary under the policy.[19] The

COLLATERAL ASSIGNMENT METHOD

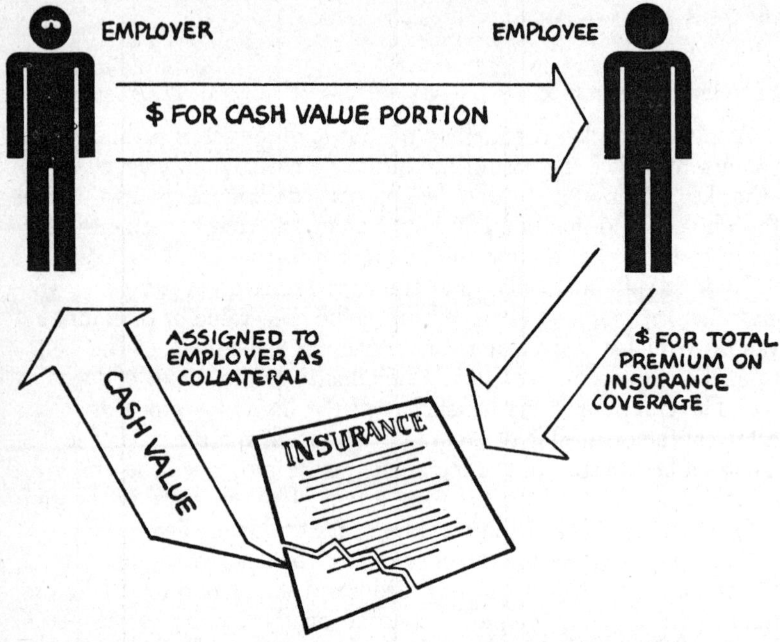

AT DEATH OF EMPLOYEE, CASH VALUE REPAID
TO EMPLOYER, BALANCE TO EMPLOYEE'S
BENEFICIARIES

deduction of premium payments is also disallowed when the key-man insurance is assigned to a creditor as collateral for a loan.

Since key-man insurance is purchased to benefit the corporation in the event of a key man's death, it is not insurance that should generally be purchased to provide insurance dollars to a shareholder's estate. However, when the shareholder either owns all the stock or the shareholder's shares are subject to purchase by the corporation at his or her death, the shareholder's estate can be the eventual recipient of the insurance proceeds received by the corporation. For example, the insurance can be paid to the shareholder's estate (a) upon liquidation of the corporation, or (b) upon redemption of the stockholder's stock if there is another shareholder with a small amount of stock.

A owns 99 shares; B, an unrelated employee, owns 1 share. Corporation AB, Inc., buys $300,000 of key-man insurance on

A. A can agree with AB, Inc., that at his death, the corporation will buy his stock for $300,000.

Thus A can in a very meaningful way get the benefit of key-man insurance purchased by the corporation.

Remember: Before making the decision of how your corporation can help you purchase the best life insurance coverage for you, be sure to study the relevant tax brackets, alternative insurance-company policies and options available in buying insurance.

chapter 24
Tax Shams

On the advice of Mr. Charlatan, a traveling tax adviser, Dr. R. Goodell paid $5,000 for a "special" trust to which he and his wife assigned all their worldly possessions. He also irrevocably committed his corporation to pay 28 percent of its income to this trust, in exchange for services to be provided the corporation by Dr. Goodell.

The special trust was much like the family trust discussed in Chapter 10. It was established to benefit family members and contained many typical trust provisions. It even named his wife as trustee. However, it created units of beneficial interest, which represented all the income interests of the trust. The units of beneficial interest were given to Dr. Goodell's children, who were in a lower income-tax bracket than Dr. Goodell.

One of the tipoffs that there was something wrong with the trust was that it contained language that said essentially the following: "This is a private document and cannot be shown to anyone outside Dr. Goodell's immediate family."

When the IRS audited Dr. Goodell's corporation, it looked into the payment of monies to the special trust that had been established. The IRS made the determination that Dr. Goodell had made an improper assignment of income and assessed him deficiency taxes, penalties for fraud and interest for all the years income had been paid from the corporation to the trust.

Unfortunately there are thousands of taxpayers who have adopted the main corollary to Dr. Goodell's approach to tax planning: pretend the tax system permits all types of devious schemes to avoid the payment of taxes; you just have to pay enough to make these schemes work. Also, most taxpayers who wind up in Dr. Goodell's plight have followed corollary number two: do not seek confirmation from a competent professional of a tax-planning idea, because most professionals either (a) are secretly working for the IRS, or (b) do not know enough to understand a good idea when they see one.

No credentials are required for anyone to hold himself or herself out as a tax expert. Most of these so-called tax specialists have some valid tax-planning ideas to offer, but they also have certain ideas to offer that are entirely without merit. Tax-planning ideas that have no legitimacy and are destined to fail will be referred to as *tax shams*.

Tax shams fall into two basic categories. Category one consists of those concepts that are antithetical to the very essence of our tax system, such as the attempted assignment of earned income or the use of the barter system to avoid the recognition of income. Category two consists of valid tax-planning ideas that are defective because they are improperly set up, such as the interest-free demand loan that is never evidenced by a promissory note.

Assignment of Earned Income

Just as people have unsuccessfully attempted to manufacture wings so that they could fly like the birds, they have also unsuccessfully attempted to have someone else taxed on income they have earned. In the 1930 landmark case of *Lucas* v. *Earl*,[1] the Supreme Court held that income is taxed to the person who earns it, even if there is an anticipatory assignment of that income. And the law has not changed one iota since 1930.[2]

Thus it is not possible to arrange for earned income to be taxed to children via the mechanism of a trust as Dr. Goodell attempted to do. To permit this would defeat the very essence of our tax system and would enable every taxpayer to substantially reduce his tax liability by setting up trusts to receive income.

However, unearned or passive income, such as dividends, interest or rents, can be assigned by a complete transfer of the income-producing property. If Dr. Goodell personally owned equipment used in his practice and transferred the equipment to an irrevocable trust, then his corporation could have properly paid a *fair* rental value to the trust for the use of the equipment. In this case, the rental payments are an ordinary and necessary expense of Dr. Goodell's professional corporation and not an invalid assignment of income. Yet, if *excess* rentals were paid to the trust for the equipment leased to Dr. Goodell's professional corporation, the same result would be created as though there had been an assignment of income. You can imagine what the response of the IRS would be to such a situation.

The Worldwide Church Approach

Another very popular tax sham has been the establishment of mail-order ministries that have been established merely to avoid taxes. For a cost of about fifty dollars, you can apply for a charter in a mother church (such as the Universal Life Church) and set up an organization

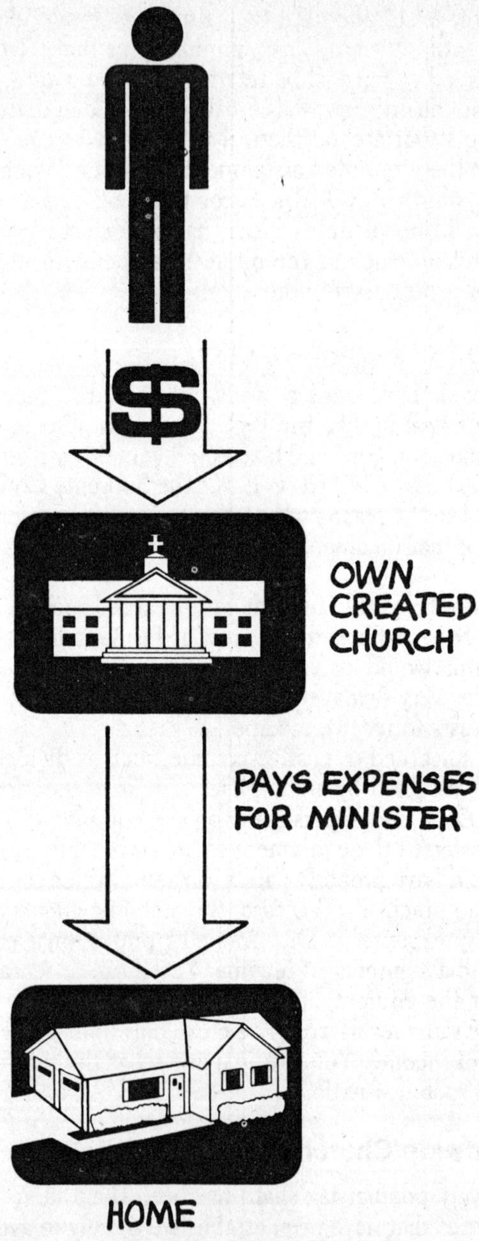
$
OWN
CREATED
CHURCH
PAYS EXPENSES
FOR MINISTER
HOME
YOU LIVE RENT FREE
(UNTIL THE IRS FINDS OUT)

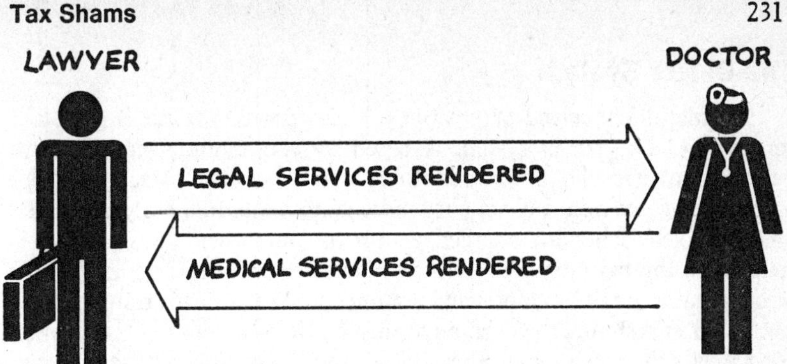

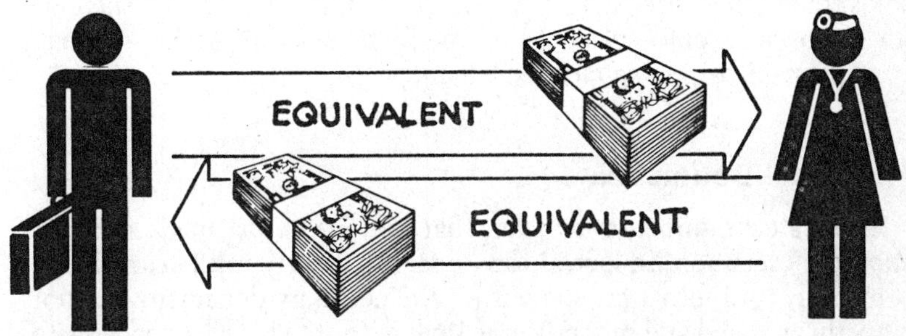

IN THE EYES OF THE IRS
THERE IS NO DIFFERENCE

that can have every appearance of being tax exempt. Your purpose in doing this might be to allow you to deduct your contributions to your church and then use the church's money to provide your living expenses (so-called parsonage expenses in the church system).

As you might expect, the IRS will not permit you to deduct a contribution to an organization that has been set up primarily for your benefit.[3] Section 501 of the Internal Revenue Code grants an exemption to a church-type organization "no part of the net earning of which inures to the benefit of any private shareholder or individual." When there is no real basis for an individual being given all the rights and privileges of a genuine minister, the IRS will simply disregard the shell of the charitable organization, disallow the putative charitable contribution and assess taxes and penalties.[4]

The Barter System

The final ill-conceived tax-savings device we will examine is the barter system. The barter system is based on the spurious notion that where no cash exchanges hands, there is no income. Instead of cash credits being given in exchange for merchandise, nonmonetary units are credited to the seller and charged against the purchaser. Thus each participant in the barter system essentially has her or his own ledger sheet of debits and credits, against which are recorded her or his transactions in the barter system. However, anytime a participant sells a product or a service, whether cash is paid or not, it is exactly the same for income-tax purposes as though cash were received.[5] Any student of taxation learns early in the first tax course that when a lawyer and a doctor exchange services (or any two people, for that matter), each has income equal to the value of what has been received (see Figure 33). The same principle holds true in the barter system. If this were not the case, would there be any reason we would not all be on the barter system? Again, avoiding taxes through barter is a clear tax sham.

Technical Deficiencies

There are a number of tax plans that turn into tax shams because of improper execution. In fact, it can be said that every valid tax plan can potentially turn into a tax sham if (a) the necessary documents are not properly prepared and properly executed, or (b) the facts are inadequate to support the tax plan.

Let's take a look at some of the more common problems:

1. In an interest-free demand-loan situation, the note is made low-interest-bearing or there is no note created at all and a gift is thus created.[6]
2. Money is borrowed for the purpose of purchasing tax-free municipal bonds or a single-premium deferred annuity, and interest on the borrowing thus becomes nondeductible.[7]
3. Prepayment of a monthly mortgage is made too far in advance, and thus the interest charges are disallowed in the year in which the prepayments are made.[8]
4. Loan payments, including principal and interest, are made with future borrowings, and thus no deduction is allowed for the interest paid.[9]
5. In a gift and loan-back situation, the donor does not have the capacity to make a gift (because of having to borrow money from the bank to make the gift), and thus the whole transaction fails.

6. In an equipment lease, there is a sufficiently close relationship between the lessor and lessee to destroy the ability of the lessor to
   take the investment tax credit, and thus the investment tax credit
   may be completely lost.[10]
7. A doctor is denied an investment tax credit because his corporation was the first user of equipment, not he.[11]
8. A limited partner is denied her share of partnership losses because
   the partnership has too many corporate characteristics and is
   taxed as a corporation.[12]
9. An individual dies in 1982. His estate is denied the unlimited
   marital deduction because his marital deduction trust was not
   amended since the 1981 act, and thus unnecessary estate taxes
   have to be paid.[13]

In nearly all these situations, the tax problems that were created
could have been avoided by obtaining proper tax counseling. This
brings us to the final chapter, about whom you need to recruit to help
you with your tax planning.

chapter 25

Whom Do You Trust?

Regan purchased a will and living trust through the mail from a business that purported to take care of all his tax-planning needs, from accounting to investments to legal work.

Regan took the will and trust to a notary public to be properly signed. Unfortunately the notary signed where Regan was supposed to sign and Regan witnessed the notary's signature. Whose will was it?

The selection of professionals who will be responsible for carrying out your tax plan is extremely important. Each professional has a distinct role to play, but it is your responsibility to limit the influence any one person has on you. For example, you should no more let your accountant sell you life insurance than you should have your financial adviser provide you with legal documents.

Document Preparation

The preparation of documents, especially wills and trusts, must be done by an attorney who is in the private practice of law. The most important reason for this is to ensure that you have the work done by an individual who has a special background for this type of thing and is subject to the jurisdiction of your state bar. Also, it is an unauthorized practice of law for anyone, whether a lawyer or not, to prepare legal documents as part of a business operation that does anything other than practice law. The improper marketing of legal services can only lead to the kind of result that Regan experienced.

Rule No. 1—Avoid anyone who offers a package of combined professional services. Find a competent attorney to prepare your legal documents.

Selecting an Attorney

There are generally four ways an individual may select an attorney. First, the attorney may be recommended by another professional (such as an accountant or life-insurance underwriter) or a friend. Second, the attorney may be a cocktail-party acquaintance or a friend of the family. Third, the attorney possibly has advertised in the Yellow Pages or elsewhere. Fourth, the attorney may be recommended by a lawyer-referral service conducted by the local bar association. Of these, the professional recommendation is the most valuable source. The recommending professional will know that his or her reputation is on the line when he or she leads you to an attorney. If the attorney fails to do a professional job at a fair price, the referring professional knows he or she will lose your confidence.

Do not do business with an attorney just because of what the attorney claims either directly or through an advertisement. Seek confirmation of the attorney's abilities and specific area or areas of expertise through your accountant, trust officer or life underwriter.

Rule No. 2—Rely on the advice of other professionals in making your selection of an attorney. Make certain that you select an attorney who specializes in the area or areas of concern to you.

Evaluating Your Current Attorney

Suppose you have an attorney who did a satisfactory job for you on your home purchase or personal injury case. Should you use the same attorney for your tax-planning work? The answer is probably no, but you should consult with him anyway. If he does not have a strong background in tax-planning work, he can refer you to another attorney who does. If your attorney indicates that he can take care of your tax needs, find out what limitations, if any, he has. You do not want an attorney who thinks he can be all things to all people to work for you in the very refined and complex area of tax planning. You need a specialist.

Rule No. 3—Seek the advice of your current attorney in finding a tax specialist, but do not expect a generalist to perform the open-heart surgery that you need.

Nonattorney Tax Advisers

What about the nonattorney professionals who have a great deal of knowledge about tax matters? Before you employ a nonattorney to work with you on tax matters, you must determine what an adviser will do that will add to what your attorney has done or will eventually have to do for you, what the fee will be and how that fee will be computed. A number of service professionals (they generally call themselves financial planners or advisers) offer a complete financial and estate analysis for a fee ranging from $500 to $5,000, with a typical charge in the $1,000 range. Yet if you avail yourself of such a service, you will still have to employ an attorney to implement whatever estate-planning recommendations are made. If a nonattorney adviser has done a good job, his recommendations for estate planning would be the same as your estate planning specialist attorney would make as part of his estate planning service to you. In other words, do not put yourself in a position where you pay twice for essentially the same service.

One of the things nonattorney professionals may charge for is the calculation to the penny of your estate settlement costs (probate fees, administrative costs and estate taxes). Since estate settlement costs vary dramatically based on appraisals of property, date of death and estate planning, the exact calculation of estate settlement costs is of dubious value. Finally, find out how and how much you will be charged for the services to be rendered. You should expect to pay on an hourly basis for the services to be provided, not on a percentage of taxes saved and not a fixed fee unless that fee can be related to the number of hours you expect the adviser to spend.

Rule No. 4—Do not pay an adviser to do what an attorney will have to do as part of normal estate planning or tax services. If you do employ someone to render tax or financial services, determine how and for what you will be charged.

Selecting a Trustee

If your estate plan includes a trust, you must select a trustee. The trustee plays the very important role of investing, managing and distributing your trust assets. Thus the selection of your trustee is a very important task.

Unless you have good reasons to the contrary, a bank should serve as your trustee. Banks do not become disabled, die or lose interest. Plus they are skilled and experienced in trust matters. If you do select a bank as trustee, make certain the bank's trust department is large enough to indicate more than a passing interest in trust business. A modest-size trust department will have assets of at least $250,000,000.

There are two reasons you might opt for a nonbank trustee: lack of the personal touch and costs. If you are concerned about a bank's nonfamiliarity with your family situation, you could appoint your spouse, eldest child or most trusted friend as a co-trustee with the bank. If you are concerned about costs, you could appoint an individual as sole trustee. However, do not name your spouse as sole trustee unless your attorney is certain that the trust is drafted in such a manner that such appointment will not cause inclusion of all of the trust assets in your spouse's estate at his or her death. Also, if you do name an individual trustee, name a backup trustee in case the individual trustee is unable to serve or to continue to serve as trustee.

If you want to establish a trust (such as a Clifford Trust or a Minor's Trust as discussed in Chapters 2 and 3) for income-tax savings, you may be tempted to name your spouse or yourself as trustee. However, you must check with your attorney as to whether the document will permit either you or your spouse to serve as trustee. In most cases, you must have a nonrelated trustee if the trust is to benefit more than one person or will enable the trustee to hold funds after the beneficiary has attained age twenty-one.

Accountants

Much of what we have said about attorneys applies to the selection of accountants. However, unlike attorneys, accountants do not have any rigorous licensing requirements and an unqualified person, who may be nothing more than a bookkeeper, can hold himself or herself out as an accountant. If you are looking for an accountant who can render valuable tax advice, generally you should only deal with a certified public accountant (CPA) who has been required to pass a series of tests and satisfy an experience requirement in order to obtain certification.

The Team Approach

Having raised some suspicions about tax-oriented nonattorney professionals, let us put things in perspective. It is important to understand that there is a very important and significant role for different advisers to play in almost any tax-planning decision you make. As a matter of professional courtesy and respect, your attorney should consult with your accountant and life underwriter on nearly all matters pertaining to your personal-, estate- and business-tax planning. And on your estate planning, your trust officer, if you have one or need one, should also be brought into the picture. The flip side of this professional courtesy and respect also holds true. Suppose, for example, you happen to be discussing a possible tax shelter with your accountant. In such a case, your attorney should be consulted for an opinion before you proceed with the shelter. In any event, keeping your professionals involved and up to date with what you are doing will improve the value of the services you receive. Sometimes people who have an inadequate plan for overall tax savings have only themselves to blame because they want to save costs and thus do it on their own without seeking the advice of competent professionals.

Rule No. 5—Use the services of your professionals to help you evaluate every major tax-planning strategy. Keep all your professionals fully apprised of your tax-planning status.

The world is full of qualified, caring professionals who can and should make a real difference in your life. It is your responsibility to find such people to work with you and to give them every opportunity to help you develop the proper tax-planning habit. The correct use of professionals can enable you to set realistic and attainable goals and to improve the quality of your life.

Newsletter

If enough of you are interested, I will publish a newsletter. Please write me at Buechner, Haffer & O'Connell Co., L.P.A., Suite 1405, 105 East Fourth Street, Cincinnati, Ohio 45202, to let me know your opinion of this book and whether you would like to receive a newsletter based on its format.

Appendixes

Introduction to Appendixes

Many of the documents that follow are legal documents that have been developed over the years by trust officers and attorneys in Cincinnati. I am responsible for some of the language in each, although it would be presumptuous for me to claim a copyright interest in these documents. Any attorney reading this book should feel free to use any of the language in these documents, and any nonattorney should feel free to give this language to his or her attorney to use in the preparation of documents.

These documents have not been updated to reflect the 1982 Act. There are, however, only a few changes necessary.

1. The marital deduction trust (Appendix F) possibly should be changed to provide for the $100,000 limitation on the estate deduction for qualified-plan assets (§6.9).

2. The profit-sharing plan (Appendix H) will need to be updated to provide for loan limitations, new Social Security integration rules, and cutbacks in maximum contributions. Also, if the plan is a topheavy one, it should provide for a new vesting schedule and minimum benefits.

New Tax Rate Schedules

**MARRIED INDIVIDUALS FILING JOINT
RETURNS AND SURVIVING SPOUSES**

(1)   For taxable years beginning in 1982.—

If taxable income is:	The tax is:
Not over $3,400	No tax.
Over $3,400 but not over $5,500	12% of the excess over $3,400.
Over $5,500 but not over $7,600	$252, plus 14% of the excess over $5,500.
Over $7,600 but not over $11,900	$546, plus 16% of the excess over $7,600.
Over $11,900 but not over $16,000	$1,234, plus 19% of the excess over $11,900.
Over $16,000 but not over $20,200	$2,013, plus 22% of the excess over $16,000.
Over $20,200 but not over $24,600	$2,937, plus 25% of the excess over $20,200.
Over $24,600 but not over $29,900	$4,037, plus 29% of the excess over $24,600.
Over $29,900 but not over $35,200	$5,574, plus 33% of the excess over $29,900.
Over $35,200 but not over $45,800	$7,323, plus 39% of the excess over $35,200.
Over $45,800 but not over $60,000	$11,457, plus 44% of the excess over $45,800.
Over $60,000 but not over $85,500	$17,705, plus 49% of the excess over $60,000.
Over $85,600	$30,249, plus 50% of the excess over $85,600.

(2)   For taxable years beginning in 1983.—

If taxable income is:	The tax is:
Not over $3,400	No tax.
Over $3,400 but not over $5,500	11% of the excess over $3,400.
Over $5,500 but not over $7,600	$231, plus 13% of the excess over $5,500.
Over $7,600 but not over $11,900	$504, plus 15% of the excess over $7,600.
Over $11,900 but not over $16,000	$1,149, plus 17% of the excess over $11,900.
Over $16,000 but not over $20,200	$1,846, plus 19% of the excess over $16,000.
Over $20,200 but not over $24,600	$2,644, plus 23% of the excess over $20,200.
Over $24,600 but not over $29,900	$3,656, plus 26% of the excess over $24,600.
Over $29,900 but not over $35,200	$5,034, plus 30% of the excess over $29,900.
Over $35,200 but not over $45,800	$6,624, plus 35% of the excess over $35,200.
Over $45,800 but not over $60,000	$10,334, plus 40% of the excess over $45,800.
Over $60,000 but not over $85,600	$16,014, plus 44% of the excess over $60,000.
Over $85,600 but not over $109,400	$27,278, plus 48% of the excess over $85,600.
Over $109,400	$38,702, plus 50% of the excess over $109,400.

(3)   For taxable years beginning after 1983.—

If taxable income is:	The tax is:
Not over $3,400	No tax.
Over $3,400 but not over $5,500	11% of the excess over $3,400.
Over $5,500 but not over $7,600	$231, plus 12% of the excess over $5,500.

If taxable income is: The tax is:
Over $7,600 but not over $11,900 .... $483, plus 14% of the excess over $7,600.
Over $11,900 but not over $16,000 .... $1,085, plus 16% of the excess over $11,900.
Over $16,000 but not over $20,200 .... $1,741, plus 18% of the excess over $16,000.
Over $20,200 but not over $24,600 .... $2,497, plus 22% of the excess over $20,200.
Over $24,600 but not over $29,900 .... $3,465, plus 25% of the excess over $24,600.
Over $29,900 but not over $35,200 .... $4,790, plus 28% of the excess over $29,900.
Over $35,200 but not over $45,800 .... $6,274, plus 33% of the excess over $35,200.
Over $45,800 but not over $60,000 .... $9,772, plus 38% of the excess over $45,800.
Over $60,000 but not over $85,600 .... $15,168, plus 42% of the excess over $60,000.
Over $85,600 but not over $109,400 .... $25,920, plus 45% of the excess over $85,600.
Over $109,400 but not over $162,400 ...... $36,630, plus 49% of the excess over $109,400.
Over $162,400 .... $62,600, plus 50% of the excess over $162,400.

HEADS OF HOUSEHOLDS

(1)   For taxable years beginning in 1982.—

If taxable income is: The tax is:
Not over $2,300 .... No tax.
Over $2,300 but not over $4,400 .... 12% of the excess over $2,300.
Over $4,400 but not over $6,500 .... $252, plus 14% of the excess over $4,400.
Over $6,500 but not over $8,700 .... $546, plus 16% of the excess over $6,500.
Over $8,700 but not over $11,800 .... $898, plus 20% of the excess over $8,700.
Over $11,800 but not over $15,000 .... $1,518, plus 22% of the excess over $11,800.
Over $15,000 but not over $18,200 .... $2,222, plus 23% of the excess over $15,000.
Over $18,200 but not over $23,500 .... $2,958, plus 28% of the excess over $18,200.
Over $23,500 but not over $28,800 .... $4,442, plus 32% of the excess over $23,500.
Over $28,800 but not over $34,100 .... $6,138, plus 38% of the excess over $28,800.
Over $34,100 but not over $44,700 .... $8,152, plus 41% of the excess over $34,100.
Over $44,700 but not over $60,600 .... $12,498, plus 49% of the excess over $44,700.
Over $60,600 .... $20,289, plus 50% of the excess over $60,600.

(2)   For taxable years beginning in 1983.—

If taxable income is: The tax is:
Not over $2,300 .... No tax.
Over $2,300 but not over $4,400 .... 11% of the excess over $2,300.
Over $4,400 but not over $6,500 .... $231, plus 13% of the excess over $4,400.
Over $6,500 but not over $8,700 .... $504, plus 15% of the excess over $6,500.
Over $8,700 but not over $11,800 .... $834, plus 18% of the excess over $8,700.
Over $11,800 but not over $15,000 .... $1,392, plus 19% of the excess over $11,800.
Over $15,000 but not over $18,200 .... $2,000, plus 21% of the excess over $15,000.
Over $18,200 but not over $23,500 .... $2,672, plus 25% of the excess over $18,200.
Over $23,500 but not over $28,800 .... $3,997, plus 29% of the excess over $23,500.
Over $28,800 but not over $34,100 .... $5,534, plus 34% of the excess over $28,800.
Over $34,100 but not over $44,700 .... $7,336, plus 37% of the excess over $34,100.
Over $44,700 but not over $60,600 .... $11,258, plus 44% of the excess over $44,700.
Over $60,600 but not over $81,800 .... $18,254, plus 48% of the excess over $60,600.
Over $81,800 .... $28,430, plus 50% of the excess over $81,800.

(3) For taxable years beginning after 1983.—

If taxable income is: **The tax is:**

Not over $2,300 .... No tax.
Over $2,300 but not over $4,400 .... 11% of the excess over $2,300.
Over $4,400 but not over $6,500 .... $231, plus 12% of the excess over $4,400.
Over $6,500 but not over $8,700 .... $483, plus 14% of the excess over $6,500.
Over $8,700 but not over $11,800 .... $791, plus 17% of the excess over $8,700.
Over $11,800 but not over $15,000 .... $1,318, plus 18% of the excess over $11,800.
Over $15,000 but not over $18,200 .... $1,894, plus 20% of the excess over $15,000.
Over $18,200 but not over $23,500 .... $2,534, plus 24% of the excess over $18,200.
Over $23,500 but not over $28,800 .... $3,806, plus 28% of the excess over $23,500.
Over $28,800 but not over $34,100 .... $5,290, plus 32% of the excess over $28,800.
Over $34,100 but not over $44,700 .... $6,986, plus 35% of the excess over $34,100.
Over $44,700 but not over $60,600 .... $10,696, plus 42% of the excess over $44,700.
Over $60,600 but not over $81,800 .... $17,374, plus 45% of the excess over $60,600.
Over $81,800 but not over $108,300 .... $26,914, plus 48% of the excess over $81,800.
Over $108,300 .... $39,634, plus 50% of the excess over $108,300.

UNMARRIED INDIVIDUALS (OTHER THAN SURVIVING SPOUSES AND HEADS OF HOUSEHOLDS)

(1) For taxable years beginning in 1982.—

If taxable income is: **The tax is:**

Not over $2,300 .... No tax.
Over $2,300 but not over $3,400 .... 12% of the excess over $2,300.
Over $3,400 but not over $4,400 .... $132, plus 14% of the excess over $3,400.
Over $4,400 but not over $6,500 .... $272, plus 16% of the excess over $4,400.
Over $6,500 but not over $8,500 .... $608, plus 17% of the excess over $6,500.
Over $8,500 but not over $10,800 .... $948, plus 19% of the excess over $8,500.
Over $10,800 but not over $12,900 .... $1,385, plus 22% of the excess over $10,800.
Over $12,900 but not over $15,000 .... $1,847, plus 23% of the excess over $12,900.
Over $15,000 but not over $18,200 .... $2,330, plus 27% of the excess over $15,000.
Over $18,200 but not over $23,500 .... $3,194, plus 31% of the excess over $18,200.
Over $23,500 but not over $28,800 .... $4,837, plus 35% of the excess over $23,500.
Over $28,800 but not over $34,100 .... $6,692, plus 40% of the excess over $28,800.
Over $34,100 but not over $41,500 .... $8,812, plus 44% of the excess over $34,100.
Over $41,500 .... $12,068, plus 50% of the excess over $41,500.

(2) For taxable years beginning in 1983.—

If taxable income is: **The tax is:**

Not over $2,300 .... No tax.
Over $2,300 but not over $3,400 .... 11% of the excess over $2,300.
Over $3,400 but not over $4,400 .... $121, plus 13% of the excess over $3,400.
Over $4,400 but not over $8,500 .... $251, plus 15% of the excess over $4,400.
Over $8,500 but not over $10,800 .... $866, plus 17% of the excess over $8,500.
Over $10,800 but not over $12,900 .... $1,257, plus 19% of the excess over $10,800.
Over $12,900 but not over $15,000 .... $1,656, plus 21% of the excess over $12,900.
Over $15,000 but not over $18,200 .... $2,097, plus 24% of the excess over $15,000.

If taxable income is: The tax is:

If taxable income is:	The tax is:
Over $18,200 but not over $23,500	$2,865, plus 28% of the excess over $18,200.
Over $23,500 but not over $28,800	$4,349, plus 32% of the excess over $23,500.
Over $28,800 but not over $34,100	$6,045, plus 36% of the excess over $28,800.
Over $34,100 but not over $41,500	$7,953, plus 40% of the excess over $34,100.
Over $41,500 but not over 55,300	$10,913, plus 45% of the excess over $41,500.
Over $55,300	$17,123, plus 50% of the excess over $55,300.

(3) For taxable years beginning after 1983.—

If taxable income is:	The tax is:
Not over $2,300	No tax.
Over $2,300 but not over $3,400	11% of the excess over $3,400.
Over $3,400 but not over $4,400	$121, plus 12% of the excess over $3,400.
Over $4,400 but not over $6,500	$241, plus 14% of the excess over $4,400.
Over $6,500 but not over $8,500	$535, plus 15% of the excess over $6,500.
Over $8,500 but not over $10,800	$835, plus 16% of the excess over $8,500.
Over $10,800 but not over $12,900	$1,203, plus 18% of the excess over $10,800.
Over $12,900 but not over $15,000	$1,581, plus 20% of the excess over $12,900.
Over $15,000 but not over $18,200	$2,001, plus 23% of the excess over $15,000.
Over $18,200 but not over $23,500	$2,737, plus 26% of the excess over $18,200.
Over $23,500 but not over $28,800	$4,115, plus 30% of the excess over $23,500.
Over $28,800 but not over $34,100	$5,705, plus 34% of the excess over $28,800.
Over $34,100 but not over $41,500	$7,057, plus 38% of the excess over $34,100.
Over $41,500 but not over $55,300	$10,319, plus 42% of the excess over $41,500.
Over $55,300 but not over $81,800	$16,115, plus 48% of the excess over $55,300.
Over $81,800	$28,835, plus 50% of the excess over $81,800.

MARRIED INDIVIDUALS FILING SEPARATE RETURNS

(1) For taxable years beginning in 1982.—

If taxable income is:	The tax is:
Not over $1,700	No tax.
Over $1,700 but not over $2,750	12% of the excess over $1,700.
Over $2,750 but not over $3,800	$126, plus 14% of the excess over $2,750.
Over $3,800 but not over $5,950	$273, plus 16% of the excess over $3,800.
Over $5,950 but not over $8,000	$617, plus 19% of the excess over $5,950.
Over $8,000 but not over $10,100	$1,006, plus 22% of the excess over $8,000.
Over $10,100 but not over $12,300	$1,468, plus 25% of the excess over $10,100.
Over $12,300 but not over $14,950	$2,018, plus 29% of the excess over $12,300.
Over $14,950 but not over $17,600	$2,787, plus 33% of the excess over $14,950.
Over $17,600 but not over $22,900	$3,661, plus 39% of the excess over $17,600.
Over $22,900 but not over $30,000	$5,728, plus 44% of the excess over $22,900.
Over $30,000 but not over $42,800	$8,852, plus 49% of the excess over $30,000.
Over $42,800	$15,124, plus 50% of the excess over $42,800.

(2) For taxable years beginning in 1983.—

If taxable income is:	The tax is:
Not over $1,700	No tax.
Over $1,700 but not over $2,750	11% of the excess over $1,700.
Over $2,750 but not over $3,800	$115, plus 18% of the excess over $2,750.
Over $3,800 but not over $5,950	$252, plus 15% of the excess over $3,800.
Over $5,950 but not over $8,000	$574, plus 17% of the excess over $5,950.
Over $8,000 but not over $10,100	$923, plus 19% of the excess over $8,000.
Over $10,100 but not over $12,300	$1,322, plus 23% of the excess over $10,100.
Over $12,300 but not over $14,950	$1,828, plus 26% of the excess over $12,300.
Over $14,950 but not over $17,600	$2,517, plus 30% of the excess over $14,950.
Over $17,600 but not over $22,900	$3,312, plus 35% of the excess over $17,600.
Over $22,900 but not over $30,000	$5,167, plus 40% of the excess over $22,900.
Over $30,000 but not over $42,800	$8,007, plus 44% of the excess over $30,000.
Over $42,800 but not over $54,700	$13,639, plus 48% of the excess over $42,800.
Over $54,700	$19,351, plus 50% of the excess over $54,700.

(3) For taxable years beginning after 1983.—

If taxable income is:	The tax is:
Not over $1,700	No tax.
Over $1,700 but not over $2,750	11% of the excess over $1,700.
Over $2,750 but not over $3,800	$115, plus 12% of the excess over $2,750.
Over $3,800 but not over $5,950	$241, plus 14% of the excess over $3,800.
Over $5,950 but not over $8,000	$542, plus 16% of the excess over $5,950.
Over $8,000 but not over $10,100	$870, plus 18% of the excess over $8,000.
Over $10,100 but not over $12,300	$1,248, plus 22% of the excess over $10,100.
Over $12,300 but not over $14,950	$1,732, plus 25% of the excess over $12,300.
Over $14,950 but not over $17,600	$2,395, plus 28% of the excess over $14,950.
Over $17,600 but not over $22,900	$3,137, plus 33% of the excess over $17,600.
Over $22,900 but not over $30,000	$4,886, plus 38% of the excess over $22,900.
Over $30,000 but not over $42,800	$7,584, plus 42% of the excess over $30,000.
Over $42,800 but not over $54,700	$12,960, plus 45% of the excess over $42,800.
Over $54,700 but not over $81,200	$18,315, plus 49% of the excess over $54,700.
Over $81,200	$31,300, plus 50% of the excess over $81,200.

ESTATES AND TRUSTS

(1) For taxable years beginning in 1982.—

If taxable income is:	The tax is:
Not over $1,050	12% of taxable income.
Over $1,050 but not over $2,100	$126, plus 14% of the excess over $1,050.
Over $2,100 but not over $4,250	$273, plus 16% of the excess over $2,100.
Over $4,250 but not over $6,300	$617, plus 19% of the excess over $4,250.
Over $6,300 but not over $8,400	$1,006, plus 22% of the excess over $6,300.
Over $8,400 but not over $10,600	$1,468, plus 25% of the excess over $8,400.
Over $10,600 but not over $13,250	$2,018, plus 29% of the excess over $10,600.
Over $13,250 but not over $15,900	$2,787, plus 33% of the excess over $13,250.
Over $15,900 but not over $21,200	$3,661, plus 39% of the excess over $15,900.
Over $21,200 but not over $28,300	$5,728, plus 44% of the excess over $21,200.

If taxable income is: The tax is:
Over $28,300 but not over $41,100 .... $8,852, plus 49% of the excess over $28,300.
Over $41,100 .... $15,124, plus 50% of the excess over $41,100.

(2) For taxable years beginning in 1983.—

If taxable income is: The tax is:
Not over $1,050 .... 11% of taxable income.
Over $1,050 but not over $2,100 .... $115, plus 13% of the excess over $1,050.
Over $2,100 but not over $4,250 .... $252, plus 15% of the excess over $2,100.
Over $4,250 but not over $6,300 .... $574, plus 17% of the excess over $4,250.
Over $6,300 but not over $8,400 .... $923, plus 19% of the excess over $6,300.
Over $8,400 but not over $10,600 .... $1,322, plus 23% of the excess over $8,400.
Over $10,600 but not over $13,250 .... $1,828, plus 26% of the excess over $10,600.
Over $13,250 but not over $15,900 .... $2,517, plus 30% of the excess over $13,250.
Over $15,900 but not over $21,200 .... $3,312, plus 35% of the excess over $15,900.
Over $21,200 but not over $28,300 .... $5,167, plus 40% of the excess over $21,200.
Over $28,300 but not over $41,100 .... $8,007, plus 44% of the excess over $28,300.
Over $41,100 but not over $53,000 .... $13,639, plus 48% of the excess over $41,100.
Over $53,000 .... $19,351, plus 50% of the excess over $53,000.

(3) For taxable years beginning after 1983.—

If taxable income is: The tax is:
Not over $1,050 .... 11% of taxable income.
Over $1,050 but not over $2,100 .... $115, plus 12% of the excess over $1,050.
Over $2,100 but not over $4,250 .... $241, plus 14% of the excess over $2,100.
Over $4,250 but not over $6,300 .... $542, plus 16% of the excess over $4,250.
Over $6,300 but not over $8,400 .... $870, plus 18% of the excess over $6,300.
Over $8,400 but not over $10,600 .... $1,248, plus 22% of the excess over $8,400.
Over $10,600 but not over $13,250 .... $1,732, plus 25% of the excess over $10,600.
Over $13,250 but not over $15,900 .... $2,395, plus 28% of the excess over $13,250.
Over $15,900 but not over $21,200 .... $3,137, plus 33% of the excess over $15,900.
Over $21,200 but not over $28,300 .... $4,886, plus 38% of the excess over $21,200.
Over $28,300 but not over $41,100 .... $7,584, plus 42% of the excess over $28,300.
Over $41,100 but not over $53,000 .... $12,960, plus 45% of the excess over $41,100.
Over $53,000 but not over $79,500 .... $18,315, plus 49% of the excess over $53,000.
Over $79,500 .... $31,300, plus 50% of the excess over $79,500.

Sample Short Term Irrevocable Trust Agreement

John Taxpayer
Short Term Irrevocable Trust Agreement
for
Robert Taxpayer

THIS WRITING contains all of the terms of an Irrevocable Trust Agreement made at Cincinnati, Ohio, this _________ day of _______________, 1982, by John Taxpayer, hereinafter referred to as the "Grantor," and John Taxpayer, hereinafter sometimes referred to as the "Trustee."

Section 1
Trust Property

1.1   The Grantor has delivered to the Trustee the property shown on Schedule A, attached hereto and made part hereof.

1.2   The Trustee acknowledges receipt of the property shown on Schedule A. The Trustee agrees to hold such property and any other property which may from time to time be delivered to it upon the various trusts hereinafter expressed, and to manage the trust estate and make distribution of income and principal thereof as provided herein.

Section 2
Surrender of Rights by Grantor and Additions to Trust

2.1   This Trust Agreement is irrevocable and the Grantor expressly waives and surrenders permanently all rights and powers to alter, amend, revoke or terminate this Agreement. The Grantor of interests conveyed or assigned to the Trustee under this Agreement, and all such incidents of ownership, shall be vested in and be exercisable by the Trustee in his sole discretion.

2.2   The Trustee agrees that the Grantor, his attorney-in-fact, or any other person, firm or corporation may, from time to time, add other property to the trust estate and place such property within the operation of all of the terms and conditions hereof. The Trustee agrees to accept any such property, provided that it may lawfully do so and provided that it is of the character normally acceptable by trustees generally, whether such property is conveyed or delivered to it or whether it is devised or bequeathed to it by Will.

Section 3
Distributions of Income and Withdrawal of Contributions

3.1 If the trust estate includes any income-producing assets, the Trustee shall distribute income in any manner whatsoever to or for the benefit of Grantor's son, Robert Taxpayer; provided, however, that no income payable to any beneficiary during his or her minority shall be paid or applied, directly or indirectly, to discharge in whole or in part, any legal obligation the Grantor may have for the support, education, or maintenance of such beneficiary.

Section 4
Trusts and Distributions

4.1 The residue of the trust estate and all other property which as principal or income may be or become part of the trust estate, shall be held and distributed as herein provided.

4.1.1 This Trust shall terminate ten years and one month from the date hereof or upon the death of Grantor's son, Robert Taxpayer, whichever is earlier; provided, however, that as to any transfer to this trust made subsequent to the date hereof, the trust shall terminate as to each such transfer ten (10) years and one (1) month from the date of such transfer, or on the date of death of Robert Taxpayer, whichever is earlier. Upon termination of the trust at the time or times provided in this paragraph, the Trustee shall pay over and distribute the principal of the trust then distributable to Grantor, if living, or if Grantor is then deceased, to such person or persons, including Grantor's estate, and in such proportions and in such manner as Grantor shall, by valid Last Will and Testament or Codicil thereto, specifically appoint to receive the same, or if Grantor fails to exercise such power of appointment, to Grantor's estate; and the Trustee shall pay all accrued and accumulated but undistributed income to Grantor's said son, Robert Taxpayer, if living, or if deceased, to the estate of Grantor's said son.

Section 5
General Provisions

5.1 As to each trust held hereunder, the Trustee shall have the following power and authority in addition to and without limiting the power and authority it may have under the laws of any state, which it may exercise without order of court:

5.1.1   To collect, pay and compromise debts and claims in favor of or against any trust.

5.1.2   To borrow money, including authority of the Trustee to borrow from itself in its nonfiduciary capacity.

5.1.3   To buy and sell real and personal property, publicly and privately; to give options to buy real and personal property for any length of time; to lease real and personal property for any term irrespective of the duration of administration of any trust; to mortgage real property and pledge personal property; and to execute and deliver instruments to effectuate such powers without liability on the part of any purchaser, lessee, mortgagee or pledgee to see to the application of the purchase money.

5.1.4   To retain property received by it, regardless of its character and whether or not it is such as is authorized by law for investment by fiduciaries, for such time as it deems reasonable; and to invest and reinvest the proceeds of the sale of such property, and cash, in whatever property it deems reasonable.

5.1.5   To exercise and not exercise, as it deems reasonable, rights of ownership incident to securities that it may hold, including rights to vote, give proxies and execute consents, except as to securities issued by the Trustee or its affiliate, which shall be voted as directed by Section 5.1.4.

5.1.6   To hold property in the name of a nominee.

5.1.7   To hire an independent investment adviser to advise the trustee as to the investing of the trust assets.

5.2   No person leasing or purchasing property from or lending money to or otherwise dealing with any trust, and no transfer agent requested to transfer corporate securities to or from any trust, need inquire as to the purpose of the lease, sale, loan, transfer or assignment or see to the application of the proceeds, and the receipt of the Trustee shall be a complete acquittance and discharge of such person for the amount paid.

5.3   The Trustee is authorized, in its sole discretion, to make any distribution of the trust estate in cash or in kind, or partly in cash and partly in kind, and to divide any real and personal property, whether it is legal or equitable. The Trustee may make any distribution or division at such valuations as the Trustee may in good faith establish therefor, and all persons shall be bound by the division so made.

5.4   If the Trustee has a reasonable doubt about the manner of allocating any credit or charge to principal or income under applicable law, the Trustee shall have the power, exercisable as a fiduciary in good faith: to determine whether money or property coming into its possession shall be treated as principal or income; to charge or apportion expenses or losses to principal or income; and to amortize or not to amortize both premiums and discounts on investments.

5.5   The Trustee is authorized to employ legal counsel and other agents in any matter in connection with the administration of any of the trusts, such as agents for the collection of rentals or the management or sale of any of the trust estate. The Trustee may pay such compensation and expenses in connection therewith as the Trustee deems reasonable under the circumstances.

5.6   Income or principal of any trust created under this Agreement which becomes payable or is, in the discretion of the Trustee, distributable to any beneficiary who is incapacitated or incompetent, may be paid to such beneficiary, despite his or her incapacity or incompetency, to his or her parent or parents, to the guardian or guardians of his or her person or estate, to a custodian for such beneficiary designated by the Trustee, or to any person, corporation or institution for the benefit of such beneficiary, as the Trustee deems reasonable. The receipt of any such payee shall be a complete discharge and release of the Trustee. Nothing in this Agreement shall permit any payment to be made to the Grantor, either for his own or any other person's benefit, or to any other person, corporation or institution for the Grantor's benefit.

5.7   For all purposes of the Agreement, a person shall be considered incapacitated or incompetent if under the age of eighteen (18) years, or if so declared by a court having jurisdiction, or if such person's personal physician or any two physicians selected by the Trustee shall advise the Trustee of such incapacity or incompetency in writing. Any such incapacity or incompetency established in the first instance by declaration of court may be removed only by such court or if established in the first instance by such person's personal physician or any two physicians selected by the Trustee, may be removed by either the personal physician then serving such person or any two physicians selected by the Trustee (who need not be the same two physicians who may have advised the Trustee of such person's incapacity or incompetency).

5.8   Notwithstanding any other provisions of this Agreement, unless terminated at any earlier date under other provisions hereof, all trusts herein created shall terminate twenty-one (21) years after the death of the last to die of Grantor and Grantor's issue who are living on the date of execution of this Agreement. Thereupon the Trustee shall distribute to the persons then entitled to receive income from any trust the share of the trust from which any such person is then entitled to receive income.

5.9   Notwithstanding anything herein contained to the contrary, no powers enumerated herein or accorded to Trustees generally pursuant to law shall be construed to enable the Grantor, or the Trustee, or either of them, or any other person to purchase, exchange or otherwise deal with or dispose of all or any part of the corpus or income of the trusts for less than an adequate consideration in money or money's worth, or to enable the Grantor to borrow all or any part of the corpus or income of the trusts for less than an adequate consideration in money or money's worth, or to enable Grantor to borrow all or any part of the corpus or income of the trusts, directly or indirectly, without adequate interest or security. No person, other than the Trustee, except by a properly executed proxy or power of attorney, shall have or exercise the power to vote or direct by voting of any stock or other securities of the trusts, to control the investment of the trusts either by directing investments or reinvestments or by vetoing proposed investments or reinvestments or to reacquire or exchange any property of the trusts by substituting other property of any equivalent value.

5.10   Notwithstanding anything to the contrary herein, in no event shall any of the income of the Trust be used or applied to the payment of premiums on policies of life insurance on the life of the Grantor or the Grantor's spouse.

5.11   Throughout this Agreement words used in the singular or plural shall be read in the plural or singular, and pronouns shall be read in feminine, masculine or neuter gender, as the facts or context may require to accomplish the purpose intended.

5.12   This trust has been accepted by the Trustee in the state of Ohio, and all questions pertaining to the trust and its validity and the administration thereof, and to the construction of this Agreement, shall be determined in accordance with the laws of the state of Ohio.

SECTION 6
The Trustee

6.1   References in this Agreement to the "Trustee" shall include not only John Taxpayer, but also any successor trustee. If John Taxpayer is unable to serve or to continue to serve, Thomas T. Taxpayer will appoint a successor trustee.

6.2   For his services in connection with the administration of each trust held hereunder, the Trustee shall receive no compensation.

6.3   Any Trustee acting hereunder shall have the right to resign upon thirty (30) days' notice to the Grantor, if living, and if not, to all of the beneficiaries then entitled to receive income who are legally competent and to the guardians or custodians of those who are not legally competent. Upon the resignation of any Trustee, the Trustee shall turn over the assets and administration of the trusts to the successor trustee.

6.4   Any successor or substitute Trustee shall have each and every right, privilege, power, discretion, authority and duty of the original Trustee and shall be subject to the same responsibilities. Any successor Trustee shall qualify by executing a written instrument of acceptance of the trusteeship, which shall be attached to any counterpart or copy of this Agreement. No bond shall be required of any Trustee for serving as such.

IN WITNESS WHEREOF, the Grantor and the Trustee have executed duplicates hereof, each of which shall be deemed as original, as of the day and year first above written.

____
                                              John Taxpayer

____

As to John Taxpayer

TRUSTEE:

____
                                              John Taxpayer

____

As to John Taxpayer

STATE OF OHIO, COUNTY OF HAMILTON: SS:

Before me, the undersigned, a Notary Public in and fc the said county and state, personally appeared John Taxpayer, who executed the foregoing Agreement as the Grantor and acknowledged the signing thereof to be his free and voluntary act for the uses and purposes therein contained.

IN TESTIMONY WHEREOF, I have hereunto subscribed my name and affixed my seal this _________ day of _______________, 1982.

Notary Public

STATE OF OHIO, COUNTY OF HAMILTON: SS:

Before me, the undersigned, a Notary Public in and for the said county and state, personally appeared John Taxpayer, who executed the foregoing Agreement as the Trustee and acknowledged the signing thereof to be his free and voluntary act for the uses and purposes therein contained.

IN TESTIMONY WHEREOF, I have hereunto subscribed my name and affixed my seal this _________ day of _______________, 1983.

Notary Public

Schedule A
John Taxpayer
Short Term Irrevocable Trust Agreement
for Robert Taxpayer
One Hundred Dollars ($100.00)

Sample Irrevocable Trust Agreement

**Irrevocable Trust Agreement
for
Jane Doe**

THIS WRITING contains all of the terms of an Irrevocable Trust Agreement made at Cincinnati, Ohio, this _________ day of _______________, 1981, by John Doe, hereinafter referred to as the "Grantor," and Mary Doe, hereinafter sometimes referred to as the "Trustee."

SECTION 1
Trust Property

1.1　The Grantor has delivered to the Trustee the property shown on Schedule A, attached hereto and made part hereof.

1.2　The Trustee acknowledges receipt of the property shown on Schedule A. The Trustee agrees to hold such property and any other property which may from time to time be delivered to it upon the various trusts hereinafter expressed, and to manage the trust estate and make distribution of income and principal thereof as provided herein.

SECTION 2
Surrender of Rights by Grantor and Additions to Trust

2.1　This Trust Agreement is irrevocable and the Grantor expressly waives and surrenders permanently all rights and powers to alter, amend, revoke or terminate this Agreement. The Grantor shall have no incidents of ownership with respect to any property Agreement, and all such incidents of ownership shall be vested in and be exercisable by the Trustee in her sole discretion.

2.2　The Trustee agrees that the Grantor, his attorney-in-fact, or any other person, firm or corporation may, from time to time, add other property to the trust estate and place such property within the operation of all the terms and conditions hereof. The Trustee agrees to accept any such property, provided that it may lawfully do so and provided that it is of the character normally acceptable by trustees generally, whether such property is conveyed or delivered to it or whether it is devised or bequeathed to it by Will.

Section 3
Distributions of Income and Withdrawal of Contributions

3.1 If the trust estate includes any income-producing assets, the Trustee may, in her sole discretion, accumulate income or distribute income in any manner whatsoever to or for the benefit of Grantor's oldest daughter, Jane Doe; provided, however, that no income payable to any beneficiary during his or her minority shall be paid or applied, directly or indirectly, to discharge in whole or in part, any legal obligation the Grantor may have for the support, education or maintenance of such beneficiary.

3.2 During each calendar year, Grantor's oldest daughter, Jane Doe, shall have the annual noncumulative right to withdraw assets which may have been contributed to the trust during such year. The portion of each contribution made to the trust which shall be available for withdrawal by a beneficiary shall be equal to the assets contributed to the trust up to a total of $5,000 per beneficiary. If a beneficiary is a minor, such beneficiary or his or her guardian may make such demand. A beneficiary must exercise his or her right to withdraw assets which have been contributed to the trust by delivering a written notice of his or her intention to withdraw to the Trustee within the calendar year during which such contribution was made or, in the event that the Trustee notifies the beneficiary in writing that a contribution has been made, within thirty (30) days after the date of such notice.

Section 4
Trusts and Distributions

4.1 The residue of the trust estate and all other property which as principal or income may be or become part of the trust estate, shall be held and distributed as herein provided.

4.1.1 The trust shall terminate as to the remaining principal and any undistributed income thereof on the date when Grantor's oldest daughter, Jane Doe, reaches the age of eighteen (18) years; and distribution shall be made to such person of the shares indicated on such date. If, in the sole opinion of the Trustee, the trust estate has at any time been so reduced in size as to make it uneconomical or otherwise impractical to continue to hold it in trust, the trust shall terminate and the Trustee shall distribute the principal and any undistributed income thereof to or for the benefit of the person for whom the trust is held, outright and free of trust. If the person for whom the trust is held dies before receiving distribution of all the principal and undistributed income of the trust, the trust shall terminate on the date of her death, and the principal and any undistributed income thereof shall be distributed to or for the benefit of Grantor's living children.

SECTION 5
General Provisions

5.1 As to each trust held hereunder, the Trustee shall have the following power and authority in addition to and without limiting the power and authority it may have under the laws of any state, which it may exercise without order of court:

5.1.1 To collect, pay and compromise debts and claims in favor of or against any trust.

5.1.2 To borrow money, including authority of the Trustee to borrow from itself in its nonfiduciary capacity.

5.1.3 To buy and sell real and personal property, publicly and privately; to give options to buy real and personal property for any length of time; to lease real and personal property for any term irrespective of the duration of administration of any trust; to mortgage real property and pledge personal property; and to execute and deliver instruments to effectuate such powers without liability on the part of any purchaser, lessee, mortgagee or pledgee to see to the application of the purchase money.

5.1.4 To retain property received by it, regardless of its character and whether or not it is such as is authorized by law for investment by fiduciaries, for such time as it deems reasonable; and to invest and reinvest the proceeds of the sale of such property, and cash, in whatever property it deems reasonable.

5.1.5 To exercise and not exercise, as it deems reasonable, rights of ownership incident to securities that it may hold, including rights to vote, give proxies and execute consents, except as to securities issued by the Trustee or its affiliate which shall be voted as directed by Section 5.1.4.

5.1.6 To hold property in the name of a nominee.

5.2 No person leasing or purchasing property from or lending money to or otherwise dealing with any trust, and no transfer agent requested to transfer corporate securities to or from any trust, need inquire as to the purpose of the lease, sale, loan, transfer or assignment or see to the application of the proceeds, and the receipt of the Trustee shall be a complete acquittance and discharge of such person for the amount paid.

5.3 The Trustee is authorized, in her sole discretion, to make any distribution of the trust estate in cash or in kind, or partly in cash and partly in kind, and to divide any real and personal property whether it is legal or equitable. The Trustee may make any distribution or division at such valuations as the Trustee may in good faith establish therefor, and all persons shall be bound by the division so made.

5.4 If the Trustee has a reasonable doubt about the manner of allocating any credit or charge to principal or income under applicable law, the Trustee shall have the power, exercisable as a fiduciary in good faith: to determine whether money or property coming into its possession shall be treated as principal or income; to charge or apportion expenses or losses to principal or income; and to amortize or not to amortize both premiums and discounts on investments.

5.5. The Trustee is authorized to employ legal counsel and other agents in any matter in connection with the administration of any of the trusts, such as agents for the collection of rentals or the management or sale of any of the trust estate. The Trustee may pay such compensation and expenses in connection therewith as the Trustee deems reasonable under the circumstances.

5.6 Income or principal of any trust created under this Agreement which becomes payable or is, in the discretion of the Trustee, distributable to any beneficiary who is incapacitated or incompetent may be paid to such beneficiary, despite his or her incapacity or incompetency, to his or her parent or parents, to the guardian or guardians of his or her person or estate, to a custodian for such beneficiary designated by the Trustee, or to any person, corporation or institution for the benefit of such beneficiary, as the Trustee deems reasonable. The receipt of any such payee shall be a complete discharge and release of the Trustee. Nothing in this Agreement shall permit any payment to be made to the Grantor, either for his own or any other person's benefit, or to any other person, corporation or institution for the Grantor's benefit.

5.7 For all purposes of the Agreement, a person shall be considered incapacitated or incompetent if under the age of eighteen (18) years, or if so declared by a court having jurisdiction, or if such person's personal physician or any two physicians selected by the Trustee shall advise the Trustee of such incapacity or incompetency in writing. Any such incapacity or incompetency established in the first instance by declaration of court may be removed only by such court or if established in the first instance by such person's personal physician or any two physicians selected by the Trustee, may be removed by either the personal physician then serving such person or any two physicians selected by the Trustee (who need not be the same two physicians who may have advised the Trustee of such person's incapacity or incompetency).

5.8 Notwithstanding any other provisions of this Agreement, unless terminated at any earlier date under other provisions hereof, all trusts herein created shall terminate twenty-one (21) years after the death of the last to die of Grantor and Grantor's issue who are living on the date of execution of this Agreement. Thereupon the Trustee shall distribute to the persons then entitled to receive income from any trust the share of the trust from which any such person is then entitled to receive income.

5.9 Notwithstanding anything herein contained to the contrary, no powers enumerated herein or accorded to Trustees generally pursuant to law shall be construed to enable the Grantor, or the Trustee, or either of them, or any other person to purchase, exchange or otherwise deal with or dispose of all or any part of the corpus or income of the trusts for less than an adequate consideration in money or money's worth, or to enable the Grantor to borrow all or any part of the corpus or income of the trusts for less than an adequate consideration in money or money's worth, or to enable Grantor to borrow all or any part of the corpus or income of the trusts, directly or indirectly, without adequate interest or security. No person, other than the Trustee, except by a properly executed proxy or power of attorney, shall have or exercise the power to vote or direct by voting of any stock or other securities of the trusts, to control the investment of the trusts either by directing investments or reinvestments or by vetoing proposed investments or reinvestments or to reacquire or exchange any property of the trusts by substituting other property of any equivalent value.

5.10 Notwithstanding anything to the contrary herein, in no event shall any of the income of the trust be used or applied to the payment of premiums on policies of life insurance on the life of the Grantor or the Grantor's spouse.

5.11 Throughout this Agreement words used in the singular or plural shall be read in the plural or singular, and pronouns shall be read in feminine, masculine or neuter gender, as the facts or context may require to accomplish the purpose intended.

5.12 This trust has been accepted by the Trustee in the State of Ohio, and all questions pertaining to the trust and its validity and the administration thereof, and to the construction of this Agreement, shall be determined in accordance with the laws of the State of Ohio.

Section 6
The Trustee

6.1 References in this Agreement to the "Trustee" shall include not only Mary Doe, but also any successor trustee. If Mary Doe is unable to serve or to continue to serve, Grantor will appoint a successor trustee. In no event shall Grantor be permitted to be trustee of any trust created hereunder.

6.2 For her services in connection with the administration of each trust held hereunder, the Trustee shall receive no compensation.

6.3 Any Trustee acting hereunder shall have the right to resign upon thirty (30) days' notice to the Grantor, if living, and if not, to all the beneficiaries then entitled to receive income who are legally competent and to the guardians or custodians of those who are not legally competent. Upon the resignation of any Trustee, the Trustee shall turn over the assets and administration of the trusts to the successor trustee. In no event shall Grantor be able to cause a Trustee to resign.

6.4 Any successor or substitute Trustee shall have each and every right, privilege, power, discretion, authority and duty of the original Trustee and shall be subject to the same responsibilities. Any successor Trustee shall qualify by executing a written instrument or acceptance of the trusteeship which shall be attached to any counterpart or copy of this Agreement. No bond shall be required of any Trustee for serving as such.

IN WITNESS WHEREOF, the Grantor and the Trustee have executed duplicates hereof, each of which shall be deemed as original, as of the day and year first above written.

____

John Doe

____

____

As to John Doe

____

TRUSTEE:
Mary Doe

____

____

As to Mary Doe

STATE OF OHIO, COUNTY OF HAMILTON: SS:

Before me, the undersigned, a Notary Public in and for the said county and state, personally appeared Mr. Taxpayer, who executed the foregoing Agreement as the Grantor and acknowledged the signing thereof to be his free and voluntary act for the uses and purposes therein contained.

IN TESTIMONY WHEREOF, I have hereunto subscribed my name and affixed my seal this ________ day of ________________, 1981.

____

Notary Public

STATE OF OHIO, COUNTY OF HAMILTON: SS:

Before me, the undersigned, a Notary Public in and for the said county and state, personally appeared Mrs. Taxpayer, who executed the foregoing Agreement as the Trustee and acknowledged the signing thereof to be her free and voluntary act for the uses and purposes therein contained.

IN TESTIMONY WHEREOF, I have hereunto subscribed my name and affixed my seal this ________ day of ________________, 1981.

____

Notary Public

Schedule A
Irrevocable Trust Agreement
for Jane Doe
One Hundred Dollars ($100.00)

Investing in Oil, Gas and Coal

**(Published by the Securities and
Exchange Commission, April, 1978)**

The energy crisis has focused attention on the development of additional energy resources, and one result has been a great many offerings to the public of investment opportunities involving exploration for oil, gas, and coal. The demand for these resources, coupled with a potential for a high return on such investments has created widespread interest among individual investors. Tax advantages which may accrue to investors often makes these investments appear even more attractive.

* * *

Exercise Caution in Selecting Your Investment

Most oil, gas, and coal investment opportunities, while involving varying degrees of risks to the investor, are legitimate in their conception, businesslike in their marketing, and prudent in their operations. However, as in many other investment opportunities, it is not unusual for unscrupulous promoters to attempt to take advantage of increased investor interest by engaging in fraudulent practices. As a result, the Commission and state law enforcement authorities have within the past several years instituted an increasing number of enforcement actions.

* * *

Other investigations have revealed instances in which:

- Investors' funds were used to pay for the European and Bahamian vacations of the promoter, leaving no money to pay for drilling wells.
- "Producing wells" indicated on the map which was shown to investors for the purpose of inducing them to invest had not been drilled.
- Prospective investors were told that the purchase of a fractional undivided interest was a "safe investment" without disclosing the high degree of risk.
- Prospective investors were told that the common stock being offered

would yield a 10% return and double in price within the first year, and that the investor would be able to send his children to college on a $500 investment in that stock.

- Prospective limited partners were told that "scientific equipment" designed and built by the promoter would improve the "risk-reward ration 400% in wildcat prospecting for oil and gas." No such equipment existed. The promoter, whose most relevant prior experience was working as a service station attendant, was represented to the potential investors as having engineering and business degrees as well as extensive oil and gas field experience.
- Investors were not told that a "psychic" was paid $100,000 to select sites for drilling.
- Prospective investors were not told that the amount being charged by the promoter for drilling and completion of the wells was substantially higher than rates for such services generally prevailing in the area.

The cases described above do not constitute a complete list of fraudulent practices which unscrupulous promoters may use in soliciting funds for oil, gas, and coal investments; they are merely examples of some of the patterns which have been detected during the course of investigations into these activities.

What to Watch for—"Boiler Room" Techniques

In order to attract the interest of individual investors, unprincipled promoters have revived what became known as "boiler-room" techniques when they were employed in the 1920's and again in the 1950's. Salespersons with little or no background in business or in energy exploration use high-pressure sales techniques which include unsolicited telephone calls to members of the public. Utilizing flamboyant and misleading statements, advertisements, and sales literature, these salespersons make their solicitations at hours of their own choosing. Typically, they make claims that are without foundation and predict potentially spectacular profits.

* * *

What They May Promise You—Don't be Misled

In a typical "boiler-room" sales pitch relating to oil, gas, and coal investments, potential investors may be told:

- they will be sold an interest in a well that cannot miss;
- the risks are minimal—that the exploration efforts "can't fail"—"are a lead-pipe cinch," etc.;
- a geologist in the company has given the salesperson a tip;
- the salesperson has personally invested in the venture;
- The Securities and Exchange Commission has approved the offering, an action which the Commission never takes;

- the promoter has "hit" on every well drilled so far;
- there has been a tremendous "discovery" in an adjacent field;
- a large, reputable energy company is operating or planning to operate in the area; and
- only a few interests remain to be sold and the investor should immediately send in his money in order to assure the purchase of an interest.

What They May Not Tell You—Be Certain You Know

A typical "boiler-room" sales pitch may not reveal:

- the amount of commission paid to the promoters and salespersons, including compensation in the form of interests in the venture for which the promoters or salespersons will contribute no money;
- how the funds you invest will be held. If separate accounts are not maintained for money contributed by the public investors, the investors' money may be subject to the claims of the promoters' other creditors from other projects;
- the level of experience in oil and gas drilling on the part of all persons responsible for the venture. If a company is involved, you should know the experience of its principal officers and directors and the length of time that the company has been in existence;
- the existence of any conflicts of interest arising out of undisclosed interests in the venture or its properties which are held by the promoters.

What to Do

In an effort to help prospective investors, the SEC suggests the following precautions:

1. Be particularly hesitant if the salesperson suggests sending money in the mail directly to him or her.
2. Resist pressures to make hurried, uninformed investment decisions.
3. Insist that all representations be made in writing.
4. Be skeptical of suggestions or promises of possible spectacular profits.
5. Be particularly wary of unsolicited phone calls.
6. Read carefully all prospectuses and offering circulars of sales literature. Obtain explanations of any matters you do not fully understand. Don't invest until all answers and explanations are fully understood.
7. Be cautious in assessing any representation regarding the accomplishments of the promoters in drilling other wells, since prior success is not necessarily indicative of future results.
8. Request and obtain written information about the background of all persons responsible for the venture, and if a corporation is involved, request such information about the company and its principal officers and directors.
9. Consider the risks in relation to your own financial position and needs.

Understand fully the difficulties that may be encountered in an attempt to resell the investment should you find at some future date that you need the funds which you invested. Ask yourself if you can afford the potential loss, which in some instances could exceed the amount of your investment.

What to Ask

The SEC suggests that you pose the following questions and requests to the person making the offering:

1. In case of an unsolicited telephone call or letter, ask how the caller/writer obtained your name.
2. Is the offering filed with the SEC? If so, you are entitled to a copy of a prospectus or offering circular.
3. Is the offering filed with the office of the State Securities Commission in your state or the state in which the promoters are located? If so, contact that agency for any information it may be able to provide.
4. Ask for a copy of any geological report that may have been prepared, especially if the offering is a private offering. Bear in mind, however, that such reports are not assurances of the presence of oil, gas, or coal. They often contain references to "provide reserves" or "probable reserves," which are only estimates and do not assure that total production will be substantial or that production will be at a rate that will be profitable.
5. Review the geological report with a geologist, petroleum engineer or other person who is knowledgeable and unaffiliated with the company and who can evaluate this type of investment.

Unified Transfer Tax Rate Schedules

UNIFIED TRANSFER TAX RATE SCHEDULES FOR 1982 AND 1983

1982

If the amount is:		Tentative tax[1] is:			
Over	But not over	Tax	+	%	On Excess Over
0	$ 10,000	0		18	0
$ 10,000	20,000	$ 1,800		20	$ 10,000
20,000	40,000	3,800		22	20,000
40,000	60,000	8,200		24	40,000
60,000	80,000	13,000		26	60,000
80,000	100,000	18,200		28	80,000
100,000	150,000	23,800		30	100,000
150,000	250,000	38,800		32	150,000
250,000	500,000	70,800		34	250,000
500,000	750,000	155,800		37	500,000
750,000	1,000,000	248,300		39	750,000
1,000,000	1,250,000	345,800		41	1,000,000
1,250,000	1,500,000	448,300		43	1,250,000
1,500,000	2,000,000	555,800		45	1,500,000
2,000,000	2,500,000	780,800		49	2,000,000
2,500,000	3,000,000	1,025,800		53	2,500,000
3,000,000	3,500,000	1,290,800		57	3,000,000
3,500,000	4,000,000	1,575,800		61	3,500,000
4,000,000	—	1,880,800		65	4,000,000

1983

| If the amount is: | | Tentative tax[1] is: | | | On Excess |
Over	But not over	Tax	+	%	Over
0	$ 10,000	0		18	0
$ 10,000	20,000	$ 1,800		20	$ 10,000
20,000	40,000	3,800		22	20,000
40,000	60,000	8,200		24	40,000
60,000	80,000	13,000		26	60,000
80,000	100,000	18,200		28	80,000
100,000	150,000	23,800		30	100,000
150,000	250,000	38,800		32	150,000
250,000	500,000	70,800		34	250,000
500,000	750,000	155,800		37	500,000
750,000	1,000,000	248,300		39	750,000
1,000,000	1,250,000	345,800		41	1,000,000
1,250,000	1,500,000	448,300		43	1,250,000
1,500,000	2,000,000	555,800		45	1,500,000
2,000,000	2,500,000	780,800		49	2,000,000
2,500,000	3,000,000	1,025,800		53	2,500,000
3,000,000	3,500,000	1,290,800		57	3,000,000
3,500,000	—	1,575,800		60	3,500,000

[1] The cumulated transfers to which the tentative tax applies are the sum of (a) the amount of the taxable estate and (b) the amount of the taxable gifts made by the decedent after 1976 other than gifts includible in the gross estate.

UNIFIED TRANSFER TAX RATE SCHEDULES
FOR 1984 AND 1985 AND THEREAFTER

1984

If the amount is:		Tentative tax[1] is:			
Over	But not over	Tax	+	%	On Excess Over
0	$ 10,000	0		18	0
$ 10,000	20,000	$ 1,800		20	$ 10,000
20,000	40,000	3,800		22	20,000
40,000	60,000	8,200		24	40,000
60,000	80,000	13,000		26	60,000
80,000	100,000	18,200		28	80,000
100,000	150,000	23,800		30	100,000
150,000	250,000	38,800		32	150,000
250,000	500,000	70,800		34	250,000
500,000	750,000	155,800		37	500,000
750,000	1,000,000	248,300		39	750,000
1,000,000	1,250,000	345,800		41	1,000,000
1,250,000	1,500,000	448,300		43	1,250,000
1,500,000	2,000,000	555,800		45	1,500,000
2,000,000	2,500,000	780,800		49	2,000,000
2,500,000	3,000,000	1,025,800		53	2,500,000
3,000,000	—	1,290,800		55	3,000,000

1985 and Thereafter

If the amount is:		Tentative tax[1] is:			
Over	But not over	Tax	+	%	On Excess Over
0	$ 10,000	0		18	0
$ 10,000	20,000	$ 1,800		20	$ 10,000
20,000	40,000	3,800		22	20,000
40,000	60,000	8,200		24	40,000
60,000	80,000	13,000		26	60,000
80,000	100,000	18,200		28	80,000
100,000	150,000	23,800		30	100,000
150,000	250,000	38,800		32	150,000
250,000	500,000	70,800		34	250,000
500,000	750,000	155,800		37	500,000
750,000	1,000,000	248,300		39	750,000
1,000,000	1,250,000	345,800		41	1,000,000
1,250,000	1,500,000	448,300		43	1,250,000
1,500,000	2,000,000	555,800		45	1,500,000
2,000,000	2,500,000	780,800		49	2,000,000
2,500,000	—	1,025,800		50	2,500,000

[1] The cumulated transfers to which the tentative tax applies are the sum of (a) the amount of the taxable estate and (b) the amount of the taxable gifts made by the decedent after 1976 other than gifts includible in the gross estate.

Sample Amended and Restated Trust Agreement

Amended and Restated Trust Agreement

THIS WRITING contains all the terms of a Trust Agreement made at Cincinnati, Ohio, this _________ day of _________________, 1981, by Mr. Taxpayer, hereinafter referred to as the "Grantor," and Mrs. Taxpayer and The Cincinnati Bank, a banking association organized and existing under the National Bank Act of the United States, hereinafter sometimes referred to as the "Trustee" or "Trustees."

WITNESSETH:

WHEREAS, on August 1, 1980, the Grantor entered into a Trust Agreement with The Cincinnati Bank, as Trustee; and

WHEREAS, the Grantor has reserved the right to amend the Trust Agreement under the provisions thereof, and now wishes to amend said Trust Agreement by restating its provisions in their entirety;

NOW THEREFORE, said Trust Agreement is hereby amended and restated in its entirety to read as follows:

SECTION 1
Trust Property

1.1 The Grantor has delivered to the Trustee the property shown on Schedule "A," attached hereto and made part hereof.

1.2 The Trustee acknowledges receipt of the property shown on Schedule "A." The Trustee agrees to hold such property and any other property which may from time to time be delivered to it upon the various trusts hereinafter expressed, and to manage the trust estate and make distribution of income and principal thereof as provided herein.

SECTION 2
Rights Retained by the Grantor

2.1 The Grantor reserves the following rights which he may exercise at any time during his life:

2.1.1   To revoke this Agreement or, from time to time, to amend its terms, including the right to change beneficiaries and the plan of distribution to them, provided that the duties, powers and responsibilities of the Trustee shall not be substantially increased without its written consent. Any revocation or amendment not requiring the Trustee's written consent shall be effective upon receipt by the Trustee of a writing executed by the Grantor, and any amendment requiring the Trustee's written consent shall be effective upon the execution of such consent by the Trustee.

2.1.2   To withdraw from time to time, upon ten (10) days' prior written notice to the Trustee, any or all the property comprising the trust estate.

2.1.3   To sell, assign or hypothecate any policies of insurance which may from time to time be part of the trust estate; to exercise any option or privilege granted by any of such policies; to borrow any sum in accordance with the provisions of any of such policies; and to receive all payments, dividends, surrender values, benefits or privileges of any kind which may be available under any of such policies.

2.1.4   To approve any investments, reinvestments, or changes in investments which the Trustee may from time to time recommend, provided that, if requested by the Grantor in writing the Trustee will notify the Grantor in writing of its recommendation for investments, reinvestments or changes in investments and if the Grantor fails to reply to the Trustee within five days from the date of such notice, either by telephone, telegram, mail or in person, the Trustee may proceed to make any investments, reinvestments or changes in investments about which it has notified the Grantor. The Grantor has no right to approve any investments, reinvestments or changes in investments during any period when he is incompetent or incapacitated.

2.2   The Trustee agrees that the Grantor may from time to time add other personal or real property, including policies of life insurance, to the trust estate and place such property within the operation of all of the terms and conditions hereof. The Trustee agrees that any other person, firm or corporation, including the Grantor's attorney-in-fact, may add such property to the trust estate. The Trustee agrees to accept any such property, provided it may lawfully do so and provided that it is of the character normally acceptable by trustees generally, whether such property is conveyed or delivered to it or whether it is devised or bequeathed to it by Will.

SECTION 3
Distributions During Life of the Grantor

3.1   If, at any time during the life of the Grantor, the trust estate includes any income-producing assets, the Trustee shall pay the net income of the trust to the Grantor at least quarter-annually, or in such other manner as directed by the Grantor in writing.

3.2   If the Grantor becomes incapacitated or incompetent, during the period of incapacity or incompetency the Trustee shall have full power and authority, in its sole discretion, to use the net income and, if necessary, all or any part of the principal of the trust for the maintenance and support of the Grantor, to pay it out for his use and benefit, and to do whatever it may deem necessary or proper for the Grantor's support, maintenance, medical care and comfort. During such period the Trustee shall also have the power and authority to use the net income and, if necessary, all or any part of the principal for the support, maintenance, medical care and comfort of any of the Grantor's wife and children who may be dependent upon the Grantor for support, and the Trustee may pay such income and principal directly to the Grantor's wife and children for such purposes.

SECTION 4
At the Grantor's Death—Trusts and Distributions

4.1 Upon the death of the Grantor, the residue of the trust estate, including all amounts of income not distributed to the Grantor during his life, any amounts collected by the Trustee from insurance policies on the Grantor's life, any amounts which may be payable by reason of the Grantor's participation in any plan for employees or for self-employed persons, any part of the Grantor's estate as may be distributed to the Trustee, and all other property which, as principal or income, may be or may become part of the trust estate, shall be divided, held and distributed by the Trustee as herein provided.

4.1.1 If Grantor's wife, Mrs. Taxpayer, survives him, and if the trust estate, including any additions as a result of Grantor's death, exceeds the largest amount that can pass free of federal estate tax, by the full use of the "credit amount," then the trust estate shall be divided into a Trust A ("Marital Trust") and a Trust B ("Family Trust"). The Trustee shall allocate to Trust B property having a fair market value at the date or dates of distribution which is equal to the "credit amount," reduced by the value as finally determined for federal estate-tax purposes of all other property included in Grantor's gross estate, however passing, which does not qualify for the federal estate-tax marital deduction or charitable deduction, and by any charges to principal that are not deducted in computing his federal estate tax. The balance of the trust estate, which qualifies for the marital deduction for federal estate-tax purposes, shall be allocated to Trust A and held under Section 4.2.

If any property is received by the Trustee which is excluded from Grantor's gross estate for federal estate-tax purposes, such property shall be set aside as a Special Fund of Trust B. None of the principal or income of such property shall be used to pay, or to assist Grantor's Executor in the payment of, his death taxes, expenses, debts or other obligations of his estate. Subject to these restrictions, the Special Fund shall be held, administered and distributed in the same manner as Trust B. After all such death taxes, expenses and other obligations of Grantor's estate have been paid, the Trustee is authorized to merge such Fund into Trust B, if it deems it advisable to do so.

Grantor's wife, Mrs. Taxpayer, may disclaim all or any amount or fractional part of Trust A by advising the Trustee in writing, or by other method allowed by law, of the amount or fraction of Trust A which she elects to disclaim. Property so disclaimed shall be allocated to Trust B and held under Section 4.3.

If Grantor's wife, Mrs. Taxpayer, survives him and the trust estate is less than the "credit amount," or if Grantor's wife does not survive him, the trust estate shall be allocated to Trust B and held under Section 4.3.

For all purposes of this Section, the "credit amount" shall be the largest amount that can pass by reason of Grantor's death free of federal estate tax by the full use of the unified credit for federal estate-tax purposes and the state death tax credit, but only to the extent that the state death tax credit does not increase the death tax payable by Grantor's estate, and no other credit. Grantor intends by the provisions of this Section to obtain the full use of the "credit amount" in effect at the time of his death and the unlimited marital deduction under the Economic Recovery Tax Act of 1981 to the extent provided for by the above provisions for the establishment of Trust A. This Trust Agreement shall be construed so as to further such intent.

4.2   Trust A shall be a separate trust for the sole and exclusive benefit of the Grantor's wife, Mrs. Taxpayer, and shall be held and distributed as follows:

4.2.1   The Trustee shall pay the net income of Trust A to or for the benefit of Mrs. Taxpayer at least quarter-annually during her life.

4.2.2   Mrs. Taxpayer shall have the power to withdraw, at any one time or from time to time, any part or all of the principal of Trust A, upon first giving written notice to the Trustee of her intention to withdraw.

4.2.3   If, in the sole opinion of the Trustee, the net income of Trust A is insufficient to support and maintain Mrs. Taxpayer in the manner to which she has become accustomed, considering her other income and means of support known to the Trustee, the Trustee may, in its sole discretion, distribute to her as much of the principal of Trust A as the Trustee determines is necessary for such purposes.

4.2.4   Mrs. Taxpayer shall have full power to appoint, effective at the date of her death, the entire principal and any undistributed income of Trust A or any portion thereof, either outright or in trust, to her estate, or to any person or persons or any corporation or corporations. If she exercises this general power of appointment by an appointment in trust, she may select a trustee or trustees, establish such administrative powers as she deems appropriate, create different types of interests, including the creation of new powers of appointment, and impose any lawful conditions upon any appointment.

4.2.5   Upon the death of Mrs. Taxpayer, the Trustee shall distribute the principal and any undistributed income of Trust A in such manner as she may have appointed by an instrument in writing as provided in Section 6.11. If she fails to exercise such power so as to appoint all the principal and any undistributed income of Trust A, any part remaining unappointed shall be distributed to Trust B and held and distributed as provided in Section 4.3.5.

4.3   Trust B shall be held, divided and distributed as follows:

4.3.1   Upon demand in writing by the Executor or Administrator of the Grantor's estate, the Trustee shall pay to such Executor or Administrator from Trust B an amount equal to all estate, inheritance or similar taxes due by reason of the Grantor's death which are imposed by any governmental authority, or such part thereof as the Executor or Administrator may demand from the

Trustee, or if there is no Executor or Administrator, or if the Executor or Administrator makes no demand, the Trustee shall pay directly such part of such taxes as the Trustee may lawfully be required to pay by any governmental authority. If the Trustee shall have in its possession any United States government bonds eligible for redemption at par plus accrued interest in payment of federal estate tax, the Trustee shall deliver any such bonds it may have in its possession in accordance with the directions of the Executor or Administrator of the Grantor's estate either to such Executor or Administrator or directly in payment of the federal estate-tax liability of Grantor's estate, or if there is no Executor or Administrator or no demand is made, the Trustee shall deliver such bonds directly in payment of such taxes, it being the Grantor's intention that only after all such bonds have been used for payment of such liability shall other assets be used for this purpose.

4.3.2 If the Grantor's wife, Mrs. Taxpayer, survives him, the Trustee shall pay for the benefit or directly to her, annually or more often during her life, at such times as the Trustee determines, as much of the net income of Trust B as the Trustee determines, as much of the net income of Trust B as the Trustee, in its sole discretion, determines necessary to support and maintain her in the manner to which she has become accustomed. In making any such decisions, the Trustee shall consider her other income and means of support known to the Trustee, and resolve any doubts in favor of generous and liberal support for her. Any part of the net income not paid to Mrs. Taxpayer may be paid, in the Trustee's sole discretion, annually or more often to any one or among any two or more of the Grantor's issue living on the date of payment, in such proportions or shares as the Trustee deems advisable, or the Trustee may, in its sole discretion, accumulate and add to the principal of the trust any income not paid to the Grantor's wife or issue.

4.3.3 If, in the sole opinion of the Trustee, the net income of Trust B is insufficient to support and maintain Mrs. Taxpayer in the manner to which she has become accustomed, considering her other income and means of support known to the Trustee, the Trustee may, in its sole discretion, distribute to her as much of the principal of Trust B as the Trustee determines is necessary for such purposes, provided that the Trustee shall not distribute principal of Trust B to her at any time when principal is available for distribution to her from Trust A under Sections 4.2.2 or 4.2.3.

4.3.4 Mrs. Taxpayer shall have the annual power to withdraw from the principal of Trust B up to $5,000.00, or up to an amount equal to five percent of the value of the principal of Trust B on the date as of which the exercise of the power is effective, whichever is greater. This power can only be exercised once annually by written notice executed and delivered to the Trustee at any time during a calendar year, which notice shall be effective only as of December 31 of such calendar year. The power shall not be cumulative and any notice to exercise the power for any year shall not be effective unless Mrs. Taxpayer is living on December 31 of such year. Mrs. Taxpayer shall not withdraw principal of Trust B in the exercise of this power at any time when she can withdraw principal of Trust A under Section 4.2.2.

4.3.5 Upon the death of Mrs. Taxpayer, if she survives the Grantor, or, if she does not survive the Grantor, upon the Grantor's death, the Trustee shall distribute the principal and any undistributed income of Trust B as follows:

4.3.5.1 Any part of the principal and undistributed income of Trust B shall be held and distributed as follows: If any child of the Grantor is under the age of twenty-three (23) years at the time set for distribution of Trust B, the Trustee shall continue to hold all the principal and any undistributed income of Trust B for the benefit of all the Grantor's children then living, under Section 5.1. If no child of the Grantor is under the age of 23 years at the time set for distribution of Trust B, the Trustee shall distribute the principal and any undistributed income of Trust B to the Grantor's issue who survive both the Grantor and his said wife, per stirpes, provided that if any such issue is under the age of thirty-three (33) years at the time set for distribution, his or her share shall not be distributed to him or her directly, but shall be held by the Trustee as a separate trust for his or her benefit under Section 5.2.

4.4 For the purposes of this Agreement, the Grantor's wife, Mrs. Taxpayer, shall be deemed to have survived the Grantor, any presumption of law notwithstanding, if she survives him for any period, or if there is no evidence as to the order of the deaths of the Grantor and his wife.

SECTION 5

Trust for Children and Trusts for Issue Under 33

5.1 If, pursuant to Section 4.3.5, a trust is to be held for the benefit of all of the Grantor's children under this Section 5.1, it shall be held under the following terms and conditions:

5.1.1 The Trustee shall pay so much of the net income of the trust as it deems appropriate at such times as it deems appropriate to the Grantor's children living at the date of payment to provide for their support, comfort, maintenance, education and well-being, and any such income not currently required for such purposes shall be accumulated and added to the principal of the trust. In paying the net income to the Grantor's children, the Trustee shall not be required to divide it equally among them, but may pay it unequally among them, according to their respective needs at the time of payment, and the Trustee may pay to any child at any time all, none or part of the net income of the trust so as to provide each of the Grantor's children with the best start in life that the net income is capable of providing. The word "education" when used in this Agreement may include private schooling, college or university education and, in an appropriate case, postgraduate education, and also, without limitation, all tuition, board, lodging, fees and travel expenses incidental thereto.

5.1.2 If, in the sole opinion of the Trustee, the net income payable to the Grantor's children is not sufficient to provide for their suitable support, comfort, maintenance, education and well-being, the Trustee is authorized, in its sole discretion, to pay principal of the trust for such purposes. It is the Grantor's intention that the need of the individual child, rather than equal distribution of the trust property among his children, shall be the primary consideration governing the Trustee in the exercise of its discretion, and it is the

Grantor's desire that the Trustee exercise its discretion liberally so as to provide each of the Grantor's children with a proper start in life.

5.1.3   If on the date when none of the Grantor's living children is under the age of twenty-three (23) years, there are issue of Grantor who survive to such time, the trust shall terminate, and the Trustee shall distribute the principal and any undistributed income thereof to the Grantor's issue who survive to such time, per stirpes, provided that if any such issue is under the age of thirty-three (33) years at the time set for distribution of such issue's share to him or her, his or her share shall not be distributed to him or her directly, but shall be held by the Trustee as a separate trust for his or her benefit under Section 5.2.

5.2   If, pursuant to any provision hereof, a trust is to be held for the benefit of a child or more remote issue of the Grantor under this Section 5.2, it shall be held under the following terms and conditions:

5.2.1   The trust shall terminate as to one-third of the principal thereof on the date when the person for whom the trust is held reaches the age of twenty-three (23) years; it shall terminate as to one-half of the principal thereof on the date when the person for whom the trust is held reaches the age of twenty-eight (28) years; and it shall terminate as to the remaining principal and any undistributed income thereof on the date when such person reaches the age of thirty-three (33) years; and distribution shall be made to such person of the shares indicated on such dates. If, in the sole opinion of the Trustee, the trust estate has at any time been so reduced in size as to make it uneconomical or otherwise impractical to continue to hold it in trust, the trust shall terminate and the Trustee shall distribute the principal and any undistributed income thereof to the person for whom the trust is held, outright and free of trust. If at the time the trust is established the person for whom the trust is held is over the age of twenty-three (23) years but not yet twenty-eight (28) years of age, the Trustee shall distribute directly to such person one-third of all the principal of the trust as of the date the trust is established, and the Trustee shall hold the balance of the trust estate for such person under the terms and conditions hereof. If at the time the Trust is established the person for whom the Trust is held is over the age of twenty-eight (28) years but not yet thirty-three (33) years of age, the Trustee shall distribute directly to such person two-thirds of the principal of the trust as of the date the trust is established, and the Trustee shall hold the balance of the trust estate for such person under the terms and conditions hereof. If the person for whom the trust is held dies before receiving distribution of all the principal and undistributed income of the trust, the trust shall terminate on the date of his or her death, and the principal and any undistributed income thereof shall be distributed to his or her estate.

5.2.2   During any period when the person for whom the trust is held is under the age of twenty-three (23) years, the Trustee shall pay as much of the net income of the trust as it deems appropriate at such times as it deems appropriate to provide for such person's support, comfort, maintenance, education and well-being, and any such income which the Trustee determines is not currently necessary for such purposes shall be accumulated and added to the principal of the trust.

5.2.3   After the person for whom the trust is held attains the age of twenty-three (23) years, the Trustee shall pay the net income of the trust to him or her at least quarter-annually.

5.2.4 If, in the sole opinion of the Trustee, the net income of the trust is insufficient to provide for the support, comfort, maintenance, education and well-being of the person for whom the trust is held, considering his or her other income and means of support known to the Trustee, the Trustee may, in its sole discretion, distribute to such person as much of the principal of the trust as the Trustee determines is necessary for such purposes.

5.3 Solely for purposes of investment convenience, the Trustee may hold and invest the assets of the separate trusts held under this Section 5 as a unit, without physically dividing them, until actual division becomes necessary in order to make distribution, and in such case the Trustee shall allocate to each separate trust its proportionate part of receipts and expenditures.

SECTION 6

General Provisions

6.1 As to each trust held hereunder, the Trustee shall have the following power and authority in addition to and without limiting the power and authority it may have under the laws of any state, which it may exercise without order of court:

6.1.1 To adjust and compromise debts or claims in favor of or against any trust.

6.1.2 To borrow money, including authority for a corporate Trustee to borrow from itself in its nonfiduciary capacity.

6.1.3 To sell real or personal property, publicly or privately; to give options to buy real estate for any length of time; to lease real estate for any term irrespective of the duration of any trust, with or without option to purchase; to mortgage real estate; to pledge personal property and to execute and deliver proper instruments to effectuate such powers.

6.1.4 To retain any of the original property received by it, regardless of its character or whether or not it is such as is authorized by law for investment by fiduciaries, for such time as it deems best; and to invest and reinvest the proceeds of the sale of any such property, or any cash, in such property as it deems advisable, including participation in any common trust fund established and maintained by the Trustee for collective investment of fiduciary funds, whether or not it is of the character authorized by law for investment by fiduciaries. The Trustee is authorized to retain as an asset of any trust any securities issued by a corporate Trustee or its affiliate. The Trustee may invest assets of any trust in securities issued by a corporate Trustee or its affiliate and exercise voting rights under such securities, only at the written direction of the Grantor during his lifetime or, after his death, at the written direction of the primary income beneficiary of the trust to which such securities are allocated, the parent, guardian or custodian to act for any beneficiary who is a minor or otherwise incompetent to act. The provisions of this Section 6.1.4 shall be subject to the rights reserved to the Grantor under Section 2.1.4.

6.1.5 To exercise or not exercise, as it may determine, all rights of ownership incident to any securities it may hold, including but not limited to the rights to vote on any matter and to give proxies or execute consents, except as to securities issued by a corporate Trustee or its affiliate which shall be voted as directed by Section 6.1.4.

6.1.6 To hold any property in the name of a duly appointed nominee.

6.1.7 To sell property to and to borrow funds from one trust in favor of another trust established by this Agreement as if dealing with outside interests.

6.2. No person leasing or purchasing property from or lending money to or otherwise dealing with any trust, and no transfer agent requested to transfer corporate securities to or from any trust, need inquire as to the purpose of the lease, sale, loan, transfer or assignment or see to the application of the proceeds, and the receipt of the Trustee shall be a complete discharge and acquittance of such person for the amount paid.

6.3 The Trustee is authorized, in its sole discretion, to make any distribution of the trust estate in cash or in kind, or partly in cash and partly in kind, or to divide any personal property or any real property or interest therein, whether it is legal or equitable, and the Trustee may make any such distribution or division at such valuations as the Trustee may in good faith establish therefor, and all persons shall be bound by the division so made; and if the Trustee considers it inadvisable to divide any real estate held in the trust, the Trustee may convey such real estate to the beneficiaries entitled thereto as tenants in common according to their respective interests.

6.4 If the Trustee has a reasonable doubt about the manner of allocating any credit or charge to principal or income under applicable law, the Trustee shall have the power, exercisable as a fiduciary in good faith, to determine whether money or property coming into its possession shall be treated as principal or income, provided that distributions of capital gains by regulated investment companies, capital gains on the sale of assets and stock dividends in stock of the declaring corporation shall be allocated to principal; to charge or apportion expenses or losses to principal or income; to establish and maintain reasonable reserves for depreciation, depletion, amortization and obsolescence, and if any portion of the trust estate consists of a wasting asset, to establish and maintain reasonable reserves for such asset; and to amortize or not to amortize both premiums and discounts on investments.

6.5 If there is included as an asset of the trust estate, real estate which the Grantor and his wife, Mrs. Taxpayer, were either occupying as their residence or vacation home at the time of the Grantor's death or using in their business operations, the Trustee shall continue to hold such real estate and shall permit such real estate to be occupied by Grantor's wife or by any business owned or operated by Grantor's wife. The Grantor's wife shall have the following powers with respect to such real estate.

1. The Grantor's wife may direct the Trustee to sell the real estate to the Grantor's wife for its appraised fair market value at the time of the proposed sale hereunder. The purchase price may, at the option of Grantor's wife, be paid by Grantor's wife's promissory note secured by a mortgage on the real es-

tate bearing interest at a rate not in excess of 12% per year, and not requiring any principal payments for twenty (20) years, at which time the full balance of the unpaid principal shall become due and payable; and/or

2.   The Grantor's wife may direct the trustee to sell the real estate and to purchase other such real estate which the Grantor's wife shall select. Any proceeds arising from the sale of real estate which are not applied toward the purchase of another parcel of real estate shall be added to the principal of the trust estate.

The Trustee shall not be liable for any consumption, damage, injury to or loss of any property so held. The beneficiaries of any such trust shall not be liable for any nonnegligent consumption, damage, injury to or loss of any property so held.

After the Grantor's wife's death, or in the event of her incapacity, the powers reserved herein for the Grantor's wife shall terminate and shall not be exercisable by any other individual.

6.6   The Trustee is authorized to employ legal counsel or other agents in any matter in connection with the administration of any of the trusts, such as agents for the collection of rentals or the management or sale of any of the trust estate, real or personal, and the Trustee may pay such fees, compensation and expenses in connection therewith as the Trustee deems reasonable under the circumstances.

6.7   The Trustee assumes no responsibility with respect to the validity or enforceability of any policy of insurance delivered or made payable to it hereunder, nor with respect to the payment of any premiums or other amounts that may be due or may become due on any such policy, nor does it assume responsibility for doing anything else that may be required in order to keep any such policy in force. Any insurance company which has issued a policy of insurance payable to the Trustee hereunder need not inquire into or take notice of this Agreement, nor see to the application of the proceeds of any such policy or any other amounts paid to the Trustee with respect to it, and the receipt of the Trustee shall be a complete release and discharge of the insurance company for the amount so paid and shall be binding upon every beneficiary of any trust created hereunder. If a dispute arises with respect to the collection by the Trustee of any such policy, the Trustee shall have authority to compromise such dispute in any manner it deems to be in the best interests of the trust, and the Trustee may enter into any agreement with respect to such compromise which it deems appropriate and may release any insurance company from any liability under any such policy. The Trustee need not engage in litigation to collect the proceeds due under any such policy unless and until it is fully indemnified to its satisfaction by beneficiaries of the trust from any liability which may result from such litigation, including obligations incurred by the Trustee for attorney fees, court costs and other expenses incident to such litigation.

6.8   In addition to the payment of taxes due by reason of the death of the Grantor which shall be paid by the Trustee as provided in Section 4.1.1, upon demand in writing by the Executor or Administrator of the Grantor's estate, the Trustee shall pay to his Executor or Administrator an amount equal to any cash bequests that may be contained in his Will, and all his debts, expenses of his last illness, funeral and burial expenses, expenses of administration, or such part of any such bequests, debts and expenses as the Executor or Administrator may demand from the Trustee, or if there is no Executor or Administrator or if the Executor or Administrator makes no demand, the Trustee may pay directly such bequests, debts and expenses.

6.9   In the event that the Trustee shall be designated by Grantor as the beneficiary of the death benefit under any qualified pension, profit sharing, stock bonus or Keogh plan trust, or Individual Retirement Account or similar trust or plan, in which Grantor is a participant and under which the Trustee as beneficiary may elect (with or without the consent of any other person) the mode of payment, the Trustee shall proceed in the following manner:

(a)   The Trustee shall, subject to the provisions of subparagraph (b), elect a mode of payment that will qualify the value of the death benefit for exclusion from Grantor's gross estate for federal estate-tax purposes. If more than one such mode of payment is available to the Trustee, the Trustee shall elect that mode which, in its sole discretion, appears to it to be most advantageous to this Trust and/or its then current income beneficiaries, in terms of income tax (federal, state and local) considerations and/or investment return considerations, based on the Trustee's evaluation of the facts and circumstances relevant to such considerations as they exist at the time the Trustee makes such election. The Trustee shall not use any such portion of the distribution it receives which is excludable from the Grantor's gross estate for federal estate tax purposes, for any of the purposes set forth in Sections 4.3.1 and 6.7, nor shall the Trustee use such portion of the distribution in any other manner for the benefit of the Grantor's probate estate. Such portion shall be added to the principal of Trust B after deducting the expenses, including taxes, if any, incurred in connection with the receipt of such portion, which expenses may be paid out of such portion of the distribution.

(b)   Notwithstanding the provisions of subparagraph (a), the Trustee may elect a lump sum distribution, which will subject the value of the death benefit to inclusion in Grantor's gross estate, if the Trustee shall determine in its sole discretion that such election appears to it to be the most advantageous option available to it under the plan to this Trust and/or its then current income beneficiaries, in terms of income and/or estate and/or inheritance tax (federal, state and local) considerations and/or investment return considerations, based on the Trustee's evaluation of the facts and circumstances relevant to such considerations as they exist at the time the Trustee makes such election.

Grantor recognizes that discretionary election by the Trustee of a lump sum distribution and resultant inclusion in Grantor's gross estate of the value of the death benefit may result in allocation in Trust A of a substantial portion of the death benefit (or of other assets qualifying for the marital deduction that may be selected by Trustee) as opposed to allocation of the entire death benefit to Trust B resulting from election of a mode of payment that qualified the value of the death benefit for exclusion from Grantor's gross estate, but Grantor specifically directs the Trustee not to make any adjustments between the beneficiaries of Trust A and Trust B to compensate for the shift in assets to Trust A resulting from Trustee's election of a lump sum distribution.

(c) Any election of a mode of payment made by the Trustee in good faith in the exercise of the discretionary power conferred upon it by Grantor in subparagraphs (a) and (b) shall be final and binding upon all persons whomsoever and shall be a full acquittance and discharge to the Trustee, and the Trustee shall not be liable to any person whomsoever by reason of its exercise of such discretionary power.

6.10 Income or principal of any trust created under this Agreement which becomes payable or is, in the discretion of the Trustee, distributable to any beneficiary who is incapacitated or incompetent, may be paid, in the Trustee's sole discretion, either to the beneficiary, despite his or her incapacity or incompetency, to his or her parent or parents, to the guardian or guardians of such beneficiary's person or estate, to a custodian for such beneficiary designated by the Trustee, or directly to any person, corporation or institution for the benefit of such person, and the receipt of any such payee shall be a complete discharge and acquittance of the Trustee for the amount paid.

6.11 The power of appointment granted Mrs. Taxpayer under Section 4.2.4 of this Agreement which is effective at the date of her death may be exercised by her only by an instrument or instruments in writing (other than a Will) signed in the presence of two witnesses and delivered to the Trustee prior to her death. Mrs. Taxpayer may execute any such instrument at any time during her life, either prior or subsequent to the death of the Grantor, but any such appointment shall not be effective unless she survives the Grantor. If Mrs. Taxpayer executes more than one instrument purporting to appoint the same trust property, the instrument last executed in conformity with the foregoing provisions shall be effective with respect to such property.

6.12 For all purposes of this Agreement, a person, including the Grantor, shall be considered incapacitated or incompetent if under the age of eighteen (18) years, or if so declared by a court having jurisdiction, or if such person's personal physician or any two physicians selected by the Trustee shall advise the Trustee of such incapacity or incompetency in writing. Any such incapacity or incompetency established in the first instance by declaration of court may be removed only by such court, or if established in the first instance by such person's personal physician or any two physicians selected by the Trustee, may be removed by either the personal physician then serving such person or any two physicians selected by the Trustee (who need not be the same two physicians who may have advised the Trustee of such person's incapacity or incompetency).

6.13 The words "child" or "children," when used in this Agreement, shall mean lineal descendants of the first degree only, including an adopted person or persons. The word "issue" shall mean lineal descendants of any degree, including an adopted person or persons and shall include a person conceived but not born.

6.14 Notwithstanding any other provisions of this Agreement, unless terminated at an earlier date under other provisions hereof, all trusts herein created shall terminate twenty-one (21) years after the death of the last to die of the Grantor, the Grantor's wife and the Grantor's issue who are living on the date of the termination of the Grantor's power to revoke the trusts established by this Agreement, whether such power terminates by death of the Grantor or otherwise, and thereupon the Trustee shall distribute to the persons then entitled to receive income from any trust the share of the trust from which any such person is then entitled to receive income.

6.15   After the Grantor's death, the interest of any beneficiary in any trust created hereunder shall not be subject to the claims of creditors and shall not be subject to attachment, execution or other legal process or lien brought by or in favor of a creditor or creditors of any such beneficiary, and no alienation or assignment of any interest in the subject matter of any trust, whether of principal or income, shall be binding upon the Trustee or anyone who may deal with it. If any such beneficiary shall attempt to alienate or assign his or her interest in any trust or the income therefrom, or if any creditor shall seek to attach it, execute against it or secure a lien thereon, the interest of such beneficiary in any trust and the income thereof shall cease. Thereafter the Trustee shall hold the trust until the date set for its termination hereunder, using the income or principal of the trust for the support, maintenance, and well-being of such beneficiary for his or her spouse or minor children, in such manner as the Trustee, in its sole discretion, deems best. Upon termination of such trust, the Trustee shall pay the principal and any undistributed income to the persons entitled thereto hereunder.

6.16   If the Trustee is unable to act as Trustee with respect to any real estate located outside the State of Ohio, then such person or persons or corporation as may from time to time be appointed by the Trustee in writing shall act as trustee with respect to such real property without order of court, and shall have all the powers and discretions with respect to such property as are herein given to the original Trustee and shall be paid the reasonable value of the services rendered. The Trustee may remove such appointed trustee and appoint another upon ten (10) days' written notice. Should such property be sold, exchanged or otherwise disposed of, the proceeds thereof shall be remitted to the original Trustee. Such appointed trustee may employ the Trustee as agent in the Administration of such property. No surety shall be required on the bond of any Trustee or agent acting upon the provisions of this paragraph. No periodic court account shall be required of such appointed Trustee, it being Grantor's intention to excuse any statutory accounting which may ordinarily be required. Such appointed trustee shall, however, send semi-annual statements to the current income beneficiaries and to the Trustee.

6.17   Throughout this Agreement words used in the singular or plural shall be read in the plural or singular, and pronouns shall be read in the feminine, masculine or neuter gender, as the facts or context may require to accomplish the purpose intended.

6.18   This trust has been accepted by the Trustee in the State of Ohio, and all questions pertaining to the trust and its validity and the administration thereof, and to the construction of this Agreement, shall be determined in accordance with the laws of the State of Ohio.

6.19 (a) Grantor retains the right to direct the Trustee in writing to employ any investment counsel for the supervision of the investments of the trust, or of any separate fund. After Grantor's death the same persons having the right to remove the Trustee pursuant to Section 7.3 of this Trust shall have the right, during the periods of time designated in said Section to direct the Trustee to employ investment counsel, or to discontinue such employment or to change investment counsel, as the case may be, affecting the portion of the trust to which such person's right of Trustee removal pertains.

(b) If investment counsel is employed, the Trustee shall follow the written recommendations or instructions of such counsel, without liability for any neglect, omission, misconduct, mistake or default of such investment counsel and shall not be liable or responsible to any person whomsoever for any loss or depreciation of the value of the trust estate, or of any separate fund, by reason of having followed the advice of investment counsel.

(c) At any time when investment counsel has not been designated to act hereunder, either with respect to the entire trust estate or with respect to a separate share thereof, the Trustee shall have the responsibility for making investments, reinvestments and changes in investments of the trust estate, or such separate share, as the case may be.

(d) The fees of investment counsel shall be charged against income of the trust estate.

(e) During any period when investment counsel is serving hereunder, either with respect to the entire trust estate or a separate share thereof, the compensation to which the Trustee is entitled as to the trust estate or such separate share, as the case may be, shall be that which is provided for in the Trustee's then current schedule of fees for serving as Trustee without investment responsibilities, and the Trustee shall have no duty, during such period, to make investment recommendations concerning the assets of the trust estate, or such separate share, as the case may be, to any person whomsoever.

6.20 The renunciation, surrender, release or disclaimer by any beneficiary of any interest(s) of his or hers in any trust created by this Trust Agreement shall accelerate all other interests therein (including other interests which may be held by him or her) in the same manner as would have his or her death at the same time, but only as to such renounced, surrendered, released or disclaimed interest(s).

SECTION 7

The Trustee

7.1 Any individual Trustee may at any time, by a signed instrument delivered to the corporate Trustee, delegate to it any or all powers and discretion under this instrument, including the power to assign or convey any trust property on behalf of the trust, either for a specified time or until the delegation is revoked by similar instrument. Any person dealing in good faith with the corporate Trustee may rely without inquiry upon the corporate Trustee's certificate with respect to any delegation.

7.2   All records, books of account and accountings in connection with the administration of the trust or trusts created herein shall be prepared solely by the corporate Trustee. The corporate Trustee shall also be responsible for the care and safekeeping of all monies or securities included in any such trust. Except as provided in Section 6.19, authority and responsibility for the investment and reinvestment of the corpus and income of the trust where necessary shall rest with the corporate Trustee, and in making any such investment or reinvestment, the corporate Trustee shall not be required to obtain the consent or signature of any individual Trustee. The individual Trustee shall be relieved of all liability with regard to duties specifically delegated to the corporate Trustee. Unless delegated to the corporate Trustee, as herein provided, all other duties or discretions shall be performed or made by the co-Trustees jointly.

Any corporate Trustee serving hereunder shall receive such compensation for its services as is provided for in its schedule of fees from time to time in effect. Any individual Trustee serving hereunder shall receive no compensation for his services. Such compensation shall be charged against the income of the trust estate except for compensation payable upon distribution of principal, which shall be charged against principal.

7.3   Upon the written request of the Grantor during his life, any trustee acting hereunder shall resign as trustee as of the date fixed in the request, which shall not be earlier than thirty (30) days after the date of the request, and any trustee acting hereunder shall have the right to resign upon thirty (30) days' notice to the Grantor, if living, and if not, to all the beneficiaries then entitled to receive income who are legally competent and to the guardians or custodians of those who are not legally competent. Upon the resignation of any trustee, voluntarily or involuntarily, the Trustee shall turn over the assets and administration of the trusts then held hereunder, to such natural person or bank or trust company authorized to do business under the laws of any state or under the National Bank Act of the United States as may be selected by the Grantor, if living, or if not, by such beneficiaries or their beneficiaries or their guardians or custodians. After the death of the Grantor, Mrs. Taxpayer shall have the same right the Grantor had during his lifetime to require a corporate Trustee to resign and to designate another bank or trust company as corporate Trustee. After the death of the Grantor, and his wife, Mrs. Taxpayer, all the beneficiaries then entitled to receive income who are legally competent and the guardians or custodians of those who are not legally competent shall collectively have the same right which the Grantor had during his lifetime, to require a Trustee to resign and to designate another bank or trust company as Trustee.

7.4   References in this Agreement to the Trustee shall include the co-Trustees, Mrs. Taxpayer and The Cincinnati Bank and any successor trustee or co-trustee. Any successor or substitute trustee shall have each and every right, privilege, power of discretion, authority and duty of any original trustee and shall be subject to the same responsibilities. No bond shall be required of any trustee for serving as such.

7.5 Upon the payment and delivery to any successor Trustee of all the property and assets of the Trust Estate, and after full settlement of accounts, the responsibilities and liabilities of the resigning or removed Trustee shall terminate. No successor Trustee shall be required to investigate the acts of any predecessor Trustee, nor be responsible for any of the acts or omissions of any predecessor Trustee.

IN WITNESS WHEREOF, the Grantor and the Trustee have executed duplicates hereof, each of which shall be deemed an original, as of the day and year first above written.

____
Mr. Taxpayer

____

As to Mr. Taxpayer

____
Mrs. Taxpayer

____

As to Mrs. Taxpayer

THE CINCINNATI BANK

By _______________________________
Trust Officer

____

As to The Cincinnati Bank

STATE OF OHIO, COUNTY OF HAMILTON: SS:

Before me, the undersigned, a Notary Public in and for the said county and state, personally appeared Mr. Taxpayer, who executed the foregoing Agreement as the Grantor, and acknowledged the signing thereof to be his free and voluntary act for the uses and purposes therein contained.

IN TESTIMONY WHEREOF, I have affixed my hand and official seal this _______ day of _______________, 1981.

____
Notary Public

STATE OF OHIO, COUNTY OF HAMILTON: SS:

Before me, the undersigned, a Notary Public in and for the said county and state, personally appeared Mrs. Taxpayer, who executed the foregoing Agreement as the Trustee, and acknowledged the signing thereof to her free and voluntary act for the uses and purposes therein contained.

IN TESTIMONY WHEREOF, I have affixed my hand and official seal this
_________ day of _________________, 1981.

____

Notary Public

STATE OF OHIO, COUNTY OF HAMILTON: SS:
   This _________ day of _________________, 1981, came before me,
_________________, who being by me duly sworn says that he is a Trust Officer
of The Cincinnati Bank and that said writing was signed by him in behalf of
said bank by its authority duly given. And the Trust Officer acknowledged the
said writing to be the act and deed of said bank.

____

Notary Public

Schedule A
Trust Agreement
Mr. Taxpayer
Ten Dollars ($10.00)

Sample Super Irrevocable Trust Agreement

Super Irrevocable Trust Agreement

THIS WRITING contains all the terms of an Irrevocable Trust Agreement made at Cincinnati, Ohio, this _________ day of _______________, 1982, by Robert W. Buechner, hereinafter referred to as the "Grantor," and The Cincinnati Bank, hereinafter sometimes referred to as the "Trustee."

SECTION 1
Trust Property

1.1 The Grantor has delivered to the Trustee the property shown on Schedule A, attached hereto and made part hereof.

1.2 The Trustee acknowledges receipt of the property shown on Schedule A. The Trustee agrees to hold such property and any other property which may from time to time be delivered to it upon the various trusts hereinafter expressed, and to manage the trust estate and make distribution of income and principal thereof as provided herein.

SECTION 2
Surrender of Rights by Grantor and Additions to Trust

2.1 This Trust Agreement is irrevocable and the Grantor expressly waives and surrenders permanently all rights and powers to alter, amend, revoke or terminate this Agreement. The Grantor shall have no incidents of ownership with respect to policies of insurance or any other property or interests conveyed or assigned to the Trustee under this Agreement, and all such incidents of ownership shall be vested in and be exercisable by the Trustee in its sole discretion.

2.2 The Trustee agrees that the Grantor, his attorney-in-fact, or any other person, firm or corporation may, from time to time, add other property to the trust estate and place such property within the operation of all the terms and conditions hereof. The Trustee agrees to accept any such property, provided that it may lawfully do so and provided that it is of the character normally acceptable by trustees generally, whether such property is conveyed or delivered to it or whether it is devised or bequeathed to it by Will.

SECTION 3

Distributions During Life of the Grantor

3.1   If, at any time during the life of the Grantor, the trust estate includes any income producing assets, the Trustee shall apply the net income of the trust to pay any premiums which are due or may become due on any policies of insurance held hereunder. Any net income of the trust remaining after the payment of such premiums shall be paid at least annually to the Grantor's wife if she is living and if not to the Grantor's children who are living on the date of payment, per capita.

3.2   If during the life of the Grantor the income of the trust is not sufficient to fully pay premiums which may become due on any policies of insurance held hereunder, the Trustee shall notify the Grantor of the amount necessary to pay such premiums and the date as of which such premiums are due. If neither the Grantor nor any other person remits such amount, the Trustee may, in its sole discretion, sell any assets of the trust other than such policies of insurance, and apply the sale proceeds to the payment of such premiums, or the Trustee may borrow the amount necessary to pay such premiums, using assets of the trust, including such policies of insurance, as collateral, or the Trustee may convert any such policies into paid up insurance, or the Trustee may exercise any other right or option available under such policies or as a result of the ownership of such policies to provide for or defer payment of the premiums thereon. Notwithstanding anything herein to the contrary, the Trustee shall not be liable for the lapse of any policies caused by the nonpayment of premiums if such nonpayment is caused by the inadequacy of Trust assets to pay such premiums.

3.3   During each calendar year, the Grantor's wife shall have the annual noncumulative right to withdraw any assets which have been contributed to the trust during such year, but not exceeding the lesser of (a) the sum excludable in calculating taxable gifts of present interests in property under Section 2503(b) of the Internal Revenue Code (said sum presently being $10,000) as it hereafter may be amended or (b) the sum which is excludable from lapses of powers of appointment under Internal Revenue Code Section 2041(b) (2) (A), (said sum presently being $5,000), as it hereafter may be amended.

As long as Grantor's wife is living, if the assets contributed to the trust in any calendar year exceed the foregoing amount which is subject to withdrawal by Grantor's wife, then the Grantor's issue, per capita, shall have the annual, noncumulative right to withdraw, pro rata, the excess amount. If Grantor's wife is not living, Grantor's issue shall have the annual, noncumulative right to withdraw, pro rata, the entire amount of assets contributed to the trust during any calendar year; provided, however, whether or not Grantor's wife is living, any issue of Grantor shall not be entitled to withdraw from the trust during any calendar year assets having a value exceeding the lesser of (i) the sum excludable in calculating taxable gifts of present interests in property under Section 2503(b) of the Internal Revenue Code (said sum presently being $10,000) as it may be amended, or (ii) the sum which is excludable from lapses of powers of appointment under Internal Revenue Code Section 2041 (b) (2) (A) (said sum presently being $5,000), as it hereafter may be amended.

If the amounts contributed during any year exceed the amounts which may be withdrawn from the foregoing provisions, the Grantor's wife may withdraw from such assets additional amounts, provided that in any event the total amounts withdrawable by her in each calendar year shall not be in excess of the sum under Section 2041 (b) (2) (A) as aforesaid as it may be amended.

For purposes hereof, assets contributed to the trust shall include, but shall not be limited to, cash as well as life insurance policies (or any interest therein) assigned to the trust. Furthermore, the payment of a premium (on a policy of life insurance or any interest therein owned by the trust) directly to the company which issued the policy, which payment is made by any person or entity other than the Trustee, shall be deemed to be a contribution of an asset to the trust as of the date of payment.

A beneficiary must exercise the right to withdraw a contribution by delivering a written notice to the Trustee at any time during the calendar year of the contribution, whether before or after the contribution is made, but in no event later than December 31 of the calendar year in which the contribution was made. If a beneficiary is a minor, such beneficiary or his natural or legal guardian (other than Grantor) may give notice of withdrawal. In the event that the Trustee notifies the beneficiary in writing that a contribution has been made, the beneficiary must exercise the right to withdraw by delivering written notice of his or her intention to withdraw to the Trustee within thirty (30) days after the date of such Trustee's notice.

The Trustee may satisfy the exercise of a right of withdrawal by selecting cash or other assets in kind, including insurance policies or interests therein, or proceeds from the sale of policies.

3.4 During Grantor's lifetime, the Grantor's wife, Angela H. Buechner, shall have the power to appoint all or any part of the trust estate; provided however, that such power may be exercised only to, or for the benefit of, the Grantor or any of the Grantor's issue, but not including Grantor's wife, Angela H. Buechner. Such power shall be exercised in writing and shall set forth such terms and conditions, whether it be in trust or otherwise, as the Grantor's wife may specify.

SECTION 4
At the Grantor's Death—Trusts and Distributions

4.1 Upon the death of the Grantor, the residue of the trust estate, including any amounts collected by the Trustee from insurance policies on the Grantor's life and all other property which as principal or income may be or become part of the trust estate, shall be held and distributed as herein provided.

4.2 If the Grantor's wife survives him, the Trustee shall pay to her, annually or more often during her life, at such time as the Trustee determines, as much of the net income of the trust as the Trustee, in its sole discretion, determines necessary to support and maintain her in the manner to which she has become accustomed. In making any such decisions, the Trustee shall consider her other income and means of support known to the Trustee, and resolve any doubts in favor of generous and liberal support for her. Any part of the net income not paid to the Grantor's wife may be paid, in the Trustee's sole discretion, annually or more often to any one or among any two or more of the Grantor's next of kin living on the date of payment, in such proportions or shares as the Trustee deems advisable, or the Trustee may, in its sole discretion, accumulate and add to the principal of the trust any income not paid to the Grantor's wife or next of kin.

4.3 If, in the sole opinion of the Trustee, the net income of the trust is insufficient to support and maintain the Grantor's wife in the manner to which she has become accustomed, considering her other income and means of support known to the Trustee, the Trustee may, in its sole discretion, distribute to her as much of the principal of the trust as the Trustee determines is necessary for such purposes.

4.4 Upon the death of Angela H. Buechner, if she survives the Grantor, or, if she does not survive the Grantor upon the Grantor's death, the Trustee shall distribute the principal and any undistributed income of the trust estate to the Grantor's issue, per stirpes, provided that if any of the Grantor's issue is under the age of twenty-five (25) years at the time set for distribution of such share to him or her, his or her share shall not be distributed to him or her directly but shall be held by the Trustee as a separate trust for his or her benefit under Section 5.1. If no child of the Grantor is under the age of twenty-five (25) years at the time set for distribution of the trust estate, the Trustee shall distribute the principal and any undistributed income of the trust estate to the Grantor's issue who survive both the Grantor and his said wife, per stirpes, provided that if any such issue is under the age of thirty (30) years at the time set for distribution, his or her share shall not be distributed to him or her directly, but shall be held by the Trustee as a separate trust for his or her benefit under Section 5.2.

SECTION 5
Trusts for the Grantor's Children and Trusts for Issue Under 30

5.1 If, pursuant to Section 4.4, a trust is to be held for the benefit of any of the Grantor's issue under this Section 5.1, it shall be held under the following terms and conditions:

5.1.1 The Trustee shall pay so much of the net income of the trust as it deems appropriate at such times as it deems appropriate to the Grantor's children living at the date of payment to provide for their support, comfort, maintenance, education and well-being, and any such income not currently required for such purposes shall be accumulated and added to the principal of the trust. In paying the net income to the Grantor's children, the Trustee shall not be required to divide it equally among them, but may pay it unequally among them, according to their respective needs at the time of payment, and the

Trustee may pay to any child at any time all, none or part of the net income of the trust so as to provide each of the Grantor's children with the best start in life that the net income is capable of providing. The word "education" when used in this Agreement may include private schooling, college or university education and, in an appropriate case, postgraduate education, and also, without limitation, all tuition, board, lodging, fees, travel expenses and other expenses incidental thereto.

5.1.2   If, in the sole opinion of the Trustee, the net income payable to the Grantor's children is not sufficient to provide for their suitable support, comfort, maintenance, education and well-being, the Trustee is authorized, in its sole discretion, to pay principal of the trust for such purposes. It is the Grantor's intention that the need of the individual child, rather than equal distribution of the trust property among his children, shall be the primary consideration governing the Trustee in the exercise of its discretion, and it is the Grantor's desire that the Trustee exercise its discretion liberally so as to provide each of the Grantor's children with a proper start in life.

5.1.3   On the date when none of the Grantor's living children is under the age of twenty-five (25) years, the trust shall terminate, and the Trustee shall distribute the principal and any undistributed income thereof to the Grantor's issue who survive to such time, per stirpes, provided that if any issue is under the age of thirty (30) years at the time set for distribution, his or her share shall not be distributed to him or her directly, but shall be held by the Trustee as a separate trust for his or her benefit under Section 5.2.

5.2   If any issue of the Grantor who is entitled to all or any share of the principal and undistributed income of any trust established hereunder is under the age of thirty (30) years at the time set for distribution to him or her, his or her share shall not be distributed to him or her directly, but shall continue to be held by the Trustee as a separate trust for his or her benefit as follows:

5.2.1   The trust shall terminate as to one-half of the principal thereof on the date when the person for whom the trust is held reaches the age of twenty-five (25) years; and as to the remaining principal and any undistributed income thereof on the date when such person reaches the age of thirty (30) years; and distribution shall be made to such person of the shares indicated on such dates. If at the time the trust is established the person for whom the trust is held is over the age of twenty-five (25) years but not yet thirty (30) years of age, the Trustee shall distribute directly to such person one-half of all the principal of the trust as of the date the trust is established, and the Trustee shall hold the balance of the trust estate for such person under the terms and conditions hereof. If, in the sole opinion of the Trustee, the trust estate has at any time been so reduced in size as to make it uneconomical or otherwise impractical to continue to hold it in trust, the trust shall terminate and the Trustee shall distribute the principal and any undistributed income thereof to the person for whom the trust is held, outright and free of trust. If the person for whom the trust is held dies before receiving distribution of all the principal and undistributed income of the trust, the trust shall terminate on the date of his or her death, and the principal and any undistributed income thereof shall be paid to his or her estate.

5.2.2 During any period when the person for whom the trust is held is under the age of twenty-five (25) years, the Trustee shall pay as much of the net income of the trust as it deems appropriate at such times as it deems appropriate to provide for such person's support, comfort, maintenance, education and well-being, and any such income which the Trustee determines is not currently necessary for such purposes shall be accumulated and added to the principal of the trust.

5.2.3 After the person for whom the trust is held attains the age of twenty-five (25) years, the Trustee shall pay the net income of the trust to him or her at least quarter-annually.

5.2.4 If, in the sole opinion of the Trustee, the net income of the trust is insufficient to provide for the support, comfort, maintenance, education and well-being of the person for whom the trust is held, considering his or her other income and means of support known to the Trustee, the Trustee may, in its sole discretion, distribute to such person as much of the principal of the trust as the Trustee determines is necessary for such purposes.

5.3 Solely for purposes of investment convenience, the Trustee may hold and invest the assets of the separate trust held under this Section 5 as a unit, without physically dividing them, until actual division becomes necessary in order to make distribution, and in such case the Trustee shall allocate to each separate trust its proportionate part of receipts and expenditures.

5.4 Notwithstanding the foregoing provisions of this Section 5, if at any time when there is established or held a trust for any of the Grantor's issue under the age of thirty (30) years under Section 5.1, there is a trust for such person or persons which has, in the sole opinion of the Trustee, substantially the same provisions under a Trust Agreement dated September 25, 1981, established by Grantor, then the share allocated to the trust for such person or persons under this Agreement shall be added to the trust for such person or persons under the Trust Agreement of the Grantor, and held, managed and distributed in all respects as a part thereof.

SECTION 6

General Provisions

6.1 As to each trust held hereunder, the Trustee shall have the following power and authority in addition to and without limiting the power and authority it may have under the laws of any state, which it may exercise without order of court:

6.1.1 To collect, pay and compromise debts and claims in favor of or against any trust.

6.1.2 To borrow money, including authority of the Trustee to borrow from itself in its nonfiduciary capacity.

6.1.3 To buy and sell real and personal property, publicly and privately; to give options to buy real and personal property for any length of time; to lease real and personal property for any term irrespective of the duration of administration of any trust; to mortgage real property and pledge personal property; and to execute and deliver instruments to effectuate such powers without liability on the part of any purchaser, lessee, mortgagee or pledgee to see to the application of the purchase money.

6.1.4 To retain property received by it, regardless of its character and whether or not it is such as is authorized by law for investment by fiduciaries, for such time as it deems reasonable; and to invest and reinvest the proceeds of the sale of such property, and cash, in whatever property it deems reasonable, including participation in any common trust fund established and maintained by the Trustee for collective investment of fiduciary funds, whether or not it is of the character authorized by law for investment by fiduciaries. The Trustee is authorized to retain as an asset of any trust any securities issued by its affiliate. The Trustee may invest assets of any trust in securities issued by it or its affiliate and exercise voting rights under such securities only at the written direction of the primary income beneficiary or beneficiaries of the trust to which such securities are allocated, the parent, guardian or custodian to act for any beneficiary who is a minor or otherwise incompetent to act. Notwithstanding the foregoing, under no circumstances shall the Grantor have the authority to direct the Trustee as to the investment of trust assets in securities issued by it or its affiliate or as to the exercise of voting rights under such securities.

6.1.5 To exercise and not exercise, as it deems reasonable, rights of ownership incident to securities that it may hold, including rights to vote, give proxies and execute consents, except as to securities issued by the Trustee or its affiliate which shall be voted as directed by Section 6.1.4.

6.1.6 To hold property in the name of a nominee.

6.1.7 In the event of the Grantor's death, to purchase assets from the estate of the Grantor at their fair market value in such quantities as the Trustee deems advisable, and to loan funds or assets belonging to the trust estate to the Grantor's estate upon such terms and conditions and in such manner as the Trustee deems advisable (and if at such time Angela H. Buechner is serving as Trustee hereunder and as Executor or Administrator of the Grantor's estate, she may deal with herself in exercising the powers granted herein in each such capacity as if dealing with outside interests).

6.2 No person leasing or purchasing property from or lending money to or otherwise dealing with any trust, and no transfer agent requested to transfer corporate securities to or from any trust, need inquire as to the purpose of the lease, sale, loan, transfer or assignment or see to the application of the proceeds, and the receipt of the Trustee shall be a complete acquittance and discharge of such person for the amount paid.

6.3 The Trustee is authorized, in its sole discretion, to make any distribution of the trust estate in cash or in kind, or partly in cash and partly in kind, and to divide any real and personal property whether it is legal or equitable. The Trustee may make any distribution or division at such valuations as the Trustee may in good faith establish therefor, and all persons shall be bound by the division so made.

6.4 If the Trustee has a reasonable doubt about the manner of allocating any credit or charge to principal or income under applicable law, the Trustee shall have the power, exercisable as a fiduciary in good faith: to determine whether money or property coming into its possession shall be treated as principal or income; to charge or apportion expenses or losses to principal or income; and to amortize or not to amortize both premiums and discounts on investments.

6.5   The Trustee is authorized to employ legal counsel and other agents in any matter in connection with the administration of any of the trusts, such as agents for the collection of rentals or the management or sale of any of the trust estate. The Trustee may pay such compensation and expenses in connection therewith as the Trustee deems reasonable under the circumstances.

6.6   Any insurance company which has issued a policy of insurance payable to the Trustee hereunder need not inquire into or take notice of this Agreement, nor see to the application of the proceeds of any such policy or any other amounts paid to the Trustee with respect to it, and the receipt of the Trustee shall be a complete release and discharge of the insurance company for the amount so paid and shall be binding upon every beneficiary of any trust created hereunder. If a dispute arises with respect to the collection by the Trustee of the proceeds of any such policy, the Trustee shall have authority to compromise such dispute in any manner it deems to be in the best interest of the Trust, and the Trustee may enter into any agreement with respect to such compromise which it deems appropriate and may release any insurance company from any liability under any such policy. The Trustee need not engage in litigation to collect the proceeds due under any such policy unless and until it is fully idemnified to its satisfaction by beneficiaries of the trust from any liability which may result from such litigation, including obligations incurred by the Trustee for attorney fees, court costs and other expenses incident to such litigation.

6.7   Income or principal of any trust created under this Agreement which becomes payable or is, in the discretion of the Trustee, distributable to any beneficiary who is incapacitated or incompetent may be paid to such beneficiary, despite his or her incapacity or incompetency, to his or her parent or parents, to the guardian or guardians of his or her person or estate, to a custodian for such beneficiary designated by the Trustee, or to any person, corporation or institution for the benefit of such beneficiary, as the Trustee deems reasonable. The receipt of any such payee shall be a complete discharge and release of the Trustee. Except as provided in Section 3.4, nothing in this Agreement shall permit any payment to be made to the Grantor, either for his own or any other person's benefit, or to any other person, corporation or institution for the Grantor's benefit.

6.8   For all purposes of the Agreement, a person shall be considered incapacitated or incompetent if under the age of eighteen (18) years, or if so declared by a court having jurisdiction, or if such person's personal physician or any two physicians selected by the Trustee shall advise the Trustee of such incapacity or incompetency in writing. Any such incapacity or incompetency established in the first instance by declaration of court may be removed only by such court or if established in the first instance by such person's personal physician or any two physicians selected by the Trustee, may be removed by either the personal physician then serving such person or any two physicians selected by the Trustee (who need not be the same two physicians who may have advised the Trustee of such person's incapacity or incompetency).

6.9   The word "issue" shall mean Grantor's lineal descendants of any degree. References in this Agreement to the Grantor's "wife" shall mean Angela H. Buechner, but if her marriage to the Grantor terminates prior to the Grantor's death by court decree, or if they are living apart from each other under a separation agreement executed by them, whether or not such agreement was approved by any court, then for all purposes of this Agreement the Grantor's wife shall be deemed to have died on the date such decree is entered or such separation agreement is executed, and she shall not thereafter be entitled to any benefit hereunder or have authority to exercise any right or power available to the Grantor's wife under any of the provisions hereof.

6.10   Notwithstanding any other provisions of this Agreement, unless terminated at any earlier date under other provisions hereof, all trusts herein created shall terminate twenty-one (21) years after the death of the last to die of the Grantor's wife and the Grantor's issue who are living on the date of execution of this Agreement. Thereupon the Trustee shall distribute to the persons then entitled to receive income from any trust the share of the trust from which any such person is then entitled to receive income.

6.11   Notwithstanding any provisions of this Agreement to the contrary, the following provisions shall be applicable if any of the assets of this trust are included in the Grantor's gross estate for federal estate tax for any reason:

6.11.1   The Trustee shall pay to the executor or administrator of the Grantor's estate such sum as may be required for the payment of any estate, inheritance or similar taxes imposed by any governmental authority by reason of his death and by reason of the inclusion of any of the assets of this trust in the Grantor's gross estate for federal estate-tax purposes, over and above the amount of such taxes which would have been payable upon his death from his estate had none of the assets of this trust been included in the determination of such taxes.

6.12   Notwithstanding anything herein contained to the contrary, no powers enumerated herein or accorded to the Trustee generally pursuant to law, singly or as a whole, shall be construed:

(a)   To enable Grantor to become a Trustee hereunder, to enable the Grantor to directly or indirectly vote any securities which may at any time be given to any trust hereunder, or to exercise any power of appointment with respect to this trust, or

(b)   To enable the Grantor to borrow any part of the assets or funds of any trust hereunder, directly or indirectly, unless such loan provides for at least such security and such interest as a commercial bank would deem to be adequate under the then circumstances and unless such loan is made by and with the continuing consent of any independent Trustee or

(c)   To permit any trust distribution which would discharge any legal obligation of Grantor (including the support or education of a beneficiary hereunder) or

(d) To enable the Grantor to reacquire any trust property by substituting other property of equal value.

6.13 (a) After Grantor's death the person or persons having the right to remove the Trustee pursuant to Section 7.3 of this Trust shall have the right, during the periods of time designated in said Section, to direct the Trustee to employ investment counsel, or to discontinue such employment or to change investment counsel, as the case may be, affecting the portion of the trust to which such person's right of Trustee removal pertains.

(b) If investment counsel is employed, the Trustee shall follow the written recommendations or instructions of such counsel, without liability for any neglect, omission, misconduct, mistake or default of such investment counsel and shall not be liable or responsible to any person whomsoever for any loss or depreciation of the value of the trust estate, or of any separate fund, by reason of having followed the advice of investment counsel.

(c) At any time when investment counsel has not been designated to act hereunder, either with respect to the entire trust estate or with respect to a separate share thereof, the Trustee shall have the responsibility for making investments, reinvestments and changes in investments of the trust estate, or such separate share, as the case may be.

(d) The fees of investment counsel shall be charged against income of the trust estate.

(e) During any period when investment counsel is serving hereunder, either with respect to the entire trust estate or a separate share thereof, the compensation to which the Trustee is entitled as to the trust estate or such separate share, as the case may be, shall be that which is provided for in the Trustee's then current schedule of fees for serving as Trustee without investment responsibilities, and the Trustee shall have no duty, during such period, to make investment recommendations concerning the assets of the trust estate, or such separate share, as the case may be, to any person whomsoever.

6.14 Throughout this Agreement words used in the singular or plural shall be read in the plural or singular, and pronouns shall be read in feminine, masculine or neuter gender, as the facts or context may require to accomplish the purpose intended.

6.15 This trust has been accepted by the Trustee in the State of Ohio, and all questions pertaining to the trust and its validity and the administration thereof, and to the construction of this Agreement, shall be determined in accordance with the laws of the State of Ohio.

SECTION 7

The Trustee

7.1 References in this Agreement to the "Trustee" shall include not only The Cincinnati Bank, but also any successor trustee.

7.2 For its services in connection with the administration of each trust held hereunder, any corporate Trustee shall receive such compensation as is provided for in its current schedule of fees effective from time to time. Unless the

Grantor otherwise directs, such compensation shall be charged against the income of each trust except for compensation on principal distributions which shall be charged entirely against the principal. Any individual trustee shall serve without compensation from the trust.

7.3   Upon the written request of Grantor's wife during her life, The Cincinnati Bank or any Trustee then acting hereunder shall resign as Trustee as of the date fixed in the request, which shall not be earlier than thirty (30) days after the date of the request, and any Trustee acting hereunder shall have the right to resign upon thirty (30) days' notice to the Grantor, if living, and if not, to all the beneficiaries then entitled to receive income who are legally competent and to the guardians or custodians of those who are not legally competent. Upon the resignation of any Trustee, voluntarily or involuntarily, the Trustee shall turn over the assets and administration of the trusts then held hereunder to such individual or to such bank or trust company authorized to do business under the laws of any state or under the National Bank Act of the United States as may be selected by the Grantor's wife, if living, or if not, by the trust beneficiaries or their guardians or custodians. Notwithstanding anything herein to the contrary, neither Grantor nor Grantor's wife shall be permitted to be sole Trustee under this Trust.

7.4   Any successor or substitute Trustee shall have each and every right, privilege, power, discretion, authority and duty of the original Trustee and shall be subject to the same responsibilities. Any successor Trustee shall qualify by executing a written instrument of acceptance of the trusteeship which shall be attached to any counterpart or copy of this Agreement. No bond shall be required of any Trustee for serving as such.

IN WITNESS WHEREOF, the Grantor and the Trustee have executed duplicates hereof, each of which shall be deemed an original, as of the day and year first above written.

____

Robert W. Buechner

_____________   _______________

____

As to Robert W. Buechner

TRUSTEE:

____

The Cincinnati Bank

____

____

As to the Cincinnati Bank

STATE OF OHIO, COUNTY OF HAMILTON: SS:

Before me, the undersigned, a Notary Public in and for the said county and state, personally appeared Robert W. Buechner, who executed the foregoing Agreement as the Grantor and acknowledged the signing thereof to be his free and voluntary act for the uses and purposes therein contained.

IN TESTIMONY WHEREOF, I have hereunto subscribed my name and affixed my seal this _________ day of _________________, 1982.

____
Notary Public

STATE OF OHIO, COUNTY OF HAMILTON: SS:

Before me, the undersigned, a Notary Public in and for the said county and state, personally appeared The Cincinnati Bank, who executed the foregoing Agreement as the Trustee and acknowledged the signing thereof to be his free and voluntary act for the uses and purposes therein contained.

IN TESTIMONY WHEREOF, I have hereunto subscribed my name and affixed my seal this _________ day of _________________, 1982.

____
Notary Public

Schedule A
Super Irrevocable Trust Agreement
Robert W. Buechner
Ten Dollars ($10.00)

Sample Profit Sharing Plan

XYZ Company, Inc.
Profit Sharing Plan

This agreement is made in Cincinnati, Ohio, effective the first day of August 1982, by and between XYZ Company, Inc., an Ohio corporation ("Employer") and Mr. Owner and Mrs. Owner ("Trustees").

WHEREAS, the Board of Directors of the Employer have authorized and directed the establishment of this Plan for the benefit of eligible employees of the Employer effective August 1, 1982; and

WHEREAS, this Plan is and has been designated by the Employer as a Plan intended to qualify under Sections 401 and 501 of the Internal Revenue Code of 1954, as amended, and to conform to the provisions of the Employee Retirement Income Security Act of 1974, as amended;

NOW, THEREFORE, in consideration of the premises and of the provisions hereinafter contained, it is agreed as follows: the XYZ Company, Inc., Profit Sharing Plan is hereby adopted effective as of August 1, 1982, as follows:

SECTION 1
Definitions

As used in this Plan, the following terms shall have the meaning hereinafter set forth, unless the context shall require otherwise.

Persons and Entities

1.01   "Trust" shall mean this Agreement, dated _________________, 1982.

1.02   "Trustee" or "Trustees" shall mean Mr. Owner and Mrs. Owner, appointed under this Trust and any successor trustee or trustees under this Trust.

1.03   "Trust Year" shall mean the twelve-month period ending the same day as the corporation's fiscal year.

1.04   "Employer" shall mean XYZ Company, Inc. (an Ohio corporation), and any successor of such Employer as provided in Section 12.03.

1.05   "Employee" shall mean a person who is currently employed by the Employer but shall not include any employee who is a member of a collective bargaining unit which has negotiated in good faith with Employer for retirement benefits.

1.06   "Participant" shall mean each Employee who has met the requirements for participation provided in Section 3.01.

1.07   "Beneficiary" shall mean one or more persons designated by a Participant to receive benefits from this Trust upon the death of such Participant.

1.08 "Committee" shall mean the Administrative Committee appointed by the Employer as provided in Section 10.

1.09 "Investment Manager" shall mean any fiduciary (other than the Trustee or the Employer) who has the power to manage, acquire, or dispose of any asset of this Trust; who is (a) registered as an investment adviser under the Investment Advisors Act of 1940; (b) is a Bank, as defined in that Act; (3) or is an insurance company qualified to manage, acquire, or dispose of assets of qualified retirement Trusts in more than one state; and who has acknowledged in writing that it is a fiduciary with respect to this Trust.

Insurance Terms

1.10 "Insurer" shall mean any life insurance company duly qualified to do business in the State of Ohio.

1.11 "Policy" shall mean an ordinary life insurance contract issued by an Insurer.

1.12 "Qualified Joint and Survivor Annuity" shall mean an annuity for the life of a Participant with a survivor annuity for the life of his spouse which is equal to 50% of the annuity payable during the joint lives of the Participant and his spouse, and which is the actuarial equivalent of a single life annuity for the life of the Participant.

Benefits

1.13 "Accrued Benefit" shall mean the balance of each Participant's account which represents Employer contributions allocated to such account as provided in Section 5. A Participant's right to his Accrued Benefit shall be nonforfeitable upon and after the attainment of age 65 ("Normal Retirement Age").

Compensation

1.14 "Compensation" shall mean the basic or regular rate of nondeferred remuneration paid or accrued to a Participant during any Trust Year, including overtime pay, bonuses, and commissions.

Service

1.15 "Years of Service" or "Year of Service" shall mean the twelve-consecutive-month period commencing on the date of hire of an Employee (or on the date of rehire of an Employee who terminated his employment prior to becoming a Participant), if he has completed at least 1000 Hours of Service during such twelve-month period, and any other succeeding twelve-month period beginning on the anniversary of a Participant's date of hire in which he completes at least 1000 Hours of Service. For a reemployed Employee who has incurred or will incur a Break in Service, the computation period for Years of Service shall begin on the day that the Employee first completes an Hour of Service after reemployment. "Date of hire" as used herein shall mean the first day that an Employee completes an Hour of Service.

1.16   An Hour of Service shall mean:

(1) each hour for which an Employee is paid, or entitled to payment, for the performance of duties for the Employer during the applicable computation period.

(2) each hour for which an Employee is paid, or entitled to payment, by the Employer on account of a period of time during which no duties are performed (irrespective of whether the employment relationship has terminated) due to vacation, holiday, illness, incapacity (including disability), layoff, jury duty, military duty or leave of absence. Notwithstanding the preceding sentence, (a) no more than 501 Hours of Service are required to be credited under this paragraph (2) to an Employee on account of any single continuous period during which the Employee performs no duties (whether or not such period occurs in a single computation period); (b) an hour for which an Employee is directly or indirectly paid, or entitled to payment, on account of a period during which no duties are performed is not required to be credited to the Employee if such payment is made or due under a plan maintained solely for the purpose of complying with applicable workmen's compensation, or unemployment compensation or disability insurance laws; and (c) Hours of Service are not required to be credited for a payment which solely reimburses an Employee for medical or medically related expenses incurred by the Employee. Calculation of Hours of Service for all Employees under this paragraph shall be made pursuant to Labor Regs. §2530. 200b-2(b) and (c) which are incorporated herein by reference.

For purposes of this paragraph (2), a payment shall be deemed to be made by or due from the Employer regardless of whether such payment is made by or due from the Employer directly, or indirectly through, among others, a trust fund or insurer, to which the Employer contributes or pays premiums and regardless of whether contributions made or due to the trust fund, insurer or other entity are for the benefit of particular Employees or are on behalf of a group of Employees in the aggregate.

(3) each hour for which back pay, irrespective of mitigation of damages, is either awarded or agreed to by the Employer. The same Hours of Service shall not be credited both under paragraph (1) or paragraph (2), as the case may be, and under this paragraph (3). The hours shall be credited to the Employee for the computation period or periods to which the award or agreement pertains, rather than the computation period in which the award, agreement or payment is made.

Each full-time Employee will be credited with 45 Hours of Service for each week for which the Employee would be required to be credited with at least one Hour of Service. Each part-time Employee will have his or her Hours of Service calculated pursuant to Labor Regs. §2530. 200b-2(a), which is set forth herein.

1.17   "Break in Service" shall mean any twelve-month period described in Section 1.15 herein during which an employee does not complete more than 500 Hours of Service. "Pre-Break Service" shall mean Years of Service prior to a Break in Service. "Post-Break Service" shall mean Years of Service after a Break in Service.

Dates

1.18 "Effective date" shall mean August 1, 1982.

1.19 "Entry date" shall mean August 1, 1982, and each August 1 thereafter.

1.20 "Normal Retirement Date" shall mean the end of the Trust Year coincident with or immediately following attainment of age 65.

1.21 "Age" shall mean actual chronological age.

Statutes

1.22 "IRC" shall mean Internal Revenue Code. "IRS" shall mean Internal Revenue Service.

1.23 "ERISA" shall mean the Employee Retirement Income Security Act of 1974.

Limitations on Benefits

1.24 "Defined Contribution Fraction" shall mean a fraction, the numerator of which is the total, for all years of employment with Employer of the forfeitures and annual contributions (including the lesser of one-half of Employee voluntary contributions or Employee voluntary contributions in excess of 6% of Compensation) allocated to the account of a Participant in Employer's defined contribution plans and the denominator of which is the sum, for each year of employment with Employer, of the lesser of $45,475 (or such other amount determined by the IRS based upon increases for the cost of living, pursuant to IRC 415(d), or 25% of such Participant's compensation.

1.25 "Defined Benefit Fraction" shall mean a fraction, the numerator of which is the projected annual retirement benefit of a Participant as of the close of any Trust Year payable from the Employer's Pension Plan (assuming Compensation as defined in such plan to continue until retirement at the then current level), if any, and the denominator of which is the lesser of $136,425 (or such higher amount determined by the IRS, based upon increases in the cost of living, pursuant to IRC 415 (d), or 100% of such Participant's average Compensation for the highest 3 consecutive Trust Years during which he or she is a Participant.

SECTION 2

Preliminary Matters

2.01 *Exclusive Benefit of Employees.* This Trust is created for the exclusive benefit of Employees of the Employer and their beneficiaries, and, except as set forth in Section 2.02, 2.03, or 2.04, no part of the corpus or income of this Trust shall be used for or diverted to the Employer. This Trust shall be interpreted and administered in a manner consistent with the requirements of the IRC and ERISA.

Wherever in this Trust discretionary powers are given to any person, or wherever any interpretation may be necessary, such powers shall be exercised and such interpretation shall be made in a nondiscriminatory manner with uniform and consistent application to all Employees similarly situated.

2.02 *Failure of Qualification.* The Employer shall cause this Trust as amended to be submitted to the IRS for a determination of its status as a qualified pension plan and trust, and until a favorable determination shall have been received by the Employer from the IRS, no Participant shall have any vested interest in any asset of this Trust attributable to Employer contributions. If the IRS shall determine that this Trust does not qualify for the first Trust Year, the Employer shall promptly so notify the Trustee in writing. Upon receipt of such notice from the Employer, the Trustee shall return all contributions made by the Employer.

In the event that the IRS shall determine that the Trust does qualify for the first Trust Year, this Section shall be inoperative and of no effect, except that any Participant who shall have terminated his employment, died, or become disabled prior to such determination, or any Beneficiary, shall be entitled to receive any benefits to which he would have been otherwise entitled under this Trust.

2.03 *Mistake of Fact.* Employer contributions made upon the basis of a mistaken factual assumption shall be repaid by the Trustee to the Employer upon receipt by the Trustee, within one year from the date of such contributions, of a certificate signed by two members of the Committee and stating such mistaken factual assumption and requesting the return of such contributions.

2.04 *Disallowance of Deductions.* Employer contributions determined by the IRS or by final judgment of a court of competent jurisdiction not to be deductible expenses under Section 404 of the IRC shall be repaid by the Trustee to the Employer upon receipt by the Trustee of evidence satisfactory to it of such IRS determination or final judgment within one year from the date of such IRS determination or final judgment, as the case may be.

2.05 *Governing State.* This trust shall be governed by the laws of the State of Ohio.

SECTION 3

Eligibility and Participation

3.01 *Eligibility Requirements.* Any Employee shall be eligible to participate on the Entry Date which coincides with or immediately precedes completion of one Year of Service and attainment of at least Age twenty-five. No Employee who terminates employment for any reason other than death or disability shall be eligible to receive an allocation of a contribution to his or her account unless such Employee is employed on the last day of the Trust year for which such contribution is made.

3.02 *Determination of Eligibility.* The decision of the Employer shall be final as to the eligibility of employees for participation in this Trust.

3.03 *Notice to Employees.* The Employer shall notify its Employees of the establishment of this profit-sharing plan and shall deliver a summary plan description describing this Trust to each Employee within ninety days of the qualification of this Trust by the IRS.

3.04 *Reentry of Terminated Participant.* If a former Participant whose employment shall have terminated shall be rehired as an Employee, he shall become a Participant on the Entry Date which coincides with or immediately precedes the date of his reemployment.

3.05 *Leave of Absence.* A leave of absence, not in excess of two years, granted as such by the Employer for reasons of maternity, illness, injury, disability, or educational purposes, shall not constitute a termination under Section 6.03 provided that the Employee shall return to the service of the Employer within thirty days after the expiration of such leave.

The account of a Participant who is on such leave of absence shall share in the allocation of income, expense and investment appreciation and depreciation as provided in Sections 4 and 5 and shall share in the allocation of contributions to the extent that the Participant receives Compensation from the Employer in any Trust Year.

SECTION 4
Contributions

4.01 *Employer Contributions.* The Employer shall determine, by resolution adopted on or before the last day of each Trust Year, the amount out of current and accumulated profits to be contributed to this Trust, not to be less than 1% or more than 15% of the Compensation paid or otherwise accrued during such Trust Year to all Participants, plus any amount available as a credit carryover from a prior Trust Year in which less than the maximum allowable amount was contributed, with the total Employer contribution, including credit carryovers from prior Trust Years, not to exceed 25% of the Compensation paid or otherwise accrued during such Trust Year to Participants.

4.02 *Form of Contributions.* The Employer's contribution shall be paid to the Trustee in cash.

4.03 *Time of Employer Contribution.* The Employer shall make its contributions for each Trust Year to the Trustee on any date or dates which the Employer may select, provided that the total contributions for each Trust Year shall be paid within the time prescribed by Section 404 of the IRC, as amended.

4.04 *Participant Contributions.* Participants are not required to contribute to this Trust.

4.05 *Voluntary Participant Contributions.* Each Participant may contribute to this Trust in each Trust Year any amount not exceeding 10% of his Compensatio₁ Such voluntary contributions shall be maintained in a separate account for the Participant (hereinafter called Voluntary Contribution Account) and a Participant's rights in his or her Voluntary Contribution Account shall be nonforfeitable at all times.

A Participant's contributions shall be transmitted to the Trustee of the Fund by the Employer within 60 days after the date on which the contribution was made. A Participant's contributions may be withdrawn by the Participant upon 30 days written notice to the Trustees.

SECTION 5
Allocation and Valuation

5.01 *Accounts.* The Trustee shall maintain a separate account for each Participant to which the Employer shall instruct the Trustee to credit or debit all appropriate amounts, including investment appreciation and depreciation, income, expenses, contributions, forfeitures, and distributions. The Employer and the Trustee shall keep records which shall indicate the account balance of each Participant.

5.02 *Allocation of Contributions.* The Employer's contribution for each Trust Year shall be allocated in the following manner: first, the Employer's contribution shall be allocated to the account of each Participant according to the ratio of the compensation of a Participant in excess of $16,000.00 to the compensation of all Participants in excess of $16,000.00 up to 7% of a Participant's compensation in excess of $16,000.00. Second, the Employer's contribution shall be allocated to the account of each Participant according to the ratio that such Participant's Compensation bears to the Compensation of all Participants for each Trust Year.

5.03 *Application of Forfeitures.* Amounts forfeited for each Trust Year shall be allocated to the accounts of Participants in the same manner as Employer contributions.

5.04 *Limitation on Contributions.* In no event shall annual contributions to a Participant's account in the Trust cause the Defined Contribution Fraction to exceed 1.0 or cause the Defined Contribution Fraction plus the Defined Benefit Fraction to exceed 1.4. In such event, the amount consisting of Employer contributions and forfeitures to the account of such Participant shall be allocated and reallocated to other Participant's accounts in accordance with the plan formula for allocating Employer contributions and forfeitures to the extent that such allocations do not cause the additions to any other Participant's account to exceed the lesser of the maximum amount. If after making the reallocation provided by the preceding sentence, there is any amount remaining which cannot be reallocated because of the limitations on annual additions, such amount shall be allocated to a suspense account as forfeitures and held therein until the next succeeding day on which forfeitures could be applied under this Trust. Notwithstanding any other provisions in this Section, the Employer shall not knowingly contribute any amount that would cause an allocation to the suspense account as of the date the contribution is allocated. If the contribution is made prior to the date as of which it is to be allocated, such contributions shall not exceed an amount that would cause an allocation to the suspense account if the date of contribution were an allocation date.

5.05 *Annual Valuation.* The Trustee, as of the last business day of the Trust Year, and at such other times as the Employer may direct, and prior to the allocation of contributions and forfeitures as provided in this Section, shall determine the fair market value of the Trust assets and the amount of income and expenses for such Trust Year and shall report such fair market value, income, and expenses to the Employer in writing. The resulting investment appreciation or depreciation, income, and expenses of the Trust fund shall then be debited or credited to each Participant's account in the same ratio as each account bears to the aggregate of all such accounts. After allocation of such credits or debits to each account, contributions and distributions, if appropriate, shall be allocated to each account as set forth in this Section.

SECTION 6
Benefits

6.01 *Retirement Benefit.* Each Participant who shall retire at his Normal Retirement Date shall be entitled to a benefit equal to his or her Accrued Benefit and his or her Voluntary Contribution Account, if any, as of his or her Normal Retirement Date.

6.02 *Deferred Retirement.* If a Participant shall continue in active employment following his or her Normal Retirement Date, he or she shall continue to participate in this Trust. Upon his or her actual retirement, such Participant shall be entitled to his or her Accrued Benefit and his or her Voluntary Contribution Account, if any, as of the last business day of the Trust Year coincident with or next following his or her actual retirement date.

6.03 *Cash Out Termination Benefit.* Upon termination of a Participant's employment prior to his or her Normal Retirement Date, such Participant shall, at the discretion of the Committee, be entitled to a cash out termination benefit equal to the nonforfeitable portion of his or her Accrued Benefit as of the last business day of the Trust Year coincident with or prior to the date of such termination. In the event that such cash out termination benefit equals the Accrued Benefit of such Participant, or in the event that such cash out termination benefit is less than the Accrued Benefit of such Participant but equals or is less than $1,750, or in the event that such cash out termination benefit is less than the Accrued Benefit of such Participant but is more than $1,750 and such Participant consents in writing to receive such cash out termination benefit, then, in the Committee's sole discretion, such cash out termination benefit plus the Participant's Voluntary Contribution Account, if any, shall be paid to such Participant as provided in Section 6.09, subject to the right of repayment as provided in Section 7.04. In the event the Committee does not permit the cash out payment or in the event that such termination benefit is more than $1,750 and the Participant entitled to receive such termination benefit refuses to consent in writing to receive such cash out termination benefit, then the Accrued Benefit and his or her Voluntary Contribution Account, if any, of such Participant shall be retained in this Trust for the benefit of such Participant and shall be paid to such Participant (or his beneficiary or personal representative) as a death benefit at the death of such Participant or a retirement benefit on the date which would have been such Participant's Normal Retirement Date had he or she continued to be employed by the Employer. Any determination made hereunder by the Committee shall be made in a manner that does not discriminate in favor of highly compensated employees, shareholders or officers.

6.04 *Disability Benefit.* A Participant whose employment shall be terminated prior to Normal Retirement Date as a result of a medically determinable physical or mental impairment which may be expected to result in death or to be of long duration and which renders him or her incapable of performing his or her normal duties for the Employer, all in the opinion of a doctor selected by the Committee, shall be entitled to a cash benefit equal to his or her Accrued Benefit and his or her Voluntary Contribution Account, if any, as of the last business day of the Trust Year coincident with or next following the date of such termination.

6.05 *Death Benefit.* Upon the death of a Participant, his or her designated beneficiary or his or her estate, as the case may be, shall be entitled to a death cash benefit equal to his or her Accrued Benefit and his or her Voluntary Contribution Account, if any, as of the last business day of the Trust Year coincident with or next following the date of his or her death. The Committee, upon consultation with the Beneficiary, if any, shall direct the Trustee as to the form of any payment hereunder.

6.06 *Designation of Beneficiary.* Each Participant shall designate his or her primary Beneficiary on a form provided by the Employer and such designation may include contingent Beneficiaries. The designation may be changed at any time by filing a new form, and the most recent designation shall govern. In the absence of an effective written designation, the estate of the Participant shall be deemed to be the designated Beneficiary. The Trustee shall name itself beneficiary of all Policies.

6.07 *Benefit Options.* The Committee shall direct the Trustee to make payment of any benefit provided under this Section 6, subject to the forfeitures provided in Section 7. Any benefit paid under this Section 6 shall be distributed by the Trustee in cash or in kind in such manner subject to Section 6.08 as the Committee shall determine in its sole discretion to be in the best interest of the Participant or his or her beneficiary or personal representative, after consultation with the same, in accordance with one or more of the following methods or in any combination thereof:

a. *Qualified Joint and Survivor Annuity.* By the purchase and delivery to the Participant of a Qualified Joint and Survivor Annuity.

b. *Annuity.* By the purchase and delivery to the Participant of an individual annuity contract or of an annuity of any type or form available.

c. *Lump Sum.* In a lump sum or single payment of cash or property.

d. *Equal Installments with Interest.* In substantially equal annual, semi-annual, quarterly or monthly installments of principal, plus accrued interest at a rate of not less than that paid by the bank selected by the Trustees upon regular passbook savings accounts, over a certain period.

e. *Installments from the Trust Fund.* In annual, semi-annual, quarterly or monthly fixed amounts payable from the account of the Participant which account shall continue to share proportionately in income, expense, appreciation and depreciation of the Trust assets as provided in Section 5.01 hereof, but such Participant (or his or her Beneficiary or personal representative) shall not share in any Employer contributions to the Trust (including forfeitures) made with respect to Trust Years after the Trust Year of such Participant's termination of employment for any reason.

6.08 *Discretion of Committee.* In exercising its discretion in determining the method of payment, the Committee may consider the preference of the Participant (or his or her Beneficiary or personal representative) reported to the Committee in writing on or before such Participant's actual date of termination of employment. Notwithstanding any settlement options contained in this Trust, the benefits payable to the Beneficiary of any Participant must be incidental to the primary purpose of distributing accumulated funds to the Participant, and if the Participant's designated Beneficiary or survivor is other than such Participant's spouse, the present value of the benefits payable to the Beneficiary or the Survivor shall not exceed 49% of the present value of the benefits payable to the Participant and his Beneficiary or Survivor. Notwithstanding anything to the contrary herein, in the event a Participant is married for a one (1) year period preceding any of the following described events and (a) begins to receive payments under the Trust on or after Normal Retirement Age, (b) dies on or after Normal Retirement Age while still in the employ of the Employer, or (c) separates from service on or after attaining Normal Retirement Age and after satisfying the eligibility requirements for payment of benefits under the Trust and thereafter dies before beginning to receive such benefits, then the pension benefit or death benefit, as the case may be, payable to such Participant shall be in the form having the effect of a Qualified Joint and Survivor Annuity with such Participant's eligible spouse, unless such Participant has elected in writing before his annuity starting date (after having received a written explanation of the terms and conditions of the Qualified Joint and Survivor Annuity with his or her eligible spouse and the effect of an election not to take such annuity) not to take such Qualified Joint and Survivor Annuity with his or her eligible spouse.

The written explanation referred to in this section shall be furnished by the Committee not less than nine months before the Participant attains Normal Retirement Age, at which time the Committee shall also furnish the Participant with a retirement application form which shall describe in plain language the terms and conditions of the forms of benefits available under this Trust and which shall provide for the Participant to indicate his retirement date, selection of benefit form and his beneficiary or contingent annuitant.

The completed retirement application form should be returned to the Committee no later than ninety (90) days prior to the Participant's benefit commencement date. If a subsequent retirement application form is filed after the first form and prior to the applicable benefit commencement date, any previous forms shall be deemed annulled. No election under this section or any other section of the Trust shall become effective until it has been received in writing by the Committee.

6.09 *Payment of Benefits.* Payment of benefits hereunder shall commence within sixty days after Normal Retirement Date, or within sixty days after the last business day of the Trust Year next following the date of death, disability, actual deferred retirement or termination of employment, as the case may be;

however, in no event shall cash out termination benefits be paid later than one year after termination of employment. At the request of a disabled Participant, or the Beneficiary or estate of a deceased Participant, or a retired Participant who submits evidence of financial hardship (such as extraordinary financial demands on account of catastrophic losses, severe illness or injury) to the Committee, the Committee, in the Committee's sole discretion, may advance the date when benefits hereunder are otherwise payable.

SECTION 7
Nonforfeitable Accrued Benefits

7.01 *Nonforfeitable Accrued Benefit.* If a Participant's employment with the Employer is terminated for any reason except Disability, Death, Retirement at Normal Retirement Date, or Deferred Retirement under this Trust, his service for such period of employment shall cease and he shall retain the right to receive the nonforfeitable portion of his Accrued Benefit. The nonforfeitable portion of his Accrued Benefit shall be equal to a percentage of his Accrued Benefit, determined as follows:

10% per Year of Service

7.02 *Forfeiture.* The nonforfeitable portion of the Accrued Benefit of a Participant shall not be forfeited for cause. At the last business day of the Trust Year during which a Participant's right to repay a cash out termination benefit expires as provided in Section 7.04 or during which a Break in Service occurs, the value of any forfeitable Accrued Benefit of a Participant shall be forfeited and applied in a manner consistent with Section 5.03.

7.03 *Leave of Absence.* A leave of absence as set forth in Section 3.05 shall not be construed as a termination of employment, provided that a Participant on such leave shall return to employment within the time prescribed. If a Participant shall not so return, he shall be deemed to have terminated his employment on the date which is the later of (1) the effective date of the beginning of his leave of absence and (2) ten months prior to the effective date of the termination of his leave of absence.

7.04 *Accrued Benefit after Reemployment.* In the event that a cash out termination benefit is paid as provided in Section 6.03 and in the event of the reemployment of such Participant prior to a Break in Service, then such Participant, upon becoming a Participant after reemployment as provided in Section 3.04, may repay the amount of such cash out termination benefit to the Trustee and upon such repayment prior to a Break in Service or within two years after the date of reemployment if there is no Break in Service such Participant shall be fully reinstated as a Participant in this Trust as if he or she had not terminated his or her employment and retain all rights to Accrued Benefits prior to the termination of his or her employment. In the event of a Break in Service prior to reemployment of such Participant, then such Participant, upon reemployment, may become a Participant as provided in Section 3.04, but shall not have the right to repay such termination benefit and retained Accrued Benefits prior to the termination of employment.

7.05 *Service after Break in Service.* If a Participant incurs a Break in Service, he shall not receive credit for Post-Break Service with respect to his Accrued Benefit prior to the Break in Service. In such a case, separate accounts will be established for the Accrued Benefit prior to and after the Break in Service.

A Participant who was partially vested under Section 7.01 prior to a Break in Service shall receive credit for Pre-Break Service and Post-Break Service with respect to the Accrued Benefit after the Break in Service if he completes one Year of Service after the Break in Service.

A Participant who was not partially vested under Section 7.01 prior to a Break in Service shall not receive credit for Pre-Break Service with respect to the Accrued Benefit after the Break in Service unless the number of Years of Service prior to the Break in Service is more than the number of consecutive Breaks in Service, in which case the Participant will receive credit for Pre-Break Service and Post-Break Service with respect to the Accrued Benefit after the Break in Service.

SECTION 8

Investments

8.01 *Trust Fund.* The Trustee shall receive contributions and hold them subject to this Trust and shall invest the same as set forth in this Section 8 for the purpose of accumulating values to provide benefits to Participants.

8.02 *Investment of Accounts in Policies.* At the written request of a Participant, the Committee may, in the Committee's sole discretion, under rules uniformly and consistently applicable to all employees similarly situated, instruct the Trustee to purchase a policy or policies upon the life of such Participant, subject to the following:

a. Each policy shall provide for level premiums (which shall be a charge against the account), shall be issued on the life of the Participant whose account is so invested, and shall be dated as of an Entry Date.

b. Each Policy shall be owned by the Trustee and the Trustee shall name itself beneficiary to carry out the provisions of the Trust.

c. Investment in Policies shall be so limited that at all times the aggregate of premiums paid for Policies shall be less than one-half of the Employer contributions and forfeitures allocated to any account.

d. Dividends declared upon a Policy may be applied in any manner permitted by the Insurer including to purchase additional insurance and shall increase the account of the Participant on whose life the Policy is issued.

e. The Trustee shall pay Policy premiums as due. If a Policy premium cannot be paid from a Participant's account without violating the prohibitions of subsection c. hereof, the Trustee, before taking other appropriate action, shall afford the Participant an opportunity to purchase the Policy from the Trustee for its cash value. If the Participant shall purchase the Policy, the Trustee shall transfer such Policy to the Participant and shall add the purchase price to his account.

8.03 *Investment of Trust Funds.* In the investment, reinvestment and management of the Trust funds, the Trustee shall follow the written instructions of the Committee to the extent that they are not inconsistent with the IRC and ERISA. In following such instructions from the Committee, the Trustee shall be vested with all such rights, powers and privileges as might be lawfully exercised by any person owning similar property in his own right. Without limitation of this general grant of power, the Trustee is hereby specifically authorized and empowered:

a. To invest and reinvest in securities, real or personal property, and in common or combined trust funds maintained by any bank or trust company established pursuant to the laws of the State of Ohio or the United States.

b. To hold securities in bearer form, or in the name of the Trustee or of a nominee without indication of any fiduciary capacity, but the records of the Trustee shall at all times show that all such investments are part of the Trust fund.

c. To sell, lease, mortgage, or exchange any or all trust property, to loan money to any person, excluding the Company, and including employees of the Company and Participants in this Trust to the extent of their Accrued Benefits, upon the giving of adequate security therefor; to borrow money from any person or firm; and to make contracts concerning real or personal property, all for such consideration and upon such terms as may be considered advisable.

d. To give proxies or powers of attorney for voting or acting with respect to securities; to deposit shares or securities with, or transfer them to, protective committees or similar bodies; to join in any reorganization and to pay assessments or subscriptions called for in connection with securities held by the Trustee.

e. To compromise claims in favor of or against the Trust upon such terms as the Trustee shall deem advisable.

f. To purchase annuity contracts or life insurance policies payable to the Trust or otherwise, or to enter into group annuity contracts or contracts with the Insurer to provide all or any part of the benefits payable under this Trust.

g. To purchase life insurance whether term or whole life as a general investment of the Trust on the life of any key employee.

SECTION 9
The Trustee

9.01 *Powers.* The Trustee shall have all powers necessary for the performance of its duties under this Trust.

9.02 *Receipt of Contributions.* The Trustee shall not be responsible for the collection of Employer contributions provided for in this Trust. The Trustee shall accept and hold in Trust such contributions of money, as it may receive from time to time from the Employer, other than cash it is instructed to remit to the Insurer in payment of premiums on Policies. All such contributions shall be accomplished by written instructions from the Employer accounting for the manner in which they are to be paid or credited, the amount of each such credit that is an Employer contribution and the amount, if any, that is a Participant's contribution.

9.03 *Distributions.* On receipt of a written instruction from the Employer certifying that a Participant's benefits are payable pursuant to this Trust, the Trustee shall take such action as may be necessary to make distribution in such form and at such time as the instruction for payment so directs. However, before making any such distribution in the event of a Participant's death, the Trustee shall be furnished with any and all certificates, tax waivers and other documents which may be requested in its discretion.

9.04 *Records and Accounting.* The Trustee shall keep accurate and detailed records of all receipts, investments, disbursements and other transactions required under this Trust. Not later than sixty days after the close of each Trust Year, (or after the Trustee's resignation as provided in Section 9.09), the Trustee shall file with the Employer a written report or reports which shall indicate the receipts, disbursements, investments and other transactions effected by it during such Trust Year (or period ending with such resignation), and the assets and liabilities of the Trust at the close of such Trust Year.

9.05 *Returns and Reports.* The Employer shall furnish to the Trustee, and the Trustee shall furnish to the Employer, such information relevant to this Trust as may be required under the IRC and ERISA.

The Employer shall fulfill any obligations imposed on the Employer or the Trustee, or both, by the IRC and ERISA. Each Participant shall be given any reports required by the IRC and ERISA. To the extent that the Trustee must assume any such obligations, it may charge a reasonable fee for the service apart from its normal fee and its expenses as provided in Section 9.08.

9.06 *Appointment of Agents; Reliance on Advice.* The Trustee may retain or consult counsel, including an investment adviser, which may be the counsel to the Employer, to the Trustee, or to the Insurer, with respect to the meaning or construction of terms of this Trust, or with respect to its obligations or duties thereunder, or with respect to any claim, action, proceeding or question of law. The Trustee may engage agents to assist it in carrying out the provisions of this Trust. The Trustee may appoint the Insurer as its agent for the purposes of holding Policies and for other purposes which may be agreed upon.

9.07 *Liability of the Trustee; Reliance on Instructions.* The Trustee shall not be responsible for the purpose or propriety of any distribution made pursuant to Section 9.03 or any action or nonaction taken pursuant to the written instructions of the Employer including investment directions, as long as these instructions are made in accordance with the terms of this Trust and are not contrary to ERISA.

Communications to the Trustee shall be addressed to it at such address as the Trustee may specify in writing to the Employer from time to time. No communication shall be binding upon the Trustee until it is received by the Trustee in writing. Communications to the Employer shall be sent to such address as shall have been last sent to the Trustee in a writing which shall specifically indicate a change of address.

9.08   *Fees, Taxes and Expenses.*

a. *Fees.* The Trustee in consideration of its services under the trust shall receive reasonable compensation as the Employer agrees to pay to the Trustee; nevertheless no compensation shall be paid from this Trust to any Trustee who is an Employee. The Trustee may change such compensation at any time upon 30 days' written notice to the Employer, or may agree to waive fees.

b. *Taxes.* Any income, gift, estate and inheritance taxes and other taxes of any kind whatsoever, including transfer taxes incurred in connection with the investment, reinvestment or distribution of the assets of this Trust, that may be levied or assessed in respect to such assets or the income thereon shall, if allocable to the account or interest of specific Participants, be charged to such accounts or interests, and if not so allocable they shall be charged proportionately to the accounts or interests of all Participants, or to the Employer, as the circumstances shall require.

c. *Expenses.* All other administrative expenses incurred by the Trustee in the performance of its duties, including fees for legal services rendered to the Trustee, shall be paid by the Employer within thirty days after a statement of such expenses is rendered by the Trustee to the Employer.

d. *Collection.* All fees of the Trustee and taxes and other administrative expenses charged to this Trust shall, at the Trustee's option, be paid by the Employer to the Trustee with the amount of the first contribution for each Trust Year which is to be credited to the Trust, or by sale or liquidation of the assets credited to the Trust if no contribution is made thereto in that Year; and if the assets of the Trust are insufficient to satisfy such charges, the Employer shall pay any deficit therein to the Trustee.

9.09   *Resignation and Appointment.* The Trustee may resign at any time upon thirty days' written notice to the Employer or, if so requested in writing by the Employer, shall resign within thirty days following receipt of such request. Upon resignation by the Trustee, the Employer shall appoint a successor Trustee or Trustees. Upon receipt by the Trustee of written acceptance of such appointment of a successor Trustee(s), the Trustee shall convey, assign and deliver to such successor Trustee(s) the assets of the Trust, together with all records pertaining thereto. The Trustee is authorized, however, to reserve such assets as it may deem advisable for payment of all fees, compensation, costs and expenses, or for payment of any other liabilities constituting a charge on or against the assets of this Trust or on or against the Trustee, with any balance remaining after the payment of all such items to be paid over to the successor Trustee(s). The successor Trustee(s) shall have all right, title and interest in the assets paid over to it (them), and all power, rights and duties vested in the Trustee shall vest in such successor Trustee(s) immediately upon its (their) appointment and acceptance, and thereupon all further duties and liabilities of the Trustee who has been succeeded shall terminate except for an accounting as may be required.

9.10   *Trustee's Duty of Care.* The Trustee shall discharge its duties hereunder with the care, skill, prudence and diligence under the circumstances then prevailing that a prudent man acting in a like capacity and familiar with such matters would use in the conduct of an enterprise of a like character and with like aims, and shall diversify the investments under this Trust so as to minimize the risk of large losses, unless under the circumstances it is clearly prudent not to do so. The Trustee shall comply with any funding policy established in writing by the Employer, but the Trustee shall be solely responsible (except in the event an outside Investment Manager is appointed by the Committee or by the Trustee under Section 9.06) for the selection and retention or disposal of the investments to comply with such funding policy. It is recognized that the Trustee does not guarantee the assets of the Trust from loss or depreciation and shall be liable only for failure to discharge its duties in accordance with this section.

9.11 *Investment in Certain Funds.* In addition to all powers and authorities hereunder and under common law and statutory authority, including the Employee Retirement Income Security Act of 1974, the Trustee is further authorized and empowered to transfer all or such part of the funds of the Trust as the Trustee may deem advisable to a group, common, collective, or pooled trust fund which has been or may hereafter be established and maintained by a banking association for employee benefit trust accounts, which fund may be amended from time to time. Such group, common, collective, or pooled trust fund shall be tax exempt under Revenue Ruling 56-267 and shall contemplate the commingling for investment purposes of such Trust assets with trust assets of other employee benefit trusts. Such part or all of the funds of the Trust so transferred shall be subject to all the terms and provisions of the group, common, collective, or pooled trust fund; and such terms and provisions are adopted as, incorporated as, and declared to be a part of this Trust so long as any portion of the funds of the Trust are invested in any such trust or pooled trust fund as the Trustee may deem advisable.

Without limiting the other provisions herein, the Trustee is further expressly authorized and empowered to invest and reinvest all or such part of the Trust Funds as the Trustee may deem advisable in a group, common, collective, or pooled trust which has been or may hereafter be established and maintained by a banking association hereunder but which is not tax exempt under Revenue Ruling 56-267.

9.12 *Multiple Trustees.* In the event there shall be more than one party acting as Trustee under the Trust, the following shall apply:

a. If there shall be more than two Trustees, an odd number of Trustees shall be appointed and the decision of a majority shall control in discretionary matters.

b. The signature of only one Trustee shall be required for any action regarding a Policy.

c. No Trustee shall be liable, responsible or accountable for any action or nonaction of any other Trustee relating to responsibilities specifically delegated to such other Trustee by this Trust.

d. The Trustees may designate any one or more of them to sign checks on behalf of the Trust.

9.13 *Loans from Trustee.* If authorized at any time or from time to time by the Board of Directors of Employer, notwithstanding the provisions for distribution hereinabove set forth in Section 6, the Administrative Committee may upon written application of the Participant in its sole discretion authorize a loan or loans to such Participant in a total amount not in excess of said Participant's nonforfeitable interest in his accrued benefit; provided, however, that such loans must be available to all Participants on a reasonable equivalent basis and in the same percentage of their vested interest and that all such loans must be evidenced by the borrowing Participant's promissory note for a fixed term bearing interest at a rate comparable to the rate being charged by institutional lenders in the area of the Employer's place of business for other loans of this type. Said loans shall require regular periodic repayments by payroll deductions or otherwise and may be secured by such Participant's vested interest as the Administrative Committee, in its sole discretion, may determine.

In addition, the Administrative Committee, in its sole discretion, may set up rules under which said loans may be made, including the requirement that the Participant show "hardship." "Hardship" may be defined by the Administrative Committee.

Notwithstanding anything to the contrary herein, if approved by the Board of Directors of Employer, under rules uniformly and consistently applied, the following shall apply to employee loans:

1. Any Participant may once during each Trust year borrow any or all of such Participant's account by putting up adequate collateral to the extent such borrowing exceeds the vested portion of such Participant's account. The determination of what collateral is adequate for the nonvested portion of a Participant's account shall be made by the Committee.
2. Such borrowing shall be made at an annual interest rate of 5% per annum and repayment shall be made on an installment basis with payments paid monthly and total payments to be made over a period of time not exceeding 36 months.
3. If a borrowing occurs under these special provisions, each Participant's account will be separated and only income attributable to the assets in each Participant's account will be credited to such account.
4. Upon the activation of these provisions of the Trust, a copy of these special provisions shall be given to each Participant.

SECTION 10

Administrative Committee

10.01 *Appointment of Committee.* The Employer shall be responsible as named fiduciary and as plan administrator as those terms are defined in ERISA for the administration and operation of this Trust. The Employer shall appoint a Committee of not less than two persons who shall be officers or other employees of the Employer or any other individuals. Members of the Committee shall serve at the pleasure of the Employer and vacancies in the Committee arising by reason of resignation, death, removal, or otherwise shall be filled by the Employer.

10.02 *Powers of Committee.* The Committee shall administer this Trust and direct the Trustee with respect to all matters related to the administration and operation of this Trust. The Committee shall make such rules and regulations as it may deem necessary to carry out the provisions of this Trust. The Committee may employ Investment Managers, attorneys, accountants, and such other persons as it may deem necessary or desirable in the administration and operation of this Trust. The Committee shall determine any question arising with respect to interpretation and application of this Trust, which determination shall be binding and conclusive on all persons, including, without limitation, questions which relate to employment, compensation, eligibility, forfeitures of Accrued Benefits, and payment of nonforfeitable Accrued Benefits. Annual contributions to this Trust shall be recommended to the Employer by the Committee. The Committee shall discharge its duties and powers in conformance with the care, skill, prudence and diligence under the circumstances then prevailing that a prudent man acting in a like capacity and familiar with such matters would use in the conduct of an enterprise of a like character and with like aims.

10.03 *Accounts and Reports.* The Committee shall maintain records and accounts showing the fiscal transactions of this Trust in accordance with the provisions of the IRC and ERISA.

The Committee shall prepare, distribute, and file with the Department of Labor and the IRS all reports required under the IRC and ERISA including, without limitation, the Annual Registration required by the IRC, and the Annual Report, Plan Description and Summary Plan Description required by ERISA.

The Committee shall provide Participants and Beneficiaries with all reports and information to which they are entitled under the IRC or ERISA, including, without limitation, a Summary Plan Description, Summary Annual Report, and statement of Accrued Benefits.

10.04 *Organization and Operation of Committee.* The Committee shall appoint a Chairman and a Secretary and such other officers as it may deem advisable. The Committee shall act by a majority of its members at the time in office and such action may be taken either by a vote at a meeting or in writing without a meeting. The Committee may by such majority action authorize any one or more of its members to execute any document or documents on behalf of the Committee.

10.05 *Expenses of the Committee.* Unless otherwise determined by the Employer, the members of the Committee shall serve without compensation for services as such but all expenses of the Committee shall be paid by the Employer. Such expenses shall include any expenses incident to the functioning of the Committee, including, but not limited to, salaries of employees, fees of investment counsel, attorneys' fees, accounting charges, and other costs of administering this Trust. In no event shall a member of the Committee who is an Employee receive compensation from the Trust.

10.06 *Indemnity.* The Employer shall indemnify and hold harmless each member of the Committee from any and all claims, loss, damages, expense (including counsel fees approved by the Committee), and liability (including any amounts paid in settlement with the Committee's approval) arising from any act or omission of such member, except when the same is judicially determined to be due to the gross negligence or willful misconduct of such member. No plan assets may be used for any such indemnification.

10.07 *Claims Procedure.* In the event of the denial of any claim by any participant or beneficiary for benefit under this Trust, the Committee or the insurance carrier shall provide adequate notice in writing to such participant or beneficiary setting forth the specific reasons for such denial, specific references to pertinent plan provisions, a description of additional material or information necessary for the claimant to perfect his claim, an explanation of why such material or information is needed, and an explanation of this Trust's review procedure. The obligation of the Committee or the insurance carrier under this paragraph shall be satisfied by sending such notice by US First Class Mail to the last known address of such participant or beneficiary. Such notice shall be written in a manner calculated to be understood by the participant or beneficiary. Each participant or beneficiary whose claim is denied shall be afforded a reasonable opportunity for a full and fair review of the decision to deny such claim by the Committee or the insurance carrier. Any participant or beneficiary for whom benefits have been denied may obtain a full and fair review of such denial by the Committee or the insurance carrier by delivering a request for such review in writing to the Trustee within sixty (60) days following receipt of notice of the denial. Any participant or beneficiary requesting a review of a denial of a claim shall have the right to be represented by counsel, to review pertinent documents relating to the denial, and to submit issues and comments in writing. Within sixty (60) days after receipt of such request for review, the committee or the insurance carrier shall review or reconsider the claim of such participant or beneficiary and shall give written notice to each participant or beneficiary of its decision. In the case of benefits provided through insurance coverage, the decision of the insurance carrier shall be final. In all other cases, the decision of the Committee shall be final.

SECTION 11
The Insurer

11.01 *Protection of the Insurer.* The Insurer shall not be responsible for the validity of this Trust and shall have no responsibility for action taken or not taken by the Employer, the Committee, or Trustee.

11.02 *Employer, Committee, and Trustee Not Responsible for Acts of Insurer.* The Employer, the Committee, and the Trustee shall not be responsible for any of the following, nor shall they be liable for instituting action in connection with same:

    a. The validity of Policies or Policy provisions;
    b. Failure or refusal by the Insurer to provide benefits under a Policy;
    c. An act by a person which may render a Policy invalid or unenforceable;
    d. Inability to perform or delay in performing an act, which inability or

delay is occasioned by a provision of a Policy or a restriction imposed by the Insurer.

11.03 *Reports.* The Insurer shall conform to such reporting or disclosure requirements as may be prescribed by Federal or State regulatory authority.

SECTION 12

Amendment and Termination

12.01 *Amendment of Trust.* The Employer reserves the power to amend this Trust. No amendment shall:

a. deprive any Participant, or a Beneficiary of a deceased Participant, or any nonforfeitable Accrued Benefit to which he is entitled under the Trust with respect to contributions previously made;
b. deprive the Insurer of any of its exemptions or immunities with respect to Policies which were issued by it prior to receipt at its Home Office of notice of such amendment; or
c. expand or increase the duties or liabilities of the Trustee without its consent;
d. deprive a Participant with at least five Years of Service of his right to elect to have his vested percentage computed for the future under the former vesting schedule if a new vesting schedule is adopted.

A copy of any such amendment shall be provided to the Trustee and to the Insurer by the Employer.

12.02 *Partial or Voluntary Termination of Trust.* Upon termination of this Trust with respect to a group of Participants which constitutes a partial termination, all accounts and interest attributable to such group of Participants shall become nonforfeitable. The Employer shall have the right to terminate the Trust at any time. Such termination shall be effected by an instrument in writing delivered to the Trustee, and upon such termination all accounts and interests therein shall become nonforfeitable. The Trustee shall distribute to each Participant, or Beneficiary, as the case may be, any Accrued Benefits credited to his account.

12.03 *Involuntary Termination of Trust.* This Trust shall terminate and distribution shall be made as provided in Section 12.02 if (a) the Employer is dissolved or adjudicated bankrupt or insolvent in appropriate proceedings, or if a general assignment is made by the Employer for the benefit of creditors, or (b) the Employer should lose its identity by merger, consolidation or reorganization into one or more corporations or organizations, unless within sixty (60) days after such merger, reorganization or consolidation, such corporations or organizations elect by an instrument in writing delivered to the Trustee to continue this Trust and such continuance is approved by the Trustee.

12.04 *Discontinuance of Contributions.* In the event that the Employer shall completely discontinue its contributions to this Trust, the right to each Participant or Beneficiary, as the case may be, to his Accrued Benefit shall be nonforfeitable as provided in Section 12.02. The Employer shall direct the

Trustee in writing to make immediate distribution of the Trust assets or to make distribution in such form and upon the contingencies and under the circumstances which would have controlled such distributions if there had been no discontinuance of contributions.

SECTION 13
Concerning Other Qualified Plans

13.01 *Transfer from Other Qualified Plans.* The Employer may cause to be transferred to the Trustee all or any of the assets attributable to employer contributions held in respect to any other plan or trust which satisfies the applicable requirements of the IRC relating to qualified plans and trusts. The Employer may permit transfer of all the assets held in respect to an Individual Retirement Account which is used as a conduit for a previous lump sum distribution from a qualified plan or trust. Any such assets so transferred shall be accompanied by written instructions from the Employer, or the trustee or custodian or the individual holding such assets, setting forth the Participants for whose benefit such assets have been transferred and showing the contributions by the Employer and the current value of the assets attributable thereto. Upon receipt of such assets and instructions the Trustee shall thereafter proceed in accordance with the provisions of this Trust and all assets received by the Trustee shall be nonforfeitable in each Participant's account to which the assets are assigned.

13.02 *Transfer to Other Qualified Plans.* The Employer by written direction to the Trustee may transfer some or all of the assets held under the Trust attributable to Employer contributions to another plan or trust meeting the requirements of the IRC relating to qualified plans and trusts. However, prior to the transfer of any assets the Trustee must be satisfied that the holding of such assets is permitted by the transferee trust. Upon receipt of such written direction the Trustee shall cause to be transferred the assets so directed and, as appropriate, shall direct the Insurer to transfer any Policies held by it to the new trustees.

13.03 *Merger or Consolidation with Another Plan.* In the case of any merger or consolidation with, or transfer of assets or liabilities to, any other plan after the Effective Date, each Participant in the plan would (if the plan then terminated) receive a benefit immediately after the merger, consolidation, or transfer which is equal to or greater than the benefit he would have been entitled to receive immediately before the merger, consolidation, or transfer (if this Trust had then terminated).

SECTION 14
Miscellaneous

14.01 *Trust Neither Creates nor Modifies Contract of Employment.* This Trust shall not be construed as creating or modifying any contract of employment between the Employer and any Participant.

14.02 *No Alienation or Assignment.* The assets of this Trust shall not be subject to alienation, assignment, trustee process, garnishment, attachment, or repay advances made by the Trustee for its fees and expenses of the Trust, and no attempt to cause such assets to be so subjected shall be recognized except to such extent as may be required by law. If any Participant shall attempt to alienate or assign his interest provided by the Trust, the Trustee shall take such steps as it deems necessary to preserve such interest for the benefit of the Participant or his Beneficiary.

14.03 *Participant's Benefits Limited to Assets.* Each Participant by his participation in this Trust shall be conclusively deemed to have agreed to look solely to the assets held under this Trust for the payment of any benefit to which he may be entitled by reason of his participation.

14.04 *Notice to Employer.* Any notice from the Trustee to the Employer provided for in this Trust shall be effective if sent by First Class Mail to the Employer at the Employer's last address on the Trustee's records.

14.05 *Obligation of Trust.* This Trust, and all actions and decisions thereunder, shall be binding upon the heirs, executors, administrators, successors and assigns of any and all parties thereto, present and future.

14.06 *Waiver.* Any shareholder-Employee or highly compensated Employee of the Employer may waive out of the Trust for any Trust year. Such waiver must be in writing and shall remain in effect until revoked in writing.

IN WITNESS WHEREOF, XYZ Company, Inc., Employer, and Mr. Owner and Mrs. Owner, Trustees, have caused this Trust to be executed this __________ day of _______________, 1982.

ATTEST: XYZ COMPANY, INC.

_______________________________   By _______________________________
        Secretary   President

                                            TRUSTEES:

                                            By _______________________________
                                                    Mr. Owner

                                            By _______________________________
                                                    Mrs. Owner

Notes

Chapter 1

1. Internal Revenue Code (hereinafter I.R.C.) §61.
2. I.R.C. §62.
3. I.R.C. §161.
4. I.R.C. §213.

Chapter 2

1. I.R.C. §676.
2. I.R.C. §673.
3. I.R.C. §674.
4. I.R.C. §677(b).
5. I.R.C. §2503.
6. Treas. Reg. §25.2512–9(f).
7. I.R.C. §674(b)(7).
8. *Lester Crown v. Commissioner of Internal Revenue*, 585 F.2d 234 (1978).
9. *Shemp v. Commissioner*, 168 F.2d 598 (7th Cir. 1948).
10. *Mathews v. Commissioner*, 520 F.2d 323 (5th Cir. 1975).

Chapter 3

1. I.R.C. §2501(a)(1) and I.R.C. §2511(a).
2. I.R.C. §2503.
3. I.R.C. §2513.
4. I.R.C. §677(b).
5. I.R.C. §665.
6. I.R.C. §667.
7. I.R.C. §674.
8. See Note 4.
9. I.R.C. §674(b)(7); I.R.C. §674(c).
10. *Crummey v. Commissioner*, 397 F.2d 82 (9th Cir. 1968).
11. Rev. Rul. 74-43, 1974-1 C.B. 285.
12. I.R.C. §170.
13. I.R.C. §170(e).

Chapter 4

1. I.R.C. §446(c).
2. 1981 Economic Recovery Tax Act §101.
3. I.R.C. §63(d).
4. I.R.C. §1232(b)(1).
5. I.R.C. §1202.
6. I.R.C. §1211(b).
7. I.R.C. §1091.
8. I.R.C. §1221.
9. I.R.C. §55.
10. I.R.C. §453.
11. I.R.C. §1031.
12. I.R.C. §1031(b).
13. I.R.C. §1301–1305.
14. Id.

Chapter 5

1. I.R.C. §219.
2. I.R.C. §219(c)(2)(A).
3. I.R.C. §408(f).
4. I.R.C. §408(ın).
5. I.R.C. §72(e).
6. Id.
7. Rev. Rul. 81-225.
8. I.R.C. §115.
9. I.R.C. §403(b).
10. I.R.C. §402(a)(5), 403(a)(4) and 408(d)(3).
11. I.R.C. §163.
12. I.R.C. §164.
13. I.R.C. §1034.
14. I.R.C. §121.
15. John Dorfman, *Getting Ready for Retirement*, Financial Planning Primer from New York State Consumer Protection Board, 1981.
16. I.R.C. §535(c)(2) and (3).

Chapter 6

1. I.R.C. §101(a)(1).
2. I.R.C. §101(a)(2)
3. I.R.C. §101(a)(2)(A).
4. I.R.C. §72(e)(1)(B); Reg. §1.72-11(b)(1).
5. *Theodore H. Cohen* 39 T.C. 1055 (1963).
6. I.R.C. §264(c).
7. I.R.C. §72.

8. Private Letter Rul. 8116073 as clarified by 8121074.

9. The IRS has challenged tax-free borrowing from an annuity contract maintained by an employer. Rev. Rul. 81-126, 1981-1 C.B. 20b.

Chapter 7

1. I.R.C. §167.
2. I.R.C. §1250.
3. I.R.C. §168(b).
4. I.R.C. §1250.
5. I.R.C. §57(a).
6. Id.
7. I.R.C. §46(a)(2) and (3); I.R.C. §48(a)(3) and §48(g).
8. I.R.C. §46(c)(7).
9. I.R.C. §179.
10. I.R.C. §46(c)(7).
11. I.R.C. §46(e)(3).
12. I.R.C. §465.
13. I.R.C. §168(f)(8).
14. I.R.C. §616.
15. I.R.C. §636.
16. I.R.C. §168(f)(8).
17. I.R.C. §46(c)(7).
18. I.R.C. §613A(c).
19. I.R.C. §613A(c)(3).
20. I.R.C. §613A(c)(6).
21. I.R.C. §280.
22. I.R.C. §48(k).
23. I.R.C. §180.
24. I.R.C. §1231(b)(3).

Chapter 8

1. *United States* v. *Davis*, 370 U.S. 65 (1962).
2. I.R.C. §121.
3. I.R.C. §1034.
4. I.R.C. §1221; I.R.C. §1202.
5. Rev. Rul. 76-83, 1976-1 C.B. 213.
6. The Tenth Circuit has found that a constructive joint interest exists when property in the husband's name alone is divided between the spouses on divorce. *Collins* v. *Commissioner of Internal Revenue*, 412 F.2d 211 (CA 10, 1969) and *Imel* v. *United States*, 523 F.2d 853 (CA 10, 1975). But see *Worthy U. McKinney*, 64 T.C. 263 (1975).
7. I.R.C. §71(c)(2).
8. *Marion R. Hesse* 60 T.C. 685 (1973).
9. I.R.C. §71(a)(1); Treas. Reg. §1.71-1(b).

10. I.R.C. §71(b).
11. Rev. Rul. 73-175.
12. *Commissioner v. Lester*, 366 U.S. 299 (1961).
13. I.R.C. §2056(a).

Chapter 10

1. I.R.C. §2010; I.R.C. §2505.
2. I.R.C. §2040(b); I.R.C. §2056; I.R.C. §2053.
3. Id.
4. I.R.C. §2001.
5. I.R.C. §2033; I.R.C. §2041.
6. I.R.C. §2503.

Chapter 11

1. I.R.C. §2042(2), Regs. §20.2042-1(c)(2).
2. I.R.C. §2035.
3. I.R.C. §652.
4. F. Weisz, *Super Trust* (1980). Rockville Centre, New York. Farnsworth Publishing Company.
5. Treas., Regs. §20.2042-1(c)(1).
6. I.R.C. §264.
7. Prohibited Transaction Exemptions 77-7 and 77-8, 42 F.R. 31575, June 21, 1975.
8. Rev. Rul. 69–54; 1969-1 C.B. 221 as modified by Rev. Rul. 72-307; 1972-1 C.B. 307.
9. Treas. Regs. §1.79-1(d).
10. I.R.C. §2512.

Chapter 12

1. *May v. McGowan*, 194 F.2d 396 (2nd Cir. 1952); *Commissioner of Internal Revenue v. Child's Estate*, 147 F.2d 368 (3rd Cir. 1945).
2. I.R.C. §318.
3. I.R.C. §301.
4. I.R.C. §303.
5. I.R.C. §361.
6. I.R.C. §306.
7. I.R.C. §541.
8. I.R.C. §701; Treas. Regs. §1.701-1.
9. I.R.C. §731.
10. I.R.C. §302(b)(3).
11. I.R.C. §704(e); Treas. Regs. §1.704-1(e)(1)(ii).
12. I.R.C. §6166(b)(1)(B)(i).
13. For a more detailed discussion on family partnerships, see "Using the

Multi-Class Partnership to Freeze Asset Values for Estate Planning Purposes," by Byrle M. Abbey in the February and March, 1980, issues of the *Journal of Taxation*, published by Warren, Gorman and Lamont.

14. I.R.C. §453.
15. I.R.C. §1014(a).
16. Rev. Rul. 69-74; 1969-1 C.B. 43.
17. Rev. Rul. 55-119.
18. Rev. Rul. 80-80 I.R.C. 1981-12, 10 (3/24/80).
19. I.R.C. §6166.
20. BNA Tax Management Memorandum, February 12, 1979.

Chapter 13

1. I.R.C. §2039(c)(1). Proceeds are excluded from participant's estate if:

   1. the beneficiary receives all the assets in one taxable year
   2. the beneficiary irrevocably elects to forego the favorable lump sum tax treatment (or if the beneficiary is your spouse, she rolls the proceeds over to an IRA account)
   3. your beneficiary receives the assets in more than one taxable year

2. Your trust should provide that the trustee has the authority (a) to decide how the assets will be distributed to the trust and (b) to make that decision based on what will be most tax advantageous to your heirs.
3. I.R.C. §535(c)(3).
4. I.R.C. §534.
5. I.R.C. §2031.
6. Rev. Rul. 59-60, 1959-1 C.B. 237.
7. I.R.C. §303.

Chapter 14

1. I.R.C. §2503.
2. I.R.C. §2503(b).
3. I.R.C. §1014(a).
4. I.R.C. §676(a).
5. Rev. Rul. 156, 1953–2 C.B. 253.

Chapter 15

1. I.R.C. §2040(a).
2. I.R.C. §2032A.
3. I.R.C. §2032A(c).

Chapter 16

1. I.R.C. §2056(a).
2. I.R.C. §2055(a).

3. I.R.C. §664.
4. I.R.C. §664(d)(1).
5. I.R.C. §664(d)(2).
6. I.R.C. §642(c)(5).
7. I.R.C. §2056(a).
8. I.R.C. §2055(a).
9. I.R.C. §170(f)(2)(B).
10. I.R.C. §170(f)(2)(B).
11. I.R.C. §170(d).
12. I.R.C. §170(b)(1)(c).

Chapter 17

1. Cal. Civ. Code §687 (West 1954).
2. Cal. Civ. Code §§5107, 5108 (West 1970).
3. Cal. Civ. Code §4803 (West Supp. 1982).
4. I.R.C. §2032A(e)(10).

Chapter 19

1. *Crown* v. *Commissioner of Internal Revenue*, 67 T.C. 1060 (3-31-77), Nonacq., aff'd 585 F.2d 234 (7th Cir. 1978); *J. Simpson Dean*, 35 T.C. 1083 (1961). But see *Greenspun* v. *Commissioner of Internal Revenue*, 72 T.C. 931 (1979), which indicates there would be gross income to the recipient of an interest-free loan if the recipient invested in securities generating tax-exempt interest.
2. Rev. Proc. 74–23, 1974-1 C.B. 476.
3. Part IV of Form 2106, Employee Business Expenses.
4. I.R.C. §179.
5. I.R.C. §280A.
6. I.R.C. §274(a)(1)(A).
7. I.R.C. §274(a)(1)(B).
8. I.R.C. §274(a)(2)(C).
9. I.R.C. §1371–1379.
10. I.R.C. §46(c)(8) and (9).
11. I.R.C. §1372.

Chapter 20

1. See Rev. Rul. 60-31, 1960-1 C.B. 174.
2. Taxed under I.R.C. §61 if in cash; I.R.C. §83 if in property.
3. I.R.C. §404(a)(5); 83(h).
4. I.R.C. §401(a)(4).
5. Rev. Rul. 67-449, 1967-2 C.B. 173.
6. M. Canan, *Qualified Retirement Plans* (1977), p. 17.
7. Rev. Rul. 68-99; 1968-1 C.B. 193.

8. I.R.C. §101(a)(1).
9. Deductible under I.R.C. §162.
10. I.R.C. §243(a)(1).
11. $10,000 income × 15% = $1,500 taxable at 50% (46% federal plus 4% state) = $750 tax.
12. Rev. Rul. 71-19; 1971-2 C.B. 220.
13. Rev. Proc. 71-19, 1971-1 C.B. 698.
14. I.R.C. §404(a)(5); I.R.C. §83(h).
15. Prop. Reg. 1.61-16.
16. Revenue Act of 1978, §132.
17. ERISA §101; Dept. of Labor Regs. §2520.104-23.
18. *Goldsmith* v. *United States*, 78-1 USTC 83, 702 (Ct. Cl. Tr. Div. 1978).
19. *Dependahl* v. *Falstaff Brewing Corp.*, 491 F. Supp. 1188 (E.D. Mo. 1980) affirmed F.2d (8th C.A. 1981); cert. denied 11-2-81; No. 81-449.
20. Rickey, *Keeping Current*, Volume 11, Number 4, September 1981, American Society of CLU, Contributing Editor Louis R. Richey, J.D.
21. Department of Labor Advisory Opinion 81–11A.

Chapter 21

1. Treas. Regs. §1.401-1(a)(2) and 1.405-1(b)(1); and Rev. Rul. 69-231, 1969-1 C.B. 118.
2. I.R.C. §§404(a), 405(c) and 415.
3. I.R.C. §411.
4. I.R.C. §501.
5. I.R.C. §402(e).
6. I.R.C. §2039(c)(1).
7. I.R.C. §411(a)(2).
8. I.R.C. §401(a)(17).
9. I.R.C. §401(d)(1) and (f).
10. I.R.C. §72(m).
11. I.R.C. §415.
12. Id.
13. I.R.C. §§4975(e)(7) and 409A.
14. I.R.C. §404(a)(10).
15. I.R.C. §44G.
16. I.R.C. §415(b).
17. I.R.C. §408(k).
18. ERISA §408(b)(1) and I.R.C. §4975(d)(1) and Rev. Rul. 67-288, 1967-2 C.B. 151.
19. I.R.C. §401(a)(13).
20. I.R.C. §2039(c).
21. I.R.C. §410(a).
22. I.R.C. §410(b)(1).
23. I.R.C. §401(d)(3) and I.R.C. §410(a)(3).
24. I.R.C. §411(a).

25. I.R.C. §401(d)(2).
26. I.R.C. §408.

Chapter 22

1. I.R.C. §415(c).
2. I.R.C. §415(e).
3. I.R.C. §3121(a)(1).
4. Rev. Rul. 71-446, 1971-2 C.B. 187, as updated by Rev. Ruls. 75-480, 1975-2 C.B. 131 and 76-76.
5. Id.
6. See §7 of Rev. Rul. 71-446.
7. See table in Rev. Rul. 78-92, which superceded Table II in Rev. Rul. 71-446.
8. I.R.C. §404(a)(3) and Reg. §1.404(a)-9(b).
9. Id.
10. I.R.C. §415(c).
11. See §3.01 of Rev. Rul. 76-464, 1976-2 C.B. 115, which defines a target benefit plan as being a money purchase plan with certain characteristics.
12. Contribution limitations are set forth in I.R.C. §415(e).
13. I.R.C. §404(a)(7).
14. I.R.C. §415(c).
15. I.R.C. §404(a)(7).
16. Pension Benefit Guaranty Corporation Publication in 1977 on Voluntary Terminations.
17. I.R.C. §401(d)(6).
18. I.R.C. §408(k).

Chapter 23

1. Tax deductible to employer under I.R.C. §162 and not taxable income to employee under I.R.C. §§105 and 106.
2. I.R.C. §105.
3. I.R.C. §213.
4. I.R.C. §105(h).
5. I.R.C. §105(h)(3).
6. Treas. Reg. §1.105(11)(g).
7. I.R.C. §264(a)(1).
8. Treas. Reg. §1.79-1(a).
9. Such plans can qualify as group-term plans only if the requirements of Treas. Reg. §1.79-1(c) are met:

   1. The plan provides protection for all full-time employees (except as otherwise permitted by 3, 4 and 5 of this paragraph).
   2. Except as otherwise permitted by 3, 4 and 5 of this paragraph, the amount of protection is computed as a uniform percentage of compensation or on the basis of coverage brackets under which no bracket ex-

ceeds 2½ times the next lower bracket and the lowest bracket is at least 10% of the highest bracket. Phantom brackets should not be used. Each bracket for employees should be filled with at least one person.

3. Evidence of insurability, based on a questionnaire and not a medical exam, may be a factor with regard to an employee's eligibility or the extent of coverage.

4. If evidence of insurability is not a factor and the tests of (1) and (2) of this paragraph are not met, a plan may still qualify if it is a plan maintained by at least two employers for employees in an organization, such as a union, and participation is mandatory for employees represented by the organization.

5. Employees over age 65 may be excluded. If covered, employees over age 65 must be covered on the same basis as employees under age 65 or on a bracket basis similar to that expressed in (2) of this paragraph.

Employees may be excluded if they have worked for fewer than six months and employees who generally work less than twenty hours per week or five months during the year can be excluded as part-time employees.

10. I.R.C. §79(a) and Uniform Premium Table in Treas. Reg. §1.79-3(d)(2).
11. I.R.C. §79(b).
12. Treas. Reg. §1.79-1(d) and Rev. Rule 71-360, 1971-2 C.B. 87.
13. Rev. Rul. 69-482, 1969-2 C.B. 164.
14. Id.
15. Id.
16. I.R.C. §79.
17. Rev. Rul. 64-328, 1964-2 C.B. 11.
18. Rev. Rul. 55-747, 1955-2 C.B. 228, Rev. Rul. 66-110, 1966-1 C.B. 12, and Rev. Rul. 67-154, 1967-1 C.B. 11.
19. I.R.C. §264(a).

Chapter 24

1. *Lucas* v. *Earl*, 281 US 111(1930).
2. Rev. Rul. 75-257, 1975-2 C.B. 251.
3. Rev. Rul. 78-232, 1978-1 C.B. 69.
4. I.R.C. §507.
5. I.R.C. §83.
6. *Lester Crown* v. *Commissioner of Internal Revenue*, 585 F.2d 234 (1978).
7. I.R.C. §265(c).
8. *Thompson* v. *Commissioner of Internal Revenue*, 631 F.2d 642 (1980).
9. *Stewart* v. *Commissioner of Internal Revenue*, 41 T.C.M. 496 (1980).
10. Technical Advice Memorandum 7928004.
11. I.R.C. §48(c).
12. Treas. Reg. §301.7701-2.
13. Economic Recovery Tax Act §403(e)(3).

Index